C000215820

Not in Front of the Children

Hidden Histories in Kids TV

Greg Healey

NEW HAVEN PUBLISHING LTD

Not in Front of the Children

First Edition
Published 2018
NEW HAVEN PUBLISHING LTD
www.newhavenpublishingltd.com
newhavenpublishing@gmail.com

Cover image © John Ryan Estate
Cover design©Andy Morten
andymorten@mac.com

Not in Front of the Children

The Mary, Mungo & Midge image on the cover reproduced courtesy of the Literary Estate of John Ryan. Special thanks to the family of John Ryan and Jane Gregory and Company for their assistance.

Not in Front of the Children

Contents

Not in Front of the Children

Introduction

Things Ain't Like They Used to Be

Our love of heritage and history, nostalgia's seemingly limitless capacity to anaesthetise us against the vagaries of modern life, grows more pervasive with each passing year. What began as an upper-class rite of passage, in the shape of the European Grand Tour, has grown to become a democratised obsession with everything from battlefield reconstructions to resuscitated railway lines.

Film, music and fashion, those things once deemed as transitory fads, have also become part of what is now a multi-billion pound industry. Reissues, regurgitations and re-imaginings, the unearthing of lost archives and misremembered gems, all feed into this lucrative sector.

The nostalgia and the heritage industry is now so ingrained in our nation's life that, as is the case when anything crosses over from fringe obsession to popular movement, it is now deemed as unhealthy. Charges of escapism abound, with the cynical accusers seeking to remind nostalgiaphiles that they are fantasists, blind to the problems of the world.

Our point of departure for this book, old children's TV programmes from the late 1950s to the early 1970s, represents a particularly potent kind of nostalgia - after all, childhood memories remind us of all that we have lost on our journey to adulthood. However, hopefully we will avoid the obvious romantic pitfalls that come with this territory and be able find a different perspective on both our past and present. Although nostalgia will be embraced in all its warmth and loveliness, this will be done with an acceptance that the past can only be legitimately understood if it is approached with an open mind.

Not in Front of the Children

In the twenty first century it is, perhaps, television more than any other medium that both feeds into and promotes the fantasies of the ordinary person. Back in 1970 the medium was still relatively new. Although colour television had been launched in the UK on BBC2 in the July of 1967, with coverage of the Wimbledon tennis championships, it was not until the November of 1969 that BBC1 and ITV went over to colour.

This innovation was initially only available to half the UK population. The distribution of the new technology was patchy and it was available only in London Weekend, Thames Television, ATV, Granada and Yorkshire Television regions. Rather like the promises of HDTV and 4K TV today the viewer was offered an experience akin to actually "being there". Those living in Scotland had to wait a few weeks, until the 13th of December, for colour. In South Wales the wait for the future took them up to the 6th of April 1970 and in Northern Ireland they finally received the signal in September of 1970.

For those who owned one of the new sets, what today might be called early adopters, the BBC had launched the all colour snooker show, *Pot Black*. They judged, quite rightly, that the multi-coloured balls on the green baize would prove attractive and engaging for an audience keen to enjoy and show off their new devices. In addition to this viewers could also enjoy colour versions of the popular shows *Dad's Army* and *Z Cars*.

The first official BBC1 colour broadcast, *An Evening with Petula - Petula Clark in concert from the Royal Albert Hall*, was shown at midnight between the 14th and the 15th of November in 1969. It was preceded by the programme *Colourful One* which began at 23:40. Typically dry and of the time, it was presented by Julian Pettifer who introduced the new colour service and offered a run-down of what the viewer could expect. Analysis of the pros and cons of colour was supplied by the *Sunday Times* journalist Maurice Wiggins. Once the cautious introductions were over it was left to Yvonne Littlewood to introduce Petula and her accompaniment, Johnny Harris and his orchestra.

The timing of this event was determined by the government's Postmaster General, in what was one of the final acts of this three hundred year old office, before it was abolished in the October of 1969. This cabinet level post had responsibility for maintaining the postal service, the telegraph system and telecommunications and broadcasting.

The final Postmaster General, the man who scheduled the BBC1 colour switch on, was John Stonehouse MP. His name lives on in infamy, though not because he triggered a televisual revolution. In a coincidental pre-echo of the plot of the mid Seventies television series, *The Rise And Fall Of Reginald Perrin,* Stonehouse attempted to fake his own death in 1974 by leaving a pile of clothes on a Miami beach to give the appearance that he had gone for a swim and drowned. Under a variety of false names Stonehouse set off for Australia, transferring large sums of money as he went, in a bid to start a new, anonymous life with his mistress Sheila Buckley. Stonehouse's suspicious financial activity was spotted by a bank teller and he was reported to the police, who initially believed him to be Lord Lucan. One month after his fake demise Stonehouse was arrested and charged with various fraud offences. He was tried, found guilty and sentenced to seven years in prison. This outrageous story did not end there. In 1979, it was discovered that Stonehouse had been a spy for the Czechoslovak Socialist Republic, a communist regime, between 1962 and 1974.

Although he was only in the role for a few weeks, Stonehouse's activities could have posed a threat to national security. This was because the Postmaster General's responsibilities went beyond overseeing mail deliveries or deciding when Petula would introduce colour television to the nation. Indeed, those who settled down on their sofas at tea time the following day to watch the new all colour edition of *Star Trek* could not have known that the service they were enjoying was designed and built for a more sinister purpose.

In 1954, as the realities of the nuclear bomb and its effects gripped the government of the United Kingdom, attempts were made to prepare the country for a Soviet attack. As Duncan Campbell outlined in his book *War Plan UK*, a strategy was conceived to ensure "that in the event of an attack on the country adequate communications for the administration of the country are available up to the time of the attack and as far as possible to assist in the work of restoration afterwards." To this end "communications services must be provided in advance, routed in diverse ways, for the operational needs of the fighting services and of Civil Defence and for the dissemination of essential information." This quote by Campbell, from the dry testimonial of Mr. J. H. H. Merriman of the Post Office in 1962, highlights the hopeful desire that a network of wireless microwave communications towers would enable Britain to continue to both fight and function in the event of large scale nuclear attack from the Soviet Union. Called *Backbone* it would allow a "bomb-blasted Britain to carry on functioning throughout a prolonged nuclear battle as an airbase and support base." Originally all of *Backbone's* stations were intended to be strong concrete structures, with the aerials shielded by perspex to make them difficult to spot, but the high cost and unresolved technical difficulties "ruled out the use of reinforced concrete at every location." *Backbone* stage one ran from London-Birmingham-Manchester-Leeds and consisted of a mixture of relay towers and underground exchanges. This was augmented by a second stage that bypassed the four main cities and then further spurs to smaller cities and towns such as York,

Lancaster and Peterborough. A spur also ran down into Cornwall that terminated in the transatlantic satellite cable terminals at Porthcurno.

The microwave system had huge advantages over cabling which, as well as being vulnerable to sabotage, was difficult to repair in the aftermath of an attack. Most cables also ran along major roads and were near the major targets, like large population centres. Incidentally, even as the Post Office endeavoured to route its new network around towns and cities, because any attack would be hugely devastating, the government's advice to the population in the event of a nuclear strike was to stay put in the towns and cities. This advice would have certainly resulted in millions of casualties. At this time Britain was, to all intents and purposes, operating as an airstrip for the nuclear V-Bomber force of Valiants, Victors and Vulcans. This continued in various forms throughout the 1950s and 1960s until the roll out of the submarine launched polaris missile system in 1969.

From the very beginning of the process to build *Backbone* in 1956 the Post Office sought to deceive the public as to its purpose and nature. A combination of national security issues and concerns about reactions to the projected cost of £20 million led to intricate cover ups and deceptions that held that the network was purely for civilian purposes. By the late 1960s, however, with the cost of construction having been met under the provision of nuclear defence, the system did begin to see use as a carrier for colour television and telephone signals. In the event of an escalating international crisis this network would have reverted to the purpose it was intended for.

Whatever the reasons for the expenditure, the arrival of colour television at midnight on the 14th of November was a huge national event. Most families didn't possess a colour television but stayed up to watch the momentous broadcast anyway - and for them Petula appeared in the familiar blur of greys and blacks.

In 1971 36% of the population did not own a washing machine and 31% did not own a fridge. The General Household Survey of that year, conducted by the Office for National Statistics, revealed some startling truths about the lives of the many, even in the aftermath of the swinging sixties, with a startling 10.3% of the population still using outside toilets and 9% of the population without a bath. A 1967 survey conducted by the Halifax Building Society and Local Government found that 22% of homes had no hot water and that 65% did not have central heating. All of this paints a picture of a significant portion of the population living in conditions at odds with the shiny modern narrative of the day.

The Britain of this time faced in two directions - trapped between a glorious past of national mythologies and proud achievements and an uncertain future of new technologies and a host of long unsolved problems. This was a country in mourning for things that had and had never been, and one that grappled heroically with the challenges of building a modern state fit for the future.

Television, a new thing in people's lives that was accepted surprisingly quickly, offered its own perspective. It recorded and documented as it went, noting down reactions and reflections with an asymmetric and brilliant aplomb, across all types of programming. This is where our story begins.

Chapter One

Ivor and the Death of Steam

In 1958, when Ivor the Engine first chuffed (or pssshhht-koofed) onto the nation's flickering screens, the number of households with a television set stood at a little over eight million, out of around sixteen million in total. Black and white and, by the standards available in cinemas, of poor quality, the broadcasts they received had, however, been steadily improving. The BBC, spurred on by the public's response to the broadcasting of the Coronation of Queen Elizabeth II, and the prospect of a potential new rival in the shape of a commercial television service, upgraded its transmitters in 1953 and began what would be a slow and fitful progress toward colour broadcasting.

Sir Winston Churchill's Conservative government had introduced the Bill that proposed the introduction of commercial television in 1954, against a backdrop of fevered national debate. The perceived perils of this move, and the outrage being expressed across the land, meant that the Bill was passionately debated. Despite this, however, it was passed into law by the summer of 1954. On the 22nd of September 1955, the Independent Television Authority broadcast its first pictures, accompanied by the bizarre collision of awkward ceremonials and self-conscious hi-tech wizardry that would come to typify the establishment's approach to change over the next two decades. A short documentary, to kick the proceedings off, spoke of adding "another sentence to the long history of London," as familiar landmarks were paraded past, accompanied by a reassuring orchestral score. The message was simple: London, and by association the rest of Britain, was at the centre of everything, shored up by its history, even in this new-fangled age of commercial television. Far from being a threat, so the message went, the new medium represented an enhancement of the nation's proudest boasts such as "the rights of free speech, fair play, our own particular brand of decency and tolerance, our own particular brand of humour and common sense." Within the hour another brand would be celebrated, as a promotion for Gibb's SR Toothpaste became the first ever British television advert to be aired. Before that, however, an expectant nation sat and watched grainy images of the great and the good in full regalia, as speeches were made by the Lord Mayor, the Postmaster-General and Sir Kenneth Clark, the chairman of the Independent Television Authority.

The starting gun had been fired and there on the line, or in the airwaves at least, were Sidney Bernstein and Alfred Hitchcock with Granada Theatre Ltd, Captain Thomas Brownrigg with Broadcast Relay Services and Associated Newspapers - trading as Associated-Rediffusion, and Maurice Winnick, Lord Kemsley and Isaac Wolfson with Kemsley-Winnick Television. This was an unusual collection of retailers, engineers, impresarios and newspaper men but they would, over the next few years, begin the process of reshaping the nation. From here on in appetites would be honed for things that could be bought on hire purchase and the traditional working class aversion to debt would be broken to make way for the birth of aspirational society.

The BBC evolved to meet the challenge, growing from a curiosity that showed the great occasions of state, such as the funeral of King George VI and the Coronation of Queen Elizabeth II, to a service that both informed and entertained the family. Alongside sporting events, like the World Cup and Roger Bannister's record breaking four minute mile, came soap operas. *The Grove Family*, a simple story of hardworking middle class folk in the new age of consumerism, was the first soap and proved hugely popular. By the end of its first year, in 1954, it had built up an audience of over eight million viewers. A host of family favourites were launched during the mid-1950s, with *Dixon of Dock Green*, *This is Your Life*, *The Woodentops* and *Crackerjack* all coming to the screen. Presented by Eamonn Andrews *Crackerjack* also featured a very young Ronnie Corbett, who began his career in television on the show. BBC radio favourites, like Ray Galton's and Alan Simpson's *Hancock's Half Hour* migrated onto the new medium and, in doing so, helped create the new genre of TV sitcom. By 1960 many of the programmes that came to define BBC television for many years to come, such as *Grandstand* and *Blue Peter*, had been created.

Oliver Postgate and Peter Firmin, the men behind *Ivor the Engine*, first began working together on two projects for the new independent commercial television company, Associated-Rediffusion. At the time Postgate was a stage manager at Associated-Rediffusion, working in the children's television department on a portion of the schedule that ran between 4.45pm and 5.00pm, known as "Small Time". Between 1955 and 1966, this meagre fifteen minute offering was pretty much it for kids in the London region and any other areas that took Rediffusion's children's programming. Despite the presence of the now disgraced entertainer Rolf Harris in this slot, and an early, basic offering from Gerry Anderson called *The Adventures of Twizzle*, Postgate felt the programming to be underwhelming, and set about writing his own.

The first project of Postgate and Firmin, called *Alexander the Mouse*, was about a mouse who would be king (of the mice). Made with a new, simple, but highly effective animation system that used cardboard cut-out figures placed on a paper background and moved about using carefully attached magnets, it was filmed live. Postgate had been introduced to Firmin, who was a student of the Central School of Art and Design, by Maurice Kestelman, Central's Head of Fine Art, and their tentative relationship soon bore fruit. *Alexander the Mouse*, which Postgate describes in his autobiography as being "a bit muddled, without much action," was broadcast on "Small Time" in 1958. This was followed up by *The Journey of Ho,* another piece of charming make-do-and-mend low cost TV that was typical of this era of budget constrained experiments and discovery.

Postgate was not alone in his reservations about the output of his employer. As Janet Thurmin says in her book *Small Screens, Big Ideas: Television in the 1950s,* "the ITA expressed concern over what the Board perceived as a lack of balance in the company's original programme output." The arts were "marginalised in the schedule," and not enough time was given to the Independent Television News bulletins. It appeared that the fears expressed during the long, fevered and, at the time, still continuing debate about the merits and demerits of commercial television were being realised and that scheduling decisions were being "governed by the the 'evil' power of money". Associated-Rediffusion, driven by the needs of shareholders, appeared to be concerned only with "maximising its audience share by scheduling popular light entertainment" and was seeking to minimise its costs. Lord Reith, the former Director General of the BBC, and a man who did much to shape the ethos of broadcasting in the Britain Isles, also weighed into the debate, raising a belated motion in the House of Lords in 1962. Moving away from the diplomatic and cautious language of that place he succeeded in calling those who sought a change in the nation's broadcasting landscape a "pressure group", with motives and methods that were not "above-board, straight forward, honourable and honest." In using the term pressure group Lord Reith referred to

Professor Hugh Wilson's 1961 book *Pressure Group,* and its revelations about the "cloak and dagger" activities of the commercial television lobby. However, both Reith's speech, which was given with "a kind of controlled ferocity", and Wilson's book, were nothing more than a futile rearguard action - one that was fought long after the battle was lost.

Postgate and Firmin surfed a dual wave of technological innovation and old school inventiveness to bring *Ivor the Engine* into being, but this charming animation chimed with a national mood of nostalgia. Like all good children's television it appealed to an adult audience as well and cemented its place in the hearts of the nation through its simple, folk tale infused stories. This story of a small private railway in a far flung corner of the land, with its cast of eccentric characters, tapped into a national love of steam and the railways, and resonated with parents because it represented a safe, reassuring and familiar world that was rapidly disappearing. Modernity was on the march and traditional structures, both physical and metaphysical, were being overturned. The new medium of television, and in particular children's television, would, over the course of the coming years, prove to be a sensitive bellwether of the shifts and changes occurring in the land, reflecting attitudes to the past, present and future in its own curious but fascinating way.

Ivor the Engine captured the complex appeal of the age of steam and what it meant to communities across Britain. In doing so it also raised questions about a disruptive driver of social change that was, eventually, assimilated into the patterns of everyday life and came to be invested with a meaning beyond its prime purpose of moving people and things from A to B.

Ivor the Engine, the first real production of Postgate and Firmin's new Smallfilms Company, was broadcast in 1959 on Associated-Rediffusion. In conceiving of the show

17

Postgate asked himself what it was that "everybody could feel unashamedly sentimental about." But he didn't want "cuddly bunnies or cute dollies" and eventually hit upon the thing that every boy of his generation wanted to be - an engine driver. Whilst at drama school Postgate had been friends with a former steam engine fireman. It was to the stories he'd heard, of early mornings clearing out the firebox and waking up the engines with paper and wood, that Postgate turned. To this atmospheric mix he added his own passion for Dylan Thomas and in particular *Under Milk Wood*. Peter Firmin's highly believable idea that, being Welsh, the engine would naturally want to sing in the choir added an extra bit of magic. *Ivor the Engine* was born and it could not have been more timely.

This story of a small tank engine and his friends drew on real concerns in Britain at the time, and highlighted the passing of traditions and practices that were as much a part of the nation's folk psyche as morris dancing or mummers.

When *Ivor the Engine* aired in 1959, time had already been called on the age of steam. Just as Parliament finished fighting and fretting over the introduction of commercial television the British Transport Commission produced the 1955 document, 'Modernisation and Re-equipment of the British Railways'. Based on "approximately £1,200 million" of projected spending, this plan called for the "efficient and modernised railway system" that was "essential to the economy of the country". Track and signalling was to be improved "to make higher speed possible" using the latest technology. Steam was to "be replaced as form of motive power, electric or diesel traction being rapidly introduced," and steam-drawn passenger rolling stock was to be replaced by multiple-unit electric or diesel trains. In addition, freight services, which were suffering at the hands of a road haulage sector that had expanded greatly after World War Two, were to be "drastically remodelled" with fewer but larger facilities.

A system that had struggled with the exertions of World War One and World War Two, without adequate investment or compensation for the role played during those conflicts, was finally to be upgraded.

Notwithstanding the plan, which was reappraised in 1959, and although diesel had been around on the network for some time, steam lingered on for years. Evening Star, the last steam locomotive to be built by British Railways, entered service in 1960 and was withdrawn only five short years later as part of the big planned withdrawals between 1962 and 1966. A mainline steam ban came into effect in 1968, but like all things on this untidy Isle the death of steam was greatly exaggerated. Indeed, aside from the heritage sector, steam survived on the many private industrial networks until the 1980s. In the top left hand corner of Wales (or more correctly the middle bit) steam continued on the national network, with the 2ft narrow gauge locos and rolling stock of the Vale of Rheidol Railway continuing to operate through the years of nationalisation and on into privatisation in 1989. They still run to this day.

Preservation, and its role in keeping steam alive, cannot be ignored, but for the purposes of this section, we will do exactly that. In 1959 and right through into the 1970s, everyone believed that the days of the steam engine, that much loved and cherished national symbol, were over and that progress would not and could not be halted. The great living beasts of the steam age would henceforth only be seen as dead and rust streaked carcasses, lined up in rows awaiting the final cut of the scrap man's torch. A clean, modern and efficient future beckoned for everyone and, in making *Ivor the Engine*, Postgate and Firmin tapped into a powerful current of nostalgia that swept the land.

But if the death of steam seemed bad, much worse lay ahead. When *Ivor* returned to the nation's screens, on the BBC and in full colour in 1975, the entire railway appeared to be facing the threat of extinction. The infamous Dr Beeching had made his prescription in the 1963 report 'The Reshaping of Britain's Railways' and with it all the optimism of 'Modernisation and Re-equipment' had been swept away. Over the ensuing decade lines and stations were to close and the landscape of the nation and its railways would be changed forever. Like the Bwca of Welsh folklore that warned of impending disaster, Ivor the little Welsh engine had returned. Unfortunately, he was just little bit too late.

To understand the importance of the railway and the steam engine, and their place at the heart of the national psyche, we must look back to the dawn of that age. Forming the backbone and blood vessels of Britain's economy, from the early nineteenth century onwards, the railways transported first goods and then, when the public felt reassured that their faces wouldn't melt at the breathtaking speed of fifteen miles per hour, people. Over the next one hundred years railway expansion was rapid and exponential, as the iron road, with its fire breathing monsters, pushed into even the most remote parts of the British Isles.

Although the mainline, with its powerful passenger express locos, was the stuff of dreams for the young boys who crowded onto ends of platforms with their notebooks and cameras, it was through the local and industrial branch lines that the railway pervaded all aspects of people's lives. Sidings, spurs and unmanned crossings, tracks running along the bottom of people's gardens, iron lattice bridges and brick viaducts, engine sheds and goods sheds, these pieces of infrastructure were everywhere. Nowadays, with so much of the evidence long since swept away under road schemes, shopping centres and housing developments, it is hard to conceive of just how much railway stuff there was. If you lived in a village, a town or a big city, anywhere where there was any form of economic activity, your environment was made and marked by the railways.

Not in Front of the Children

Ivor the Engine is set on the Merioneth and Llantisilly Rail Traction Company Ltd, a made up railway somewhere in a fictitious part of the "top left-hand corner of Wales" and focusses particularly on the adventures of a small steam engine called Ivor. It is described by the Small Films Treasury website as being "not so much an invention but rather more a coagulation... patted together from a morass of memories, of the many small railways that infest the area, the works of Dylan Thomas, and an indefinable quality which might be called Welshness."

The Merioneth and Llantisilly Rail Traction Company Ltd typifies the remote railway lines that criss crossed Britain, and served towns, small halts, coal mines and gas works and carried everything from hats to livestock. Serving the community, as well as being part of the community, they were the product of the explosion of speculative ventures that marked the many railway building booms and busts of the nineteenth century. This was the unfettered free market economics of railway mania that made people rich and then, as the bubble burst, poor again.

The phenomenon of railway mania begins, perhaps, with Queen Victoria's first ever railway journey, made in the summer of 1882. This short trip, from Windsor to Paddington on the Great Western Railway, acted as a kind of celebrity endorsement and showed that this form of transport was both respectable and safe. Within two years those seeking to speculate on the new railway bug received a helping hand from Parliament when, on 6th of May 1844, Sir Robert Peel's motion, the Bank Charter Act, created confidence in the pound and the national lending rate was cut to three and a quarter percent. This cheap money led to a speculative bubble around railway building projects. Between 1844 and 1845 the number of lines granted parliamentary approval rose from 805 miles to 2700 miles. By 1946 some 272 Acts of Parliament had been passed that set up new railway companies, with a total of over 9,500 miles of line proposed. There were many of these booms and all would inevitably go bust due to variety of reasons, including an international gold crisis and an overcrowded market. These factors, plus a combination of fraud and poor management, or buy outs by competitors, meant that roughly a third of the railways approved, in what was a laissez-faire and unregulated system, never came into existence.

It was necessary to obtain an Act of Parliament to build a railway line and this was not always easy. There was, understandably, intense opposition from the landed gentry and farmers, on whose land the new routes would be built, as well as from those who held shares in turnpike roads and canal companies and those who ran stagecoaches. Once an Act was passed land could be bought by compulsory purchase order, which was, initially at least, an affront to those long established land owning vested interests for whom the railways represented a form of dangerous and destabilising revolution. However, pragmatism and the lure of monetary compensation would eventually hold sway and landowners soon began to demand eye wateringly large payments from companies seeking to build across their land. Incidentally, the canal companies were one of the biggest obstructions to the growth in railways for very particular reasons. Canals had enjoyed their own construction boom over the sixty years before the opening of the Liverpool Manchester Railway in 1830. This lucrative situation, along with their near monopoly position as carriers of bulk freight, was never going to be surrendered lightly.

Despite the benign and rather cuddly image of railways portrayed in *Ivor the Engine*, and the general affection the railways were and are still held in, the arrival of one of the new iron road ventures in your neighbourhood was never going to be an easy thing to come to terms with: if you lived in the path of a railway your home would be knocked down. When it came to entering Britain's industrial towns and cities the line of least resistance was always through areas where densely packed slums were located. Although these slums were insanitary and overcrowded they provided a roof and four walls to incredibly poor working people. If the march of progress swept through your locality and demolished your and your neighbours' homes, you would simply be turfed out onto the street with your children, your elderly relatives, and whoever else used your bed when you were at work so that you could pay the rent. This was free market economics at full tilt and there was no state welfare provision. Indeed, it was not until 1874 that social reformers secured help for those displaced by the railways with a Parliamentary order stipulating that railway companies must rehouse the poorest of those affected. This was, however, just a piece of window dressing and easily circumvented and ignored.

Despite the homelessness caused, public perception was often managed by the wholly disingenuous claim that the clearance of slums was a deliberate and positive act aimed at improving public health. Between 1859 and 1857 nearly forty thousand people were made homeless by railway construction, and its effects did not escape the attention of the writers and artists of the time. Charles Dickens described the the building of the North London Railway through Camden Town in his 1848 monthly periodical series *Dealings with the Firm of Dombey and Son: Wholesale, Retail and for Exportation* or, as it is now known, *Dombey and Son*: "Houses were knocked down; streets broken through and stopped; deep pits and trenches dug in the ground; enormous heaps of earth and clay thrown up; buildings that were undermined and shaking, propped by great beams of wood.... Everywhere were bridges that led nowhere....

temporary wooden houses and enclosures, in the most unlikely situations; carcasses of ragged tenements, and fragments of unfinished walls and arches..."

Even the dead had to give way to railways. In Leeds, as the railway forged its route into the city through the closely packed streets near the notoriously impoverished and overcrowded Mabgate area, the way ahead was barred by the cemetery of Leeds Parish church. The solution was simple: dig them up, remove the headstones and then, when the embankment and the bridge works were complete, lay the headstones up the sides of the embankment like some kind of grim crazy paving. Few with influence and money in Leeds were prepared to challenge the railway. The city was booming and transport links were needed if the city was to keep up with its neighbours in Bradford, Manchester and Liverpool.

The sheer number of men needed to build these schemes meant that the physical disruption of earthworks and streets demolished was not the only thing communities had to contend with. The most famous of this labour force were the navvies. These were hard men, who travelled from place to place along the route of the railway and did the work that lay beyond the physical scope of your ordinary local labourer. Be it blasting and tunnelling, excavating cuttings or digging the foundation pits for bridges and viaducts, the navvies (navigators, from which the word comes, refers to the origins of this workforce as the people who built the first canals) were the only ones up to the job.

By the middle of the nineteenth century they numbered more than two hundred and fifty thousand strong and moved, with their families, to where there was work to be done, often living in squalid conditions in makeshift shelters. Living on a diet of beer and beef - according to Terry Coleman's *The Railway Navvies,* the ability to drink eight pints of beer and eat two pounds of beef a day would see a man accepted by his peers - they were a raucous and unruly bunch for whom fighting and rioting was a way of life.

Drawn from a variety of communities across the British Isles and Europe, and in particular Ireland where famine had forced many off the land, their arrival must have been a shock to any community. In Victorian Britain, before the railways arrived, it was unlikely for people to travel more than a few miles beyond where they lived, and any sudden influx of strangers caused both fear and resentment. With a variety of accents and languages, and a patois-cum-slang that they developed to communicate, they were regarded with suspicion.

Despite the toil, the sweat and the intolerable conditions, navvies were known for their distinctive, dandyish, fashionable attire, and this also marked them out as strange and not to be trusted. The humdrum lives of people in towns and villages, where not much changed for generations, were upended by these exotic strangers. Of course the industrial revolution had brought about shifts in the way things were done and of course many people had moved. Many had left behind life in the country for the new and growing urban centres and jobs in industry, but still, when the railway navvies arrived in any area they came like an invading horde. People and their routines did not fair well when the navvies came to town. The new arrivals in their camps on the edge of town would still be seen as interlopers. Added to that, the temporary nature of their communities made it all but impossible to integrate them.

They were wild folk and paid no heed to the rules and social mores of respectable society. Their wages were often paid in pubs and because of their itinerant way of life they could pretty much behave as they wished. Drunkenness may have been frowned upon, but in the tightly regulated life of Victorian Britain extra-marital sex was the biggest no no of all. However, as Terry Coleman writes in *The Railway Navvies*: ".... navvies found their women where they could, and behaved in this way very much like soldiers..." And so the legend of the horny navigator, fine and strong and virile, was established. This, allied to living arrangements that saw the sexes mixed together, created the perception that the men and the women of the navvy camps were promiscuous and lacking in morals.

Viewed as degenerate and lawless and considered a threat to the social order, various attempts were made at reforming the lives lived by navvies. These usually revolved around temperance, prayer and that staple of Victorian rectitude, the singing of hymns. Unfortunately, any navvy who shifted the twenty tonnes of earth a day that was necessary to earn a good wage, would probably build up quite a thirst. As water was rarely safe to drink, particularly in the early days of railway building, beer was really the only option, though it would be stretching a point to say the choice was ever made out of health considerations.

Those who ministered to the ungodly horde were not always immune to the appeal of their lifestyles and choices. Around 1860 the Reverend Perkins was sent by the Bishop of Carlisle to preach to the navvies working on the London and North Western Railway's Ingleton branch line. Alas, the right Reverend became the tight Reverend and was soon sacked for being drunk. Methodist preachers, for whom alcohol was largely forbidden, usually faired better. However, Anglicans and non-conformists alike went about the task of saving souls with vigour, and a good indicator of their somewhat frenetic activities can be seen in the physical legacy of their chapels.

More destructive even than the military forces of the day, the railways shaped both the landscape and social fabric of the time. Once an Act of Parliament was passed and construction began, their seemingly unimpeachable ubiquity meant that they had, as Christian Wolmar writes in his book *Fire and Steam*, "the status of a quasi-state". Each of these quasi-states had their own hierarchies and bylaws, which were enforced through various means - ranging from a severe ticking off to prosecutions and fines. All manner of activities were prohibited, from trespassing and spitting, to passengers hopping off at intermediate stations to stretch their legs or jumping off moving trains to steal a march on the crowd of disembarking fellow passengers. Devised to ensure both the smooth, punctual running of trains, as well as the safety of the passengers and the staff, these bylaws built up over time, accumulating to give the railway its own particular atmosphere of order and security. Although wider Victorian society was characterised by orders that prohibited such diverse things as the beating of rugs before 8am, or being drunk in charge of a cow, the nature of the railway companies' vast properties, in the form of stations, steam sheds and goods yards, gave each their own peculiar profile.

Whatever kind of railway line, be it branch, industrial or mainline, the effect was one of concertinaing time and space. This compressed social conventions and influenced the way people operated within them. Despite the vast complexity of the various networks, human nature, the characters, the people themselves, were to the fore. A brief look at any of the vast body of memoirs and stories by and about railway people quickly makes clear that this was no faceless behemoth under whose iron hoof all humanity was crushed. Rather, the railway was an environment where bonds were forged through work and common aims; where, through rapidly emerging traditions and daily interactions, strong relationships were built.

The cast of *Ivor the Engine* would have been familiar to people who both used and worked on the railways. Jones the Steam (the driver of Ivor) and Dai Station (the station master) are distillations of typical personality types engendered by and found on the railways.

Jones the Steam, the engine driver, is a calm and practical man, solid and unfussy but with a deep affection for his engine, with whom he has developed a personal relationship. On a small railway like the Merioneth drivers would know their engines well, preserving the relationships that Cecil J. Allen speaks of in his 1928 book *Trains and Their Control* that existed in "earlier days (when) each crew had their own engine, and in the course of time a real affection was often aroused in the breast of the driver for his 'mount'." Allen goes on to state that, even in 1928, at a time now referred to as the golden age of steam when the LNER, GWR, LMS and Southern railways commanded the network as the big four, he "heard the driver apostrophise his steed in quite affectionate terms." For Allen, this situation arose because "the fact is that each locomotive, for one reason and another, is almost human in its own characteristics and idiosyncrasies." Drivers would get to know and "learn to get the best possible out of their machine." Although this intimacy would, in time, be lost to a certain extent on the bigger steam sheds, as engines and crews were rotated, the "similarity between the care of the iron horse and his brother of flesh and blood" would ensure that the connection between man and those beasts of steam and fire would remain strong.

Despite this apparent sentimentality, the nature of the job they did, and the training they received, meant that drivers and firemen were schooled in practicality and calmness. Drivers learnt on the job, gaining what Richard Hardy calls the "profound experience which made our enginemen such great individualists." This footplate experience would see the accumulated knowledge of locomotives, routes and best practices passed down the generations. This connected the drivers of the first commercially operated steam locomotive on the Middleton Railway in 1811 to the final BR mainline steam service on the Fifteen Guinea special in 1968 - and all in between. Immensely proud, the engine driver held a special place in the hierarchy of jobs, crafts and trades that made up the structure of the old working class and the industries they worked in. There would be some useful instruction for the new driver or fireman from the Inspector or the Shedmaster, but these abstract words in the ear would only become solid knowledge when tested in the real world. There were books and pamphlets that were required reading. The GWR even ran Mutual Improvement Classes for its young enginemen that ran from 1893 right up until the end of steam, on what was by then the BR Western Region, in 1968. Indeed, railway men were known as voracious readers.

The above pre-eminent training method, and the dangerous nature of a job where everyone relied on each other for safety, meant that small personal gestures were important. There is a vast body of work written by railwaymen about their experiences as they progressed through the industry, from engine cleaner to fireman to driver, and these fascinating books and diaries give an insight into those everyday gestures. Richard Hardy's story about a fellow engineman, an old hand called Bill who would come to work with his pockets stuffed with fruit, is a good example of the gentle dynamics at play between those with experience and those hoping to learn. On their route Bill informed Richard that they would be taking on water from the water-troughs between the rails (an operation carried out whilst moving at 50 mph) and that he should wait for his shout before pulling the lever. At the ready, and no doubt anxious, Hardy waited and waited as they approached the troughs and then ran over them - no instruction came so Hardy took the initiative and pulled the lever. "Bill turned his kindly if quizzical face towards me as the lever locked solid and the tank overflowed, water (and coal) cascading down onto the footplate..." As he cleaned up the mess, soaked to the skin and his feet wet, the already "wiser young man" was turned to by Bill who said: "Never mind Richard, you'll know better next time".

Away from the assistance of the shed, on a network that had to keep moving, the problem solving experience of the "practical men" of the railway, known by its members as the "Great Brotherhood of Railwaymen," was essential. All of this created a certain type of person with a certain type of disposition. Such a man is Jones the Steam.

Dai Station the station master represented another sphere of railway life - that of rules and, as Dai never tires of reminding Jones, "regulations." The railways gave our nation a universal standard time that was centrally determined, dispensing with the age old system that relied on local sunrise and sunset. All this was done to "afford the maximum speeding-up effect", as CJ Allen calls it, and create a punctual and smooth running railway. Methods that emanated from the busiest stations and lines formed the standard practices and rules of the railway and, although the officious observance of them by Dai on his sleepy branch line seems laughable, that was the reality on even the smallest of small railways.

Rules were there for a reason and had to be followed, even if the railway was bought by a "silly" aristocrat called Mrs Porty - as was the unfortunate fate of the Merioneth and Llantisilly Railway Traction Company Limited. There is something deeply sad about this collision between the long strictly observed regulations of the Merioneth and Llantisilly Railway Traction Company Limited and its new ad hoc reality under Mrs Porty. Her drunkenness and use of the railway to transport hats sent down from London sits in bleak opposition to the ordered, sensible world of Dai and

Jones. But at least her intervention kept the line from closure!

The pathos evoked by this particular storyline in *Ivor the Engine* speaks of the changing national landscape at the time. Numerous old industries were being stripped of their once respected status, as a lack of investment combined with longterm inefficiency and new competition to force them to the brink. The consequences of these changes were often quite brutal for those whose lives were turned upside down. However, these changes, and the rationalisation they brought about, did provide inspiration and impetus for all kinds of creative responses that included film, television, and literature and the emergence of the preservation and industrial heritage movements.

In 1953 the film *The Titfield Thunderbolt* was one such response and, in its own way, it explored the collisions mentioned above. Inspired by the story of the world's first volunteer run heritage railway, the Talyllyn (again in Wales), *The Titfield Thunderbolt* follows a town's desperate bid to keep their branch line open. More pantomimic than *Ivor the Engine* in the way it tackles the drama, this excellent Ealing Studios comedy offers its own charming insights into the lengths that people would go to to try and save their lines from the faceless men at the Ministry of Transport - often with shambolic results.

The archetypes of Jones and Dai are augmented by an ensemble of beautifully realised local figures, representing the various strands of a society that lingered on, even in the 1950s and 1960s. Each of these, in their own way, shed light on different aspects of the time. Mrs Porty, the very rich, very silly old lady whose paternalistic interventions saved foxes from the huntsman and Ivor's line from closure, is the quintessentially eccentric and independent spirit of provincial Britain. The particular story line in which Mrs Porty buys the railway echoes the real circumstances of at least one of the little railways of Wales as well as the fears that many on the railways felt at the time. Aside from the threat of closure that government control meant, many saw British Railways, with its new national livery and standardised practices, as replacing their own superior way of doing things that had been honed over decades of inter-company rivalry. Each of the railway companies were fiercely independent. That independence reflected a multiplicity of complex relationships that included the individual roles of people within each organisation and the interactions between different railway regions within the country. The ghost of those old firms remained long into nationalisation, surviving in some aspects right up until the railways were privatised and re-fragmented between 1994 and 1997. The BR regions, as the component parts of the rail network became known after 1947, each fought to maintain their own particular identities. Despite demands for standardisation across the land, to bring down costs and increase efficiencies, idiosyncrasies remained. The most obvious of these, and a continuation of the Great Western Railway's unique strategies, was the Western Region's pursuit of diesel hydraulic locomotion when the rest of the network invested in diesel electrics.

As tempting as it is to be misty eyed about a long lost Britain of old heavy industries, for those who lived and worked with technologies that, by the 1950s, were considered obsolete in other western countries, life was often tough and fairly short. Workplace accidents were commonplace and, if you weren't killed or rendered incapable of work by being crushed, having a limb severed or burned, it was possible that the toxic environment you worked in could prove debilitating in the longer term.

Mr Dinwiddy, the insane gold miner in *Ivor the Engine*, represents the consequences of a lifetime digging for gold. It may be that his odd and curmudgeonly demeanour is simply a result of the isolation of his trade, but it is more likely that his madness is a result of using mercury to purify his gold. Rather like the hatters of old, whose chronic mercury poisoning resulted in symptoms including pathological shyness, irritability, mania and hallucinations, gold miners were often seen as being mad. Although there was speculation that these mental conditions were brought on by the disappointment at not finding gold, it is certain that they were a direct result of processing ores. Replaced by the equally toxic cyanide in larger scale industrial mining, artisanal and small scale mines in developing nations continue to use mercury to this day. In this process mercury is mixed with gold containing materials and then heated until the mercury vaporises, leaving the gold behind. In this country the 1897 Workmen's Compensation Act failed to acknowledge or make provision for industrial diseases, but this was remedied in 1906 when poisoning by mercury, lead, phosphorus and arsenic were listed. Unfortunately, the Workmen's Compensation Act didn't mean the process was banned and workers continued to be exposed to these materials, even after 1948 when the Industrial Injuries Advisory Council was established.

Dinwiddy, self employed, artisanal and beyond the remit and protection of company or state, is a remnant of an older form of small scale industrial activity. He "knows something about rock", claims to be "educated", and his cleverly engineered though not always useful contraptions suggest that this bearded eccentric has a secret life beyond the dark, grime and insanity of his goldmine. Dinwiddy is every bit the alchemist/scientist of yore: a man who conducts secret experiments in an out-of-the-way place. In this way he connects with a magical past long before the industrial revolution, before even the 8th century when philosophy and proto-science mingled to create a tradition that spread across the ancient trade routes of Europe, North Africa and

Asia. The chrysopoeia or transmutation of base metals into gold, the creation of the elixir of immortality, panaceas capable of curing any disease and alkahest, a solvent capable of dissolving every other substance, were the elusive goals of the dark and ancient practice known as alchemy, which began in Egypt before 330 BC. At its core was the erroneous belief that all metals were made up of mercury and sulphur and that any metal could be created from another by varying the proportions of the noxious substances. Although Dinwiddy was rich, with piles of gold about the place, he never spent his wealth on anything apart from numerous pairs of boots. He was mad, but with good reason.

The mention of ancient practices and beliefs brings us to the next main character in *Ivor the Engine*, Idris the Welsh dragon. In Celtic myths dragons were believed to exist in a parallel reality, and the paths they took were important to the lines and flow of Ley energy. An abiding symbol of Wales, the first recorded mention of the dragon as being connected to the country was in the *Historia Brittonum* of AD 828. The dragon also forms the ancient battle standard of Wales and was linked by Geoffrey of Monmouth to the Arthurian legends in his *Historia Regum Britanniae* of 1129.

Idris appears when his egg hatches in Ivor's firebox (much to Dai Station's alarm) and thenceforward the activities of Jones, Ivor and friends are taken up trying to find a place for Idris to live. A home for Idris is found in Smoke Hill, which is either a small volcano or, as is more likely, a smouldering coal spoil heap of the kind that occurred when waste mining materials were piled up. These spoil tips or slag heaps often contained high levels of hydrocarbon materials which would spontaneously combust and cause underground fires. Looking every bit like a volcano, coal tip fires were still a common sight in the Welsh valleys, even in the 1950s. Extinguishing them was dangerous and difficult so they were usually left to burn themselves out. When Smoke Hill finally burns itself out the Antiquarian Society, who prove to be rather mercurial in their attitudes, hatch an ambitious plan to pipe gas to the hill to keep it heated. Eventually, however, the mood of the Antiquarians changes again, when Idris's offspring attack a statue of Saint George. As a result the dragons are forced to join Mr Dinwiddy deep underground where it is hot, even without piped and metered gas.

Another subterranean and unearthly force, the dragons in *Ivor the Engine* are essentially benign but brave creatures who signify yet another collision between the old and the new - between external and internal forces. Their attack on the statue of St George, launched because they believe they are saving one of their own from being slain, encapsulates the age old struggle between local tradition and the interference of outsiders. When threatened by the Antiquarian Society, who rather ironically label the dragons as a menace incompatible with the standards of modern society because of their attack on an old statue, the townsfolk close ranks to protect this ultimate symbol of Welshness. Unfortunately, because of this clash the dragons, who until then had been part of the wider community and even members of the local methodist choir, are forced into hiding.

Ivor the Engine is shot through with acute moments of pathos as it explores the passing of things and the sad futility of resisting change. Even as the townsfolk fight back against the forces of modernisation, there is a sense of delayed inevitability. When the dragons flee underground they do so as fugitives from the march of progress and the ignorance it fosters. When Mrs Porty buys the Merioneth and Llantisilly Railway Traction Company Limited her intervention is overshadowed by her age, her eccentricity and by the fact that a railway without a purpose, beyond the delivery of new hats, is a railway doomed to die. Of course there are small jobs to be done and there are still victories to be had over the forces of change, but the abiding sense is of an era ended and of time running out.

The character of Ivor, the steam engine who lies at the heart of the programme, reflects the bleak conundrum behind the railway's ongoing existence. Forlorn and filled with pathos and melancholy Ivor is aware of the many limits his life and existence have placed on him. In some ways it is as if his situation, that of being almost redundant, like one of the many workers from heavy industry - those who were laid off or put on short working as the economic realities of the post war world bit - gave him more time to dwell on his circumstances.

In a clever reverse of the usual situation, which sees human beings anthropomorphising railway engines, Ivor is sentient, self-aware and, most of all, desperate to be considered human. He wants to be part of the choir, an activity that is used by Postgate and Firmin to define community and togetherness, and when the townsfolk go to the seaside he wants to splash in the sea like everyone else. But alas his circumstances are fundamentally defined by the fire in his firebox (which makes the steam to bring him to life) and the rails up which he runs. The trip to the seaside encapsulates and delineates his limitations: special rails have to laid to allow him to get to the sea; when he goes into the sea his joy is curtailed when the water puts his fire out.

Both the choir (and its associations with Methodism) and the day trip were cornerstones of working class community life before World War Two. As improved living standards and the march of the consumer society meant that communal spaces, like the chapel and the pub, and mass holidays taken by train, were replaced with the sitting room and travel by car, the individual became preeminent. Indeed, Ivor was in effect marooned, clinging desperately to a past way of living that, at the time, was becoming increasingly irrelevant.

Between 1959 and 1975, when the films were remade in colour, there was a huge reduction in the rail network. Two reports by Dr Richard Beeching, 1963's *The Reshaping of Britain's Railways* and 1965's *The Development of the Major Railway Trunk Routes,* signalled a massive change in the way railways served the country. The initial report recommended that a massive 30% of all route miles be axed. This project was presented as a necessary response to the challenge posed by increased car ownership, bus use and an expanding road haulage sector. Motorways were being built and the old, winding A and B road network was being rapidly upgraded. The very nature of British society was changing as modernisation and shifts in how and where people lived undid long established patterns of life and old heavy industries gave way to high tech and service sector jobs.

The cast of *Ivor the Engine*, the local figures, the life of the town and the world the railway represented was one last backward glance at a society that was rapidly disappearing. Both in the media and in the world of academia, particularly in Britain's vibrant university sociology departments, the changes that were occurring caused consternation. Writers like Jeremy Seabrook and Brian Jackson recorded and commented on the dislocation and destruction that was being wrought. The new "material sufficiency", as Seabrook put it, produced a kind of "materialism... that hurts" - where "the competition for all this plenitude and beauty leads to great cruelty; and everywhere the talk is of violence, loneliness, family breakdown, mental illness, racism, the spoiling of human relationships." For him, through his studies, the great loss in all this change was that of human relationships. 93% of the population may have been able to watch television by the 1970s but for many the glowing box in the corner represented just another symptom of an alienated society where the superficial appeal of consumerism had supplanted deeper and more important human needs.

The country was evolving and changing but this change was untidy and rather chaotic. As the railways buckled beneath Beeching's axe and various other plans that disguised cuts as modernisation, the future of travel, which had long beckoned in the shape of the motorcar and the coach, was still an awkward pill to swallow for many people.

Post-war government policies, including steel supply rationing, that encouraged manufacturers to export the majority of cars produced were relaxed in the early years of the 1950s. On the customer side a two year moratorium on reselling, which had kept the price of second hand vehicles artificially high, was also relaxed.

For a time the British car industry had things all its own way and was able to rely on its traditional markets both at home and abroad to boost balance sheets. With the exception of Ford of Britain and General Motors, most car production was British owned in 1952. These two American companies accounted for around 29% of the market. At this time Ford offered consumers a range of models. Their top marque was the roomy and powerful six cylinder, 2.2 litre Zephyr with its modern steering column gear change and exotic styling based on the Detroit built Ford Tudor Custom. Intermediate models on offer were the Consul, the Prefect, down to the Popular and the Anglia models. At the start of the 1950s the General Motors owned Vauxhall offered the Wyvern and the Velox. Later, Vauxhall launched the Viva in 1963, a small family car aimed squarely at the promising market held by the Ford Anglia and the Morris Minor.

As the constraints caused by post war austerity were slowly loosened the challenge represented by Ford and

Vauxhall to British owned motor manufacturing was met when Lord Nuffield, latterly known as William Morris and the founder of Morris Motors Limited, merged Morris with the Austin Motor Company to create the British Motor Corporation. At its creation in 1953 the new BMC encompassed an impressive array of familiar marques, such as Morris, Austin, Wolseley, Riley and MG, and accounted for 40% of the British car market. Other British owned volume car makers at this time were Standard-Triumph and Rootes.

For all the burgeoning choice of products produced by these companies, their offerings were still beyond the reach of ordinary people, with 86% of the population having no access to a car at the start of the 1950s. Although growth in the ownership of cars accelerated through the 1960s, as that decade came to an end around 40% of households still had no access to a car.

As rail services were cut back the buses, which had been an important and growing part of the transport mix since before the war, did not fill the gaps. In 1952 42% of all passenger miles travelled were made by bus, but over subsequent years, in areas outside London, this figure would fall dramatically: 12.7 billion journeys were made by bus in 1950, falling to 9.7 billion in 1968 as car ownership increased. As with the railways, this falling demand would put pressure on the financial viability of bus services. But the proceeds from economic growth were spread unevenly in a Britain still plagued by an inequality of opportunity and riven by petty class prejudices, leaving a significant portion of the population without a shiny Ford Anglia on their driveway, or even a driveway at all.

The move to a consumer economy was not without its perils and, as successive governments would find, shifting and competing demands were not always easy to deal with. Once people had access to the purchasing power to buy the cars, the fridges and the washing machines, simply shutting off the wage/credit faucet could not be easily done - even if circumstances seemed to dictate it. When the economy was given a boost due to the Korean War (1950 - 1953), the Labour government of the day deployed budgetary measures to 'soak up' the purchasing power. This era of full employment was accompanied by pay restraint across the economy, but the government's management of demand by allowing prices to rise brought a sudden and massive spike in wage demands. A couple of years later, in 1955, the Conservative government's industrial investment boom would cause further problems when the economy, with demand running ahead of capacity, ran too hot. The chancellor of the time, Rab Butler, followed his predecessor's lead and controlled the cost of living through a rise in purchasing tax. There were also mechanisms introduced that were designed to slow or halt the pace of capital investment occurring at the time. These measures worked and became a hallmark of that government's policies over the next few years. Between 1955 and 1958 wages rose by a staggering 14%. This inflationary spike was followed by a run on sterling in 1957 and a recession in 1958, though this was a result of a global recession. Over the same period industrial output stalled and prices rose by 9%. Alongside this the manufacturing/industrial sectors stopped making the capital investment that would have allowed them to compete with the growing challenge from a resurgent Germany and Japan.

Research by Peter Scott and James Walker has shown that, at least for the Conservative government of the late 1950s and early 1960s, these intermittent policies were aimed primarily at re-establishing sterling as an international currency and the City of London as a preeminent global trading centre. With a mix of high purchase tax rates of around 66% and a tightening on the availability of credit, demand was squeezed - with disastrous consequences for the ordinary people, jobs and the domestic consumer durables industries.

The City and the banking sector were resuscitated by these moves, but given that much of the post war global economy was set to revolve around the development and manufacture of products for a new breed of consumer the policies that facilitated this do seem rather short-sighted. Indeed, it seems strange that at a time when much of the talk was about an emerging home centred affluence that would straddle the class divide, the twin motors of that paradigm, domestic manufacturing and domestic consumption, should be so carelessly squandered.

Abstract ideas with real world consequences, that saw the Trade Union movement painted as the bogey man or accused the boss class of mismanaging the economy, were all part of the daily nationwide discourse at the time. However, amongst it all, the rising prices and an economic model that increasingly placed expensive purchases at the heart of people's lives would, inevitably, have an impact. In 1950 the number of days lost was 1,389,000, but by 1960 this number was nearer 3,000,000. Ten years later, in 1970, the number had jumped to 10,980,000 and would climb to 23,909,000 by 1972. An increasingly polarised debate, founded on deeply entrenched, historic positions that placed division and mistrust between the classes at the heart of national life, fed into the decisions being made and how they were received. Despite all Britain's claims to being a modern state, perhaps, when it came down to it, very little had really changed since the dawn of the railway age.

Chapter Two

Mary, Mungo and Midge and the New Jerusalem

With its almost utopian vision of modern urban living John Ryan's 1969 animation *Mary, Mungo and Midge* was groundbreaking. Until then most children's television programmes were set in pastoral locations, reflecting an escapist ideal of the magic of childhood.

Mary, Mungo and Midge live in a modern tower block amidst a well ordered landscape of paved areas, manicured trees and carefully tended flowerbeds. All around, beyond the environs of the high-rise, is the townscape, a panorama of buildings and bustling streets which, although crowded, is presented as being benign. Mary is a little latchkey kid, Mungo is her dog and, ignoring the obvious implications a rodent infestation might have in such a building, Midge is a feral mouse who likes to play on the gas stove.

The animations were made using Ryan's own real-time technique that he called 'captions'. Involving exquisitely drawn backgrounds, onto which were laid equally beautiful cardboard cutout characters, the whole thing was controlled by a series of levers. His drawing style, now more popularly known through his *Captain Pugwash* animations, is crisp and features mildly compressed and distorted shapes in a nod to the aesthetics of modernist art. These were accompanied by a wonderful score, composed by Johnny Pearson of Pye Records' easy listening group Sounds Orchestral.

Each episode is essentially made up of set piece celebrations of modern living. Be it the local shops, the health service, the postal service, or any of those other munificent organs of a well-functioning civic society that we used to enjoy, everything is clean and functions efficiently.

Even the lifts in the tower-block work and don't smell of piss. With its steady yet authoritative narration, by the much loved BBC newsreader Richard Baker, *Mary, Mungo and Midge* resembles a work of propaganda, designed to promote the rehousing and urban renewal schemes of Britain's post war governments.

Episode one of the series is called 'The Crane' and sets up *Mary, Mungo and Midge* as both a celebration and record of the times, capturing on the way the essence of the entire thirteen episodes. As the psychedelic folk influenced jaunt of the opening theme fades away we are presented with a built up skyline. Here the new shapes of the modern town block dominate as Richard Baker opines: "A town is full of buildings, some tall, some short, some wide and some narrow." The camera pans down the side of a sleek white high-rise, set next to its identical twin, edifices of modernity above quaint pitched roofs and a funny old clock tower. Baker continues in the measured manner of a public service announcement, laying out the elements that make up the town with its streets that have many "cars and buses and lorries driving along them." The place before us is sizeable, with a river along the banks of which signs of old industry are visible like ships and boats, warehouses and dock cranes. We are then told that "there is a bridge across the river, so that the cars and buses and lorries can get to the other side" and that "the cars and buses and streets are full of people." Against this image is set, in clear contrast, the place where Mary, Mungo and Midge live: a spacious, well lit, modern place, uncluttered and uncrowded with lots of grass, trees and flowers.

Looking from their top floor view point the trio take in the panorama of the town below and see the signs of progress in a crane on a building site where new concrete flats are under construction. This is inspired by scenes that anyone would recognise in Britain in the 1960s and it is presented as a propaganda of the new. In this first episode, where Mungo and Midge (and let's not comment on the contortions necessary to see such a place as suitable for exploration) go and play on a building site, the propagators and purveyors of the high-rise revolution, the crane itself and the workmen who work on the building, are cast as funny and benign figures, but also as important parts of the life of a growing city. The message is simple: the modern tower blocks that dominate the skyline are the future and that future is good.

Whether deliberate or not, by 1969, propaganda could not have been more necessary as the image of this new build Jerusalem had become severely damaged in the eyes of the public due to a variety of complex factors. The upheaval caused, as long established communities were swept away under the ever expanding remit of slum clearance and road building, meant that strong bonds that had grown up over decades around work, the street, or down the local pub were replaced by disparate, hermetically sealed existences that brought with them a feeling of alienation. This issue was further compounded by the use of shoddy building techniques and poor materials, particularly on those estates built from 1960 onwards. *Mary Mungo and Midge* is a peculiarly succinct snapshot of an era when the establishment still viewed the aggressive modernising agenda that spawned urban motorways and brutalist, high-rise, high density housing as a panacea for the nation's ills. Its simplicity and modernist feel invokes the optimism many still felt about these solutions. At the same time, however, within the premise of the show, and through the course of the stories told, there are also troubling indicators of many of the problems that beset Britain's cities and those who lived in them at the end of the 1960s.

Like all planned utopias, the world Mary, Mungo and Midge inhabit is pulled at by subtle and disquieting currents that bubble away just beneath the shiny, well ordered surface. Mary is a latchkey kid who has to rely on her pets for companionship, apparently never seeing her parents. Her forays into the world beyond juxtapose the arm's length, immaculate and well-ordered safety of the block and the environs around her flat with the picture beyond, where everything is chaotic, threateningly close and looming dangerously large. It's not quite Ballard's *High-Rise* or *Concrete Island*, but the remoteness of her existence chimes, in the subtlest of ways, with many of the concerns writers like Brian Jackson and Richard Hoggart were examining at the time. The old high street, beyond the well-groomed precincts and clean lines of the tower block development, is still there, but due to the congestion and bustle, as well as the old fashioned appearance of the shops and buildings, it looks rather antiquated and, as a result, doomed. For the young viewer the choice presented seems stark: Which would you prefer? Open grassy spaces with trees and flowers, free from the danger of traffic? Or busy roads and crowded streets full of strangers?

The changes wrought upon the national landscape in the forty years after World War Two were huge. As the British economy struggled to both rebuild and modernise itself governments of both political hues intervened with varying degrees of success. These interventions had significant implications for the built environment and on the daily lives of ordinary people. Where people lived, where they shopped and how they went to work - nothing was left untouched by the changes.

When Conservative Prime Minister Harold Macmillan commissioned the report *The Reshaping of British Railways* (The Beeching Report) in 1960 he called for a rail industry "of a size and pattern suited to modern conditions and prospects". More fundamentally he stipulated that the railways should be got into a shape so that they were no longer reliant on state subsidies and could operate at a profit. This reshaping of the rail network dovetailed perfectly with moves, begun by Macmillan's government during the 1950s, to establish a national motorway network, foster growth in the independent haulage sector and encourage private car ownership. It would also integrate with nationwide slum clearance schemes and plans to reinvigorate tired local economies through urban renewal and redevelopment of town and city centres. Change on this scale had not been seen since the heady days of railway mania, almost one hundred years before.

It is almost impossible, looking back, to conceive of the tremendous scope and scale of railway infrastructure, and in particular the amount of space taken up in the immediate environs of town and city centres across the land. Acres were given over to all manner of facilities needed to service the railway and its associated economy. In Leeds, a stone's throw from the main banking street of Park Lane and the city's late Victorian municipal show piece of City Square, a vast swathe of land was given over to railway activity. These sprawling facilities, which had grown up as need dictated, ranged from main railway stations (three of them), goods and marshalling yards, parcel depots, sidings and engine sheds. From when they were built in the mid nineteenth century, right up until the end of the 1960s, places like this represented the beating heart of the nation's transport economy. In the decades to come, after the rationalisation and modernisation of the 1960s, this area and those adjacent would see massive change as soot stained buildings and coal and oil blackened earth was reinvented as prime real estate, given over to small businesses, corporate office space and retail.

Perhaps the biggest driver for these changes was the advent of the major road scheme. Acting on local landscapes with the same ruthless and destructive efficiency that had seen the railway rise to primacy in the nineteenth century, the motorway building program changed the face of Britain and the lives of its citizens forever.

It may be surprising to discover that plans were drawn up for a national motorway network as early as 1902. However, in what seems like a familiar tale for modern Britain, it took fifty-six years for the first eight and a quarter mile section to open. Plans for this stretch of road, located near Preston, were first drawn up in 1937 as part of a cross county motorway project and, once World War Two was over, planning permission was approved by Lancashire County Council in the mid-1940s. By 1952, due to the economic constraints of the post war era the scheme had evolved and shrunk to become a bypass scheme designed to alleviate traffic congestion in Lancaster and Preston.

Preston represents a useful archetype for many British towns and cities. Transformed during the nineteenth century because of the rapid expansion of cotton mills in the town (in no small part due to the invention of Arkwright's water powered spinning frame in the town), the population had swelled to 120,000 in 1901 from a base of 11,000 just a century before. Once known as 'Proud Preston' and recognised in the eighteenth century for being a 'pretty town' with an 'abundance of gentry', by 1901 it had developed a reputation for squalor and filth. Although filth and squalor were commonplace in Britain at the time it is worth noting that, in spite of the construction of a partial sewer system in the years after 1870, a significant portion of Preston's townsfolk still relied on earth or pail closets. This practice, which went by the charming name 'the Rochdale system', involved a bucket into which the user would defecate. The offending mound would then be sprinkled with earth, covering it until it was emptied by the local corporation's night soil man. Again, these rather medieval arrangements were not unique to Preston and could be found right across the country. Over the Pennines, in Leeds, it is believed that, even as late as 1870, there were some 30,000 non flushing earth closets or privies - each one contributing to the great many piles of human dung, known as middensteads, which could be found on the streets of the city. A particularly notorious Leeds middenstead was found in the Kirkgate area of the city, in Wellington Yard: measuring twenty one feet long, six feet wide and six feet deep, it is reputed to have claimed the life of a local drunk who, worse for wear, fell in.

At this time streets were rarely paved. What drainage there was relied on surface run off to carry away the pungent and unhealthy combination of human and animal faeces, and by-products of industrial activity that occurred in towns and cities at the time. In most places this included waste from slaughterhouses, dye works, tanneries and various small scale industrial processes, such as foundries and chemical works.

People lived close by to where they found employment, with ramshackle and overcrowded housing often thrown up cheaply and quickly. From these overcrowded settlements a river of filth would flow, washed by rainfall, into the rivers and water courses. With this in mind it is of little surprise that, in 1831, Britain suffered a major cholera epidemic, the first of many such outbreaks to occur throughout the nineteenth century. Fresh, clean water was a rarity and the few public water pumps that there were were often contaminated. As knowledge and understanding of the transmission of cholera grew throughout the century sewer systems were built and expanded alongside a greater provision of separately piped drinking water. However, for the majority of the population the provision of flushing toilets meant communal toilets, housed in blocks, that served several properties. By their very nature these were anything but sanitary.

By 1958 Preston was backed up in an altogether different way. With the town's streets clogged by cars and lorries accidents were numerous. The part motorway-come-bypass, which was completed in that year, was designed to solve this growing problem, but it also acted as a test bed for construction techniques and materials. Ironically, as the nation embraced the shiny new age of petroleum, it would be the dirty legacy of old king coal to which it turned for its physical foundations. In a piece of admirable thrift they alighted on burnt red shale colliery waste as a suitable sub-base for the new roads. This rather noxious material was in abundant supply from the large, smouldering spoil heaps that scarred the landscape of areas where coal had once been mined.

Unfortunately for the Preston road builders the stuff they used may have been in plentiful supply but it did not behave as expected. The hills of shale selected had been doused with water during World War Two to prevent their glowing embers being used as beacons for Luftwaffe bombers. These partially burnt shales, and the unusually heavy rains during the autumn of 1956 when the road's foundations were being built, resulted in the sub-base becoming saturated. It became a quagmire and almost impossible to work with. The knock on effect of this was to delay the entire project by a further six expensive months. Valuable lessons were learned about the procedures for selecting sub-base materials which would then be applied to subsequent projects.

The Preston scheme was the result of Sir James Drake's *Road Plan for Lancashire* which formed part of a county wide plan to kickstart the region's economy. Traffic and accident surveys were produced which meant that each facet of the plan had an evidentiary justification. This would be particularly helpful when objections were raised to the plan. Another important factor in the success of this and subsequent motorway projects was the Special Roads Act of 1949. This created conditions, specific to motorways, that meant that, unlike normal roads, only specified vehicles could use it; pedestrians, bicycles, horse and carts, steam traction engines and tractors would not be permitted on the new high speed network. Also all other roads would be subordinate and could be closed, moved or diverted if their routes conflicted with that of the motorway. Another important aspect of this Act stipulated that there would be no sewers, water mains, gas mains, or electricity cables laid under these routes. Motorways would never suffer from the rows of cones and cordoned off lanes that blighted your average road.

As the 1950s drew to a close the heavy machinery of the construction gangs was at work across the country. Over the coming years the impact on both urban and rural landscapes would be huge. A significant experiment, this network would be plagued by various teething troubles as kinks with drainage, hard shoulders etc were worked out once roads had opened.

The first phase of the M1, between Watford and Rugby, opened in late 1959, with the Rugby to Leeds section opening, by way of a series of extensions, between 1965 and 1968. The M1 terminated at Leeds, but in 1972 a further additional stretch was added that took the road into central Leeds. Here it linked up with what was called the Leeds South Eastern Motorway, now the M621, a spur that came from the M62 west to east trans-Pennine motorway that linked Liverpool to Hull via Manchester. The M62 was opened, as with other motorways, in stages between 1971 and 1976.

Again Leeds provides a useful example of the dramatic impact motorways and their construction had on communities. The M1 ploughed through the working class and industrial area of Hunslet on the south side of the city, dividing a proud and cohesive community in a way it never fully recovered from. Part of Hunslet Moor, an open space that had served as a cornerstone of local life, was sacrificed. The adjacent neighbourhood of Holbeck was also bludgeoned by the arrival of this asphalt and concrete invader. In his book *A Local Habitation* the Leeds born writer Richard Hoggart described the motorway as "cutting a huge swathe through" the area.

Even to this day, beneath all the now mature trees and greenery that was planted hide the scar, it is still possible to the see the impact this piece of planning had on the community. Cleaved in two, these old locales had their history and complex cultures scattered and broken. With almost symbolic callousness this slab of road fetched up right on the doorstep of Hunslet Engine Works, the home of one the world's most famous steam engine manufacturers.

The motorway planners would make a practical use of another aspect of the railway age's recently decommissioned legacy. As the M1 entered the city from a large interchange at Stourton it followed the route of the former Great Northern Railway Hunslet East to Beeston Junction line, crossing an earlier 1755 coal tramway that connected the Middleton New Pit to the River Aire. This use of a convenient alignment and the steady gradients of its track bed would see yet more of the past erased. The use of this route reduced the amount of buildings that needed to be knocked down. However, from there the M1 ploughed through an area of high density terraced housing and industry, with 400 homes and 600 industrial and business premises, by way of embankments, concrete bridges and cuttings. This was seen as being part and parcel of the slum clearances and regeneration of this area.

Unfortunately the combination of these two factors meant that Hunslet and Holbeck suffered from years of planning blight. As we shall see later on in this chapter Hunslet would continue to be plagued by negative planning decisions.

Leeds had built back to back terraced houses longer than other local authorities and as a result possessed a huge stock of this kind of property. These high numbers may have had a bearing on the city's decision to develop its pioneering "Leeds Method" in the 1950s and 1960s. Through this grants were used to improve and prolong the life of older housing. Despite this unusual and, as it turns out, fortuitous piece of accidental foresight, Leeds still demolished large tracts of back to back terraced housing.

In an attempt to alleviate problems with noise from traffic Leeds City Council used a clause in the Leeds Corporation Act to acquire, by compulsory purchase, land on either side of the motorway route. This was then piled up with banks and hills in a form of landscaping that was grassed over and planted with trees. A strange and spectacular result of these earthworks was an unnaturally high and pointed hill that, from certain angles, resembles a single giant's burial mound. The use of the clause, from the Leeds Corporation Act, did not go unnoticed in Whitehall and the "Leeds Clause" was subsequently incorporated into the Highway Act and used to great effect across the land when roads needed hiding from those people not travelling on them.

There were some for whom the arrival of the motorway had positive consequences: residents of Old Run Road were pleased to see the long established spoil heap of a quarter of a million tons of colliery waste relocated from around their homes and redeployed to make embankments on the motorway. This waste was a legacy of the area's industrial past. Mining had a long history in the area, beginning in the

Middle Ages when coal was extracted using shallow bell pits and adits, before expanding into full blown colliery working in the late eighteenth century. In 1758 the Middleton Railway, the oldest continuously working railway in the land, was established by Act of Parliament. Whether by design or accident, coal production ended in the area with the closure of Broom Pit in 1968, just before the motorways arrived.

As the M1 approached the fate of the Middleton Railway looked to be in the balance. It had become a preserved railway in 1960, the first standard gauge railway to be taken over and run by volunteers. Established by an Act of Parliament, but not part of the nationalised network, the legend goes that this unusual status meant it could not be as easily swept away under the provisions of the Special Roads Act. Incredibly, a tunnel for the railway was incorporated into the motorway plans. Middleton Railway still operates to this day.

Other parts of the nation's railway and industrial revolution heritage did give themselves up to the new transport revolution. As well as following existing alignments of railway lines the motorways around Leeds also used burnt and unburnt shale, as well as ballast and embankment material from disused railways in the area. Another large amount of colliery waste, built up over the decades from the Middleton workings, was moved and used to fill the disused Gildersome railway tunnel. In time the hole that was left was backfilled with landfill waste. Gases from this huge dumping exercise continued to be burned off well into the 1990s, long after the site closed.

The pattern of line closures followed by the use of these alignments for motorway construction was repeated across the country. From a distance of fifty years it is easy to forget what a shift this represented, with so many things, from long held jobs to old familiar landmarks, disappearing over the course of a few short years. The residents of Old Run Road may well have celebrated their new and open vista, replacing an unsightly spoil heap, but elsewhere, viaducts, bridges, stations and tunnels were closed and quickly demolished before the blades of bulldozers tore up the land. Often the promised freedoms of the open road were, for those who lived in the communities blighted by this seismic modal shift, a distant if not impossible dream.

Original planning for the motorways may have begun as far back as 1902, but once the process began, in whichever locality it occurred, the changes happened with shocking speed and violence. Often communities would find that the removal of the stopping service or the closure of the local station and its line would have profound social and economic consequences. But it wasn't just about cold hard numbers. In purely emotional terms railway workers and passengers alike found the sudden loss of things that so seemed eternal, an immutable part of the landscape, difficult to accept or get over. Aside from the sentimental, however, the reasons to fear the loss of rail services were significant: in the mid-1960s 66% of UK households were still without a car. Of course there were buses available, but these services struggled to cope with the rapid expansion in demand. For those seeking to travel further afield, the main rail arteries were in still situ, but the network of lines and stations that used to feed them were no longer there.

At this time the UK was engaged in a shift away from coal towards oil and electricity, with steam traction giving way to diesel on the railways (in lieu of the more expensive but preferred electrification schemes). The move to encourage private car use also formed part of other changes that were driven by an expansion of the role of consumer credit and spending in the economy. In respect of travel, the difficulties these changes presented cannot be underestimated. Car ownership rose from low levels at the start of the 1960s, when the majority of households still relied almost exclusively on public transport, to a point at the end of the 1960s where 60% of households owned a car. However, this still left some 40% for whom the motorway network represented an alien transport system that they had little use for.

Of course there were numerous reasons to attempt the shift away from coal. The smogs of the 1950s were a serious problem, not only in London, where the most famous and severe of them occurred in 1952, but across the country wherever there were major concentrations of population and industry. The primary cause of smog was domestic coal fires and prevailing local weather conditions. Another reason was a longstanding political nervousness about the power of the miners and their ability to disrupt the economic life of the nation. Also the increasing power of oil companies (and the broader petrochemicals industry) to lobby and influence government policy should not be underestimated.

Despite the disruption caused by three motorways descending on Leeds within the space of a few years there were surprisingly few objections. This may be due to the fact that the majority of works were concentrated in deprived areas of the city as much as any careful planning or former rail route utilisation. Poorer areas have less of a voice. Certainly Hunslet and Beeston were places of considerable dereliction and poverty. In a situation similar to that of their neighbours across the Pennines in Preston, these areas of Leeds, once thriving centres of heavy industry and manufacturing, had experienced a series of factory closures and job losses. Blighted by long term issues with poor productivity and competitiveness and under investment, the UK had struggled to cope with the challenges of the post war world. The warnings were there, even during the boom years immediately after the war, when Britain enjoyed almost exclusive access to the world market for manufactured goods. Systemic problems in the nation's manufacturing base, many of which were present as early as the 1870s, had been disguised due to the disruption and exertion of the two world wars. In the early 1950s half the country's working population were employed in manufacturing and our share of global manufacturing output stood at a smidgeon over one quarter. But this Indian summer was unsustainable: Germany and Japan were recovering with surprising rapidity from the destruction of the war and those once safe markets in the Empire would soon be lost as newly independent states sought out new partners.

Places like Hunslet and Beeston, along with countless others across the land, bore the brunt of these changes, as a once great tradition of manufacturing was lost and famous names, with their traditions, spirit and pride, all contributing to the cohesion of their surrounding communities, were cast upon the wind of change.

By the beginning of the 1970s areas like these were scenes of dereliction, designated for redevelopment. Housing would be marked as slums and cleared to make way for new concrete flats and long established shopping streets were demolished, replaced by precincts and wide treeless boulevards designed to move traffic swiftly. All this was part of a long term plan of traffic management and regeneration that would roll slowly forward, bringing with it new and unimagined problems.

Every town and city has its own stories of the destruction caused by insensitive planning of motorway routes, but perhaps the most famous is that of London's Ringways and its supporting radial routes. These concentric circular motorways were designed to alleviate traffic congestion on the capital's highways and were complemented by a series of spoke like arteries coming in and out of the city and connecting the orbital routes. Plans to reorganise the capital's transport originated before World War Two, in 1937, but were updated during the war years, eventually forming the basis of the road schemes of the 1960s. Three out of four of these planned orbital "Ringways" were built before cancellation of the final one was forced, in 1973, due to political pressure from action groups like Homes Before Roads and the London Motorway Action Group. Subsequently Homes Before Roads provided both a template and the banner under which motorways would be opposed across the country. Their high profile London campaign was bolstered by its intelligent and groundbreaking use of the media, expert evidence and witnesses and public meetings. This strategy was then deployed across the country and still forms the basis of grass roots campaigns against all kinds of developments.

Many aspects of the Greater London Council's transport scheme for new urban motorways proved particularly divisive. Its plan called for a massive expansion in road building and for cuts to public transport spending. One of the most infamous aspects of the scheme was the Westway, a three and half mile section of elevated dual carriageway designed to carry part of the A40 through west London from Paddington to North Kensington, shadowing the route of existing railway lines as much as possible. The public's attitude towards the new schemes quickly turned hostile, as a highhanded local authority misjudged the mood. Attempts by the GLC to promote it through facile public relations and advertising campaigns backfired spectacularly, in what is now widely known as the Westway Disaster. There was a perception that the GLC simply wanted to impose the scheme, rather than engage in meaningful consultation, leading to what John Davis describes as "the most heated anti-roads protest that London has ever seen," in the book *Civil Society in British History*. The whole scheme was seen as a disaster for the area of Ladbroke Grove and its residents. Even the British Road Federation, the normally pro road industry stakeholder body, said the Westway was "insensitive and socially unacceptable".

The disconnect between the slick brochures of the GLC's carefully orchestrated PR campaign and the reality of the Westway's construction was both sharp and vivid and served to supercharge political pressure on the way the scheme was scrutinised. The feeling grew that, after over ten years of unchecked growth, the tyranny of motorway building, where communities were either conned or completely ignored, had to be tackled. In 1969, with objections standing at 20,000, five years after the construction work on the Westway had begun, the Secretary of State for Local Government and Regional Planning, Mr Anthony Crosland, got to his feet in the Commons and announced that a special statutory inquiry would be conducted under "an independent chairman of high standing and repute". In this work he would be assisted by a panel of independent transportation experts and an independent planner. In turn these would be aided by Ministry inspectors to enable "the inquiry to be conducted efficiently, expertly and expeditiously". In addition the panel would be further assisted by "a number of outside assessors to help them probe and evaluate, fully and searchingly, the policies embodied in the plan, the objections made to them and possible alternative strategies." The Conservative shadow, in the shape of Mr. Peter Walker, welcomed this news. One year out from a general election it seemed that politicians of both political hues had finally woken up to how toxic urban motorways were.

The Greater London Development Plan was destined to wither, caught between the hard realities of politics and the unfolding economic problems of the early 1970s. However, although many of the worst aspects of a scheme that would have seen large areas of the capital sacrificed to the bulldozer were stopped, the cost was still high. Once the dust settled, many areas found themselves draped in ribbons of fast moving traffic, borne aloft on brutalist concrete flyovers or channelled on uncrossable tracts of road. Whatever the machinations, the Westway was built: "the largest continuous concrete structure in the country," as the Westway Trust, the charity established to enhance the 23 acres under the giant flyover, puts it.

After the Westway a potent mix of local and national activism, which grew out of an awareness of and a desire to protect both the built and natural environment, merged to create a potent force. Activism was catalysed by the emergence of a series of rallying points that allowed disparate community campaigns to support each other and gain momentum.

Alongside Homes Before Roads another group lent their weight to the various campaigns. This was the Victorian Society, which was founded in the late 1950s by the writer and broadcaster John Betjeman, the Countess of Rosse and a group of well-respected architects and critics that included Nikolaus Pevsner. Tasked with campaigning to preserve the best of Victorian and Edwardian era architecture, its activities overlapped with those of the Georgian Group, founded some twenty years before.

Although the Victorian Society responded to numerous threats to the nation's built heritage, it was the campaign to save Philip Hardwick's monumental Euston Arch, built in 1838 as the grand entrance to Euston Railway Station, the London terminus of Robert Stephenson's London to Birmingham Railway, that proved pivotal; it was a key moment in heritage campaigning that led to a host of new approaches to the threats facing Britain's built heritage as the country modernised. Unfortunately the Euston Arch campaign, which began in 1960 after the British Transport

Commission announced its plans to demolish the arch, was unsuccessful. Euston station lay at the heart of an ambitious modernisation programme that featured the electrification of the West Coast mainline and the long overdue replacement of lifts to Euston's underground station. This was just one part of a wider national jigsaw of upgraded trains, routes and stations. Despite a vigorous campaign fought by Betjeman and co the final die was cast when Harold MacMillan, a conservative Prime Minister whose fusty, gentlemanly image belied his thirst for all things modern, refused to back preserving the arch.

This rejection of the old was very much part of the zeitgeist of the times and characterised the approaches of MacMillan's administrations from 1957 to 1964 and Harold Wilson's governments from 1964 to 1970. Just as Wilson, as leader of the opposition, evoked the white heat of technology as a hallmark of his commitment to the new in 1963, so MacMillan was wedded to an agenda of renewal. Indeed, this ethos could be said to have pervaded the majority of those in positions of power over the public space, be they town planners, local councillors, ministers or Prime Ministers. According to Gavin Stamp, the writer and architectural historian, the Victorian era came to be seen as "dark and oppressive, at once sinister and ludicrous" with the built environment that that era bequeathed rejected in favour of "a clean, uncluttered modernity".

The reasons for this attitude are open to speculation: perhaps it was because of the trauma of two world wars and the loss of national confidence that accompanied Britain's inevitable demotion from its position of global imperial super power; perhaps it was a desire to reap the benefits of a new national outlook based on a more open, equal and democratic society; perhaps it was a hangover from the centrally planned national life that was needed to conduct the total war of World War Two; perhaps it was driven by

Keynesian and interventionist policies aimed at boosting domestic growth as a way of escaping the drag of post war austerity (despite MacMillan's apparent rejection of what he called the "doctrinaire nightmare" of socialist nationalisation and central planning); perhaps it was a rejection of the world of our forefathers, with all its various symbols. Whatever the reasoning, the broader modernising message appealed to the electorate and chimed with the nation as a whole, engendering a spirit of optimism that carried the country forward - all despite a progressively deteriorating economic outlook and systemic problems with both the domestic and global economies.

Regardless of the difficulties that would later emerge with this modernising agenda, and the opposition it faced at various turns, it certainly helped to carry the country forward for the ten years after 1957. The mantle of moderniser was one that Harold Wilson seized early and then used with great skill throughout his time as Prime Minister from 1964, until his shock defeat to Ted Heath in 1970.

On the second day of the Labour party autumn conference of 1969, in Brighton, a confident Wilson, still then seemingly at the height of his powers despite growing industrial unrest and chill winds in the global economy, issued a new clarion call to the party faithful and the nation at large. Painting a vision of a land swept clean of the clutter and detritus of a bygone age, whilst outlining and promising solutions to the problems created by increasing prosperity and consumerism, his speech offered action. "First, our environment. There is a two-fold task: to remove the scars of 19th century capitalism - the derelict mills, the spoil heaps, the back-to-back houses that still disfigure so large a part of our land. At the same time we have to make sure that the second industrial revolution through which we are now passing does not bequeath a similar legacy to future generations. We must deal with the problems of pollution - of the air, of the sea, of our rivers and beaches. We must also deal with the uniquely 20th century problems of noise and congestion which will increasingly disturb, unless checked, our urban life."

Of course the process he spoke of was already well under way and had been since the decade before, but his use of it shows just how much political leverage these themes still had. Where once the emphasis had been on the white heat of technology and the ineluctable forces of modernisation, a new message was emerging that talked of removing scars and healing disfiguration, evoking already popular themes of the environment, of legacy and a world bequeathed to future generations. This, in terms of rhetoric at least, speaks of change made for very different reasons. In doing this Wilson sought to co-opt the momentum of protest movements like Homes Before Roads whilst also, perhaps rather cynically, projecting back the consequences that any resistance might have onto those protesting. Also by his use of such pejorative language when speaking of surviving vestiges of nineteenth century capitalism Wilson also sought to reject any block that preservation might place on progress. It was a skilful move. You can see why the Conservative Party, and Ted Heath in particular, saw him as a tricky political operator.

The strategy known as slum clearance was not new in 1969 when Harold Wilson called for removal of the disfiguration that was back-to-back houses.

In the years after World War One slum clearance programmes were triggered by a mixture of political expediency and genuine welfare concerns, as the country struggled to make good on promises made to working people during the conflict. The spectre of political unrest and the very real fear of communist revolution certainly focussed the minds of Britain's ruling elites.

In the years before the 1914 to 1918 hostilities the great majority of new housing in towns and cities was built by private builders; however, after the hiatus of the war years the peace brought with it a new social paradigm. Prime Minister Lloyd George promised 'homes fit for heroes' and there was a concerted national push to build decent quality properties that could be rented at affordable rents.

Perhaps the most significant piece of legislation was the 1919 Addison Act which tasked local councils with the job of providing homes. This sprang from a series of social changes, most notably the Tudor Walters Report, that can possibly trace their initial impetus to the Garden City movement and principles, established by Ebenezer Howard. These sought to envisage an alternative to the industrial city by proffering a solution that combined the best of town and country living. A 1912 report, *Nothing Gained by Overcrowding* by Sir Raymond Unwin, the influential architect and town planner, who also laid out the first Garden City in Letchworth in Hertfordshire, can be seen as forming part of an emerging story with Local Government Board recommendations of the same year. The Board recommended cottages for the working classes, built "with wider frontages and grouped around open spaces which would become recreation grounds". The Board also suggested that each cottage should have three bedrooms, a large living room and a scullery fitted with a bath. The Board also recommended that each house should have its own WC, with covered access. There were five designs published, each one varying a little in size.

Although the outbreak of war suspended any further progress on actually building these new homes, the interactions of the state, in the shape of the Army, with the common man proved to be a wakeup call; when conscription drew in the ordinary working man to fight for King and Country he was found to be in a generally poor state of health and not fit for modern soldiering.

Working during the closing months of the war the Tudor Walters Committee delivered its conclusions on the best way forward for housing in the same month as the armistice, in November 1918. The importance of the document cannot be underestimated, particularly at a time when new twenty-first century pressures on housing have led for calls (and in some cases action) to lower standards that were set for council (latterly social) housing some 100 years ago.

Prescriptions were made to design and build to allow sunlight into properties, even in the winter months, with maximum lengths stipulated for terraces. A healthy flow of air through was also noted as an advantage. Local housing committees were set up and these used the Tudor Walters Report as their main guide. Generous central subsidies shared the cost of the new homes between the rents paid by the tenants, the local ratepayers and the Treasury. As the 1920s progressed the vision of the garden estate took hold and many new suburbs were constructed on the outskirts of the nation's cities. These new developments, built on what we would now call greenfield sites, offered both space and facilities, with all necessary amenities, such as schools, shops and public houses, included in the plans, as well as large gardens so tenants could grow their own veg.

The garden estates were genuinely revolutionary, and laid the groundwork for much of what was to come after World War Two. In an interesting aside, just as academics and town planners were preparing the way for homes fit for heroes and the garden suburbs, many other nations were looking to our own housing solutions as a model to be followed. In 1908, following a study of Britain's housing conditions, the German academic, economist and planner Rudolf Eberstadt observed that the "ordinary English terraced house is vastly superior to the German dwelling, economically, socially and healthwise." He also noted that, at this time, new powers were being called for, in an echo of the German status quo, to regulate "the development of towns by public authority".

It was these powers which would, when adopted, give rise to the aforementioned garden suburbs and, eventually, the drive to demolish large areas of terraced dwellings. The County of London Plan, with its Ringways and Radials, which was an echo of plans conceived by Eberstadt for Berlin as part of the Greater Berlin Competition, also sprang from these changes. Patrick Abercrombie, the architect of the County of London Plan, could also be seen as the father of the New Towns Movement and all that came from that after 1946. Regarded by some as the most influential and respected town planner in Britain, Abercrombie also planned the rebuilding of Plymouth and Coventry after World War Two.

Whatever the rights or wrongs, the seeds of the destruction of Britain's Victorian cities were sown during those years between 1900 and 1945. For Abercrombie the city, as he saw it constituted, represented nothing more than a resource from which factories, heavy industry and manufacturing could draw a work force. He wanted to change this to make the city "the centre of culture and learning, of entertainment, and the market". This sounds an awful lot like a description of any post-industrial twenty-first century British city. However, as we shall see, the situation we find ourselves in now came about as an accidental result of anything and everything else but Abercrombie's philosophies.

Slum clearance did not figure as part of the equation when the garden suburbs and cities were being built in the 1920s and would not until the Housing and Slum Clearance Act of 1930. Even then slum clearance schemes were sporadic and it was not until the large scale regeneration schemes of the 1950s, 1960s and 1970s that things began to change on a disruptive scale.

Ferocious idealism may have driven the forces of change but this change and its consequences did not go unchallenged. Even though much of the housing was overcrowded and lacked basic modern amenities the communities who lived in them were close knit and robust. During the 1960s and early 1970s rows of back to backs still marked out the hill sides and valley bottoms of many towns and cities. Many of these people were still very poor and lacked those things that were seen as defining modernity and convenience. Even by 1971 36% of the population still did not own a washing machine, whilst 31% still did not own a fridge. The General Household Survey of 1971, conducted by the Office for National Statistics, reveals some startling truths about the lives of many, even in the aftermath of the swinging sixties, with a startling 10.3% of the population still using outside toilets. 9% of the population were without a bath. A 1967 survey conducted by the Halifax Building Society and Local Government found that 22% of homes had no hot water and that 65% did not have central heating. All of this paints a picture of a significant portion of the population living in conditions at odds with the shiny modern narrative of the age.

Nowadays we have an image of these kind of houses, based mostly on those terraces that survived and through their portrayal on TV programmes like *Coronation Street*. But this fails to give an idea of the variety of solutions the nineteenth century threw up in the name of high density housing across the land. The terrace, whether it was a through terrace or back to back, is the most famous. There were also courts - where dwellings were arranged around a small communal square. Also, within each city and each area of each city, there was a multiplicity of subtle variations.

Not in Front of the Children

In his book *The English Terraced House* Stefan Muthesius outlines some of the range of details to be found in decoratively applied brickwork, stonework and woodwork that differentiated the Victorian houses of Hull, Sunderland, Manchester, Liverpool et al from each other. Within these details, as well as countless others ranging from the kind of wood a toilet seat was made from, Muthesius detects "a minutely detailed accentuation of class". In the nineteenth century, he tells us, the details present in the "small old houses" were championed and celebrated by people like Pugin and Norman Shaw. He goes on to make the point that much of the destruction of the humbler end of nineteenth century architecture came about as much due to artistic disregard rather than any "actual or presumed obsolescence". Writing in 1982, once the rubble had been cleared and the dust had long ago settled, he highlights the regret felt at "letting those houses come down," and the growing penchant of middle classes for smaller nineteenth century homes - complete with their newly designated status as antique and period. Despite this regret, and any aesthetic motivations that led to the decisions that were made, the great slum clearances were not whimsical fancies of taste. Instead they came from a long building fear that the industrial city was, as Peter Hall puts it in *Cities of Tomorrow*, "biologically unfit". The problems with the health of recruits that World War One highlighted were not new - Hall notes that during the South African War around the year 1900, only one thousand out of eleven thousand men from Manchester who came to be recruited were actually passed as fit for regular service.

When, in the years before World War One, Patrick Abercrombie noted that James Horbrecht's compact, planned city of Berlin "does not straggle out with small roads and peddling suburban houses, but slowly pushes her wide town streets and colossal tenement blocks over the open country," he was airing his own vision of the British city. The idea of the sick city and what to do with it had preoccupied the great and the good for many years. The "stunted, narrow-chested, easily wearied," town dweller of the Liberal MP Charles Masterman's 1901 book *The Heart of the Empire* was a threat to the security of the nation: too enfeebled or drunk to put in a hard day's work or for that matter defend the motherland. Whatever the eventual truth or the ideological thrust of 'homes fit for heroes', or the welfare improvements implemented in the years after both world wars, these changes must be seen, at least in part, with this in mind. It is also worth noting that, in the much changed political and economic circumstances following both World War One and Two, a fear of the newly politicised working classes and demobbed soldiers drove the implementation of many ideas that had languished for years on desks of university academics. The fear of the enemy without (the population's inability to compete in the world of commerce or fight to defend the nation in times of war) was supplanted by a fear of the enemy within (communism, political activism, upheaval, strikes, insurgency and revolution).

Although change was needed the slum clearances brought with them new problems that, for many observers, continue to plague our society today. Within all those areas of densely packed housing, with their shops, pubs and factories, that were swept away in the fulfilment of grand and overarching plans, there were communities of friends, relations and neighbours. The destruction of these places, with their complex sets of values and codes, was done with little thought for the longer term consequences. As our politicians and planners were to discover, social engineering, though neat and tidy when laid out in graphs and charts, was subject to a host of unseen "human" factors, the interactions of which could play out in a multiplicity of unimagined and chaotic ways. The order offered by modern housing developments, furnished and with all the services a community could possibly want (or a planner could imagine) and connected and bisected by high speed motorways, was, for some people at least, both superficial and illusory.

"I'll tell you what, I've noticed this with old folk that's been moved away - they don't seem to have reigned long. It's too bad rehousing old people." These lines, taken from Brian Jackson's 1968 book *Working Class Communities - Some general notions raised by a series of studies in northern England*, express just one concern amongst many others caused by the wholesale clearances of huge areas of old housing stock in the name of slum clearances and urban regeneration. Jackson's work was part of a significant canon of sociological investigations into communities where traditional values were being challenged, as whole sectors of society were reshaped by a host of factors. Alongside the regeneration plans and rehousing schemes, an increase in incomes and leisure time also had a significant impact on lives that had changed little over the course of the preceding one hundred years.

Despite the improvements many felt there were still a significant number of people living in poverty, as the growth in living standards proved to be uneven. The common view that "need and poverty ended in the 1930s, and that today," in 1965 when Jackson was writing, "the working class is affluent and moving easily into a middle class standard and style of living" was challenged as early as 1958 by Richard Titmuss in his book *Essays on the Welfare State*. Indeed, Titmuss showed that welfare services such as medical care, allowances and pensions widened the gap between manual workers and a middle class who reaped the benefits of the system more easily. Also, by citing the research of Peter Townsend, Jackson points to seven and half million people living "below an income level set by the National Assistance Board as necessary for rent, food and clothing." Whilst acknowledging that poverty was less visible and no longer as "horrifying" in areas like Attercliffe in Sheffield, Stepney and Bethnal Green in London and the Gorbals in Glasgow, Jackon notes that privation persists in "complicated pockets".

Digging further into the old working class communities still housed in areas that were or would be dubbed slums it becomes clear that many of those left behind in those areas were the old, the sick, the unemployed, the widowed, and those on low incomes with large families. The disparity between people buoyed up on the wave of affluence and the deprived, "surrounded by apparent affluence" made their poverty even more stark. Writing in the early months of 1966 Jean Stead, the Guardian's news editor, saw children from these families as "in some ways more deprived than the poor of the 1940s when there was communal poverty." Those children, who had "no vests and shoes that were too tight," were in school with other children who "will be talking about the Continental holidays they are going to have." Research conducted at the time pointed to persistent "neglect and extreme inequality" on a big scale.

As the great modernising project of the 1950s and 1960s reached its peak, with the redevelopment of town centres, rehousing schemes and a growth in consumerism fuelled by higher wages and easier consumer credit, there were many who began to question where it was all heading. Writers like Jackson foresaw problems in the clash between established working class values and established middle class values. They fretted that, through exposure to the shiny new world of consumerism and mass media, the old styles of living would come to an end, leaving in their place nothing but isolation and loneliness.

Not in Front of the Children

At the heart of those old styles of living was the extended family that "centred on mum", stretching over several nearby households, where abundant everyday support and help, from childcare, cooking and shopping to support in times of crisis like "death, accident or illness" was to be had. This family arrangement was the cornerstone of those communities and reinforced a value system that had supported the working class through the travails of the preceding decades. Against this long established scenario was placed the vastly improved material conditions of the new housing estates, with hot water, gardens and good schools, and family set ups where husband and wife were closer together. However, despite the better living conditions research showed an increase in unhappiness and loneliness and found that the extended family, that vital part of working class life, had been destroyed. The housing interventions and initiatives, well meant and much needed in many respects, had broken up those established patterns of living, and no amount of artificial stimulation by way of community centres could resuscitate what had been lost. Kinship and family had been squandered in fulfilment of a change agenda that, according to Jackson and his ilk, was based on a misunderstanding of working class society.

By the beginning of the 1970s a little over half of homes were privately owned, with semi-detached houses making up almost 50% of the housing stock. These private dwellings are what Dominic Sandbrook calls the "markers of affluence", places where people could relax and socialise with the immediate family or with their small group of friends. People were living different lives in different places and, as employment patterns changed, they did different jobs. The old occupations in heavy industries, upon which the traditional working class was built, were being replaced by office work and activities that relied on a different, even lower set of skills. Self-worth and status, which had previously been tied up with a steady accrual of skills, had to be found elsewhere, in material possessions bought on HP.

The cooperative, mutual aid of the South Wales coal fields had been used by the Labour Minister for Health, Aneurin Bevan, as the model for the 1946 National Insurance Act, enshrining the working class value of community and self-help at the heart of post war Britain and its new welfare state. By the beginning of the 1960s this paradigm was being challenged, a point noted by Bevan himself, in a speech he made not long before he died, that warned against the ills of consumerism. As that decade progressed the compact that held together those carelessly referred to as the masses disintegrated, fracturing not only community but also the collective bargaining that had underpinned the solidarity of the union movement. When the economy faltered, at the end of the 1950s and into the 1960s, the pressures and consequences of personal debt came to the fore as individual groups of workers sought their own local solutions to the threat of job loses and shorter hours. Increasing insecurity exposed the flip-side of consumer culture as more families found themselves out of work and in debt. In the final years of the 1960s a new sensitivity to inflation fed into an emerging dynamic that saw a transfer of power away from national union executive committees towards factory shop floor based shop stewards who reacted to local concerns and called unilateral strike action. For some the new reality of home ownership and the fragmented nature of people's lives were a prison much worse than anything caused by the deprivations of years gone by. They found in their new box-like homes, with their TVs and carpets and fitted formica kitchens, a kind of plastic gilded cage of superficial and unfulfilling pleasures.

An argument raged between those who advocated more traditional models, based around the terrace, and proponents of modernist solutions. A mishmash of the modernist and updated traditional approaches was found in the new towns of the 1950s and represented a very British accommodation with and incorporation of radical ideas. In the case of new towns the early tentative uses of modernist vertical buildings, inspired in part by Le Corbusier's towers set in open spaces, tended more towards the conservative Swedish point block system of flat building. Both traditional and modern methods had their positives and negatives. In the years after World War Two the apparatus that had been put in place to manage the nation's war effort, the residues of Edwardian paternalism, and ideas that had emerged from the pre-war manifestos of organisations like the Bauhaus school merged. Further ingredients added to this were the ever present British desire to save money and cut costs allied to pressures from the British construction sector and those firms who provided the materials. This awkward, mongrel chimera would, over the three decades after 1945 exert a distorting influence over the country's housing solutions, as bold and often exciting visions were subject to the grim realities of the real world.

Ebenezer Howard was the father of the Britain's Garden Cities. In the years immediately after the war several of his ideas, envisaged in his 1898 book *Tomorrow: A Peaceful Path to Real Reform* and realised in his developments at Letchworth and Welwyn Garden cities, gained broader credence. Indeed Howard's philosophy underpinned much of the recommendations made by Abercrombie and Forshaw in their 1943 County of London Plan. This was the plan that also laid out the Ringways mentioned earlier in the chapter.

The 1946 New Towns Act, fostered by the eminent paternalist and founder of the BBC Lord Reith, saw the drawing up of plans for twenty new towns. Along lines recommended by Abercrombie and Forshaw, the first four of these, Stevenage, Crawley, Hemel Hempsted and Harlow, would be built in the countryside around London. Reith stipulated that each of the new towns, which were funded by 60 year loans from the HM Treasury, would have their affairs, such as compulsory land purchasing and building, overseen by a locally based corporation. In keeping with the spirit of a time that saw the founding of the Welfare State and the National Health Service the main aim of these New Towns was to give people the very best start possible in life. This was driven by ideology and idealism as well as a desire to avoid a return to the business as usual of the years before the war; the ghosts of the Great Depression, those horror years of poverty and privation in the 1930s, still haunted both sides of the political divide.

Stevenage was the first to be designated, but the picture of how the news was received is anything but clear. In his book *Concretopia* John Grindrod mentions a "largely optimistic" response, with some 57 percent of those polled believing that it would be good for the area. Certainly, though, local opposition was strong, not least from the newly formed Stevenage Residents' Association, who saw the proposals as bordering on Stalinist. Unfortunately for those local residents and landowners of Old Stevenage who sought to stop the plans, Lewis Silkin, the Minister of Town and Country Planning, was implacable. "It's no good you jeering. It's going to be done," was his comment to a public meeting. This attitude resulted in a very British satirical response, with the town's signs being replaced by new ones bearing the name 'Silkingrad' written in Cyrillic script. It was certainly an image that sat uneasily with a place that was the setting for E. M. Foster's 1910 novel *Howards End*.

It is easy to understand the alarm of the locals in this rural town. The 1950 plan for the 'Mark One New Town', as it and others were called, promised 60,000 new homes divided across six neighbourhoods, each with their own community facilities in the shape of shops, schools, doctors' surgeries and community centres. Many who disliked it also feared it was the thin end of the wedge. They were not wrong. In 1966 this plan, which was quickly seen as not being ambitious enough, was further updated and expanded.

Despite Silkin's apparent high handedness in addressing the citizens of Old Stevenage, both his and the government's motivations were highly laudable and eminently practical. Addressing parliament during the second reading of New Towns Bill on 8th of May 1946 Silkin spoke of the "not unreasonable" expectation that More's *Utopia* of 1515 "should be translated into practical reality in 1946." Continuing, Silkin referred to Ebenezer Howard's main object of "relieving the congestion of large cities by redistributing the population in new and well-balanced towns of limited size," to be "planned as a whole and to provide for industry and residence" and with "adequate cultural and recreational facilities." The "many warnings," he said, "of the dangers of permitting unplanned and uncontrolled development to take place on the outskirts of our towns," had not been heeded before. This, Silkin said, resulted in urban spread and miles of ribbon development that extended urban sprawl, ate up miles of countryside and made the "centre of the town more and more remote from the country." The new towns were, after years of reports and consultations on the effects of this kind of expansion, and nearly thirty years after parliament first recognised the need for them, a much needed solution to the problem of overcrowded and unhealthy city life.

Later, in his foreword to Frank Schaffer's 1970 book *The New Town Story*, Silkin would write candidly about the lack of "real knowledge of the organisation and finance required," that those tasked with building the new towns had. Nothing of this nature or scale had ever been attempted before. It is unlikely that, without the attitudes and administrative infrastructure in place due to the exertions of the recent conflict, it would have or could have been carried out in the way it was. Centralised planning was still woven into the fabric of our national institutions and those who worked in them.

Britain was not only embarking on a revolution in where houses were built and how people were homed but also a revolution in how those homes were constructed. The damage wrought by bombing on many of the nation's cities fed into existing concerns about housing and this, in turn, led to the establishment of the Burt Interdepartmental Committee on House Construction in 1942. With the nation already staring bankruptcy in the face one of its prime foci was on the efficiency and economy with which the housing crisis could be solved - as well as with the rapidity with which buildings could be put up. Concerns also emerged that there would be a shortage of suitably skilled tradesmen (particularly bricklayers). To this end radical methods of construction were examined, including the use of timber and steel frames and the introduction of a limited range of standardised factory produced systems utilising reinforced concrete. In the years immediately after the war a national surplus in steel and aluminium production, allied to an acute need for diversification away from the war effort across whole sectors of the industrial economy, provided a good deal of impetus for the development of prefabricated solutions to the rehousing problem.

This early form of British industrialised building was given a helping hand by the government in the form of generous grants in a move that went some way to establishing this sector.

The majority of the solutions, and there were quite a few of them developed by all kinds of companies, proved not to be fit for purpose due to deterioration or failure. A litany of problems would eventually be examined and delineated by the Building Research Establishment, before finding their way into the 1984 Housing Defects Act. (Incidentally this Act became law four years after the government Right to Buy scheme had begun offloading council housing stock.)

Examples of these construction solutions were multifarious and include: the concrete framed and slab unit Airey house (20,000 units), designed by Edwin Airey and based on huts produced by his building firm for troops during the war; the precast reinforced concrete clad and concrete and timber framed Cornish Unit (30,000 built), with a distinctive pulled down mansard hipped roof, made by Central Cornwall Concrete & Artificial; the Reema Hollow Panel system which used prefabricated reinforced concrete panels; the Hawksley SGS which utilised a brick outer skin around a concrete frame. The list goes on. The above techniques tended to be used by local authorities in edge of town locations, but the Development Corporations that constructed New Towns also made use of system building, falling in line with a government stipulation that at least 15% of all homes were system built.

The New Towns, under the tutelage of their autonomous corporations and led by chairpeople, planners and architects with radical visions, were a genuine departure from all that had gone before. People like Frederick Gibberd, the consultant architect and planner for Harlow, and the activist and urban planner Monica Felton, the Chairperson of the Stevenage Development Corporation, led from the front, often pushing their own pet ideas. Gibberd is credited with giving the country its first modern high-rise building. Containing thirty six flats, ranged over nine storeys, it was based on the pre-war Swedish "point block" design, where apartments are laid out around a central spine that carries services and a lift shaft or stairs - the design is often said to resemble a butterfly.

When addressing the House of Commons, during the second reading of the New Towns Bill in 1946, Silkin was at pains to point out that his bill was not called the Garden Cities Bill. As construction got underway it became clear why. Though the new iteration may have had a shared lineage and heritage with Ebenezer Howard's Garden Cities they would certainly not share their look. Resolutely modern and urban, there would be no looking backward to a reimagined past, no resuscitation of a romanticised Edwardian ideal of country cottage living. Despite this promise, the New Towns, developed over the course of three distinct waves, 1946-1950, 1961-1964 and 1967-1970, made liberal use of natural environment, with green open space and trees deployed amongst the clean modern lines of the roads and buildings.

Although initially popular, with their walkways, underpasses, roundabouts, green wedges and pedestrianised precincts, these essays in civilisation, as Lord Reith called them, soon faced a backlash. Beginning as early as 1953, with searing critiques of Harlow by Gordon Cullen and J M Richards in the Architectural Review, the tide turned; a mood that was picked up on by the national press. Pithy, condemnatory phrases, like prairie planning and pram town began to circulate in popular culture, catching the public's imagination, as the new utopias were labelled as bleak places, deserts of concrete and grass, where the predominant mood was one of isolation rather than hope. The residents of Harlow may have "found themselves marooned in a desert of grass verges and concrete," as Richards wrote, but perhaps it was a little unfair to target a project that was still in the process of establishing itself. However, despite a spirited defence of Harlow by Gibberd, Cullen and Richards' words spoke to a growing debate.

Not in Front of the Children

Although certainly modern, with their open, barrier free gardens, green spaces and road layouts, along with many new building techniques, the approach to the New Town solutions of the 1950s could hardly be described as Modernist. Indeed, some of the pre-war solutions in the UK, like Quarry Hill Flats in Leeds, could be seen as much more radical even than The Lawn point block high-rise in Harlow. Designed by R.A.H. Livett, the Leeds Director of Housing, in 1934 and championed by the Labour Party councillor and vicar of Holbeck Church, the Reverend Charles Jenkinson, Quarry Hill Flats were heavily influenced by Red Vienna's fortress-like mid-rise Karl-Marx-Hof. However, unlike the Karl-Marx-Hof, the design of Quarry Hill flats came about not due to a burning desire to adhere to a particular philosophy, but rather because of a confluence of expediencies that called for quickly executable, low cost, high density housing. Quarry Hill also offered an alternative to the garden suburbs that had sprung up around the edge of Leeds in the decade before, bringing with them problems of isolation, community breakup and remoteness from people's places of work. In many ways Quarry Hill foreshadows those solutions adopted by councils from the late 1950s onwards, an alternative to New Towns or garden estates, that saw system built high-rises arrive on our city skylines.

Gibberd may have talked about landscape architecture, as he sought to defend Harlow, but his ideas did not occur in a vacuum. After World War Two, in those years of reconstruction, one of the strongest themes to emerge was the revival of the Picturesque. As architects struggled to find an appropriately British mode and style in which to respond to the challenge of renewing the nation they looked to influences and ideas from the years before the conflict began.

Not in Front of the Children

The New Picturesque, an approach fostered by those public authorities who saw in the rebuilding a chance to address age old problems, emerged out of Christopher Hussey's 1927 book *The Picturesque*. Going right to the heart of a debate that had rumbled on almost since the industrial revolution, the New Picturesque sought to heal the schism between town and country. This process, according to Helen Atkinson's paper *A "New Picturesque"?* sought to "reconcile, in the visual form, the self-image of Britain as a rural nation, with a landscape that had been dramatically transformed by modern roads, buildings, industry and war." In terms of creative practice Britain of the early 1950s was a place of playful engagement with ideas. Dogmatic theories were shied away from as being too constraining. In many ways, this is perhaps why the nation's creative life, so rich, vibrant and contradictory in both popular and high art spheres, would prove to be so exciting and groundbreaking over the ensuing years.

Within architecture the Revived Picturesque, a movement which Alan Powers describes as "an anti-theoretical theory at best", there was a partial intellectual framework. The drive to enhance the urban environment by bringing in aspects of the rural or pastoral landscape went hand in hand with moves to improve the lot of the working classes. Plant some trees, landscape a hill, drive green wedges into the heart of the cityscape, all of these aspects played an important role in the post war rebuilding programme that placed health and wellbeing at the heart of planning. This approach dovetailed with a very British interpretation of the tenets of modernism. Prewar concerns that any architectural intervention should be sensitive to the existing context held sway for quite some time after the outbreak of peace. However, as Powers notes, this approach led to an "eclecticism and mannerism" that would come to be seen as subverting the pure ideal of modernism. For some the dialectic around modernism promulgated the belief that the pre-existing urban landscape acted as a drag on society and civilisation, reminding of and reasserting the old ways. In 1925, when the Swiss-French architect, urban planner and pioneer of modernist architecture Le Corbusier wrote in his text *Urbanisme:* "Our world, like a charnel-house, lies strewn with the detritus of dead epochs," he distilled what would become a guiding tenet for the interface between Marxism, Modernism and the reshaping of the cities of the industrialised world.

Though this idea appealed to some and, perversely, could be seen as providing the justificatory framework for much of the disastrous developer led destruction of the nation's city centres in the 1950s, 60s and early 70s, various alternative strands emerged. These peculiarly British responses, in styles such as "situated modernism", "soft modernism" and "contemporary", represented an evolving accommodation between a desire to embrace new solutions, both technical and artistic, and an innate national characteristic that favoured evolutionary change over revolutionary cataclysm. In the end both approaches would leave their marks on the landscape of this country.

Initially at least, and certainly in the prewar era, where Modernist architecture was found the buildings tended to be in the style Alan Powers calls soft modernism - sensitively deployed with an eye to the surrounding buildings. And as the 1950s rolled on the lack of any defining, rigorous theory produced an ad hoc approach to styles. This, in turn, would come to create a schism between the established architects and an emerging new generation who saw in these projects everything from woolly compromises to traitorous betrayals. The claims to modernity of the British flagship architecture of the time were roundly rejected, with the New Brutalist architect Colin St John Wilson describing them as being "symptomatic of that post war loss of nerve". Underneath the banner of Le Corbusier, Aalto and Lewerentz, St John Wilson and his fellow travellers in the Independent School would emerge to have a major impact on the landscape of the UK. For them the city was a problem to be solved in a different and more robust way. However, in keeping with our national character, change, when it came, was fitful and sporadic, evolving through the push and pull of emerging acceptance and continued resistance.

Whatever the ideological drivers, the new generation of British architects, planners and developers would harness the power of industrialised building processes, marrying to it a radical outlook as they pursued a new vision for Britain. In the process much of the nation's accumulated cityscapes, that hodgepodge of unregulated and untidy growth, dictated and designed by random, local requirements, would be scrubbed clean.

The 1960s and 1970s would see the formation of awkward partnerships, as architects, whose ideas were often steeped in Marxist theory, local government officials and capitalist developers cooperated to see visions realised, boxes ticked and money made. Architect practices, like that of Peter and Alison Smithson - practitioners and proponents of New Brutalism whose work became concerned with a quest to find the essence of Modernism in architecture - explored ideas that would merge political thought and theoretical frameworks and utilise groundbreaking engineering and design. Through this work the meaning of community would be recast and reimagined, as bold solutions to the practical and intellectual problems of the modern age were sought. Beginning in the 1950s, through broad coalitions like the Independent Group of painters, sculptors, writers, critics and architects, an awkward continuum of ideas would emerge. Through a merging and de-merging of philosophies, and a co-opting of broad and disparate positions and approaches, cherished tenets would be challenged and lots of stuff would get built.

From the 1950s onwards arguments raged, both in the professional and national press, over what form the nation's ambitious programme of rehousing should take, with community and neighbourhood placed at the heart of this debate. The impulse to sweep away complex patterns of housing and replace them with grandiose schemes in the modernist style was challenged and, by turn, any attempt to reinstate more traditional modes of housing was opposed. An important interaction with this came from the aforementioned architects, Peter and Alison Smithson. This husband and wife team sought to incorporate reflections on and of the life of the surrounding locale, acknowledging history as well as physical and human geography, alongside re-imaginings of traditional streetscapes and community. The 1970 BBC documentary *The Smithsons on Housing,* which strangely echoes the opening frames of *Mary Mungo and Midge* with its views of the traffic rushing by below, offered a fascinating insight into their belief that there was a viable concrete alternative to the tower block and that it was possible to reflect the essence of a place and its people in a building's design. The programme also highlighted the difficulties they faced in building their estate at Robin Hood Gardens in Poplar, London, between 1966 and 1972, on a site that was bounded by working industry, dereliction and busy urban motorways. Their "streets in the sky" would join the list of terms, like green desert, prairie planning and pram town, that would rattle around the public consciousness, often with bad associations, as the general public attempted to get to grips with these alien housing solutions. The Smithsons' highly personal, poetic and surprisingly undogmatic approach offered yet another uniquely British solution to housing and regeneration. Under the banner New Brutalism, the epithet applied to the style by the critic and writer Reyner Banham, they did much to redefine British architecture through their bold use of reinforced concrete and sculptural form.

On the flip side, further north, back in Preston, the district of Avenham offered a glimpse of the alternative view of how architecture could navigate the complex social problem of rehousing and community. Here, James Stirling, in his partnership with James Gowan, sought to find a solution to the problem by connecting more overtly with historic norms of housing. Brick built, low-rise and terraced, this project, built between 1957 to 1961, was said to reflect the newly discovered understanding by social scientists of the vitality of traditional working class communities, whilst solving the need for improved services (remember Preston's outside lavvies). Stirling's Avenham development was almost universally condemned for its apparent regressive nostalgia for Victorian slums, with everyone from Pevsner to the *Daily Mail* lining up alongside all manner of modernist critics and practitioners.

Twin aspects, identified by Reyner Banham as "working class scene painting" and "socialist formalism", characterised the debate around rehousing and regeneration at this time. However, this theoretical tussle over form could not solve the core problem that community and place only come into being over time and through shared experience. Just as social scientists like Brian Jackson and critics like Richard Hoggart recorded, researched and represented the complex nature and structures of working class communities, many of those communities were being aggressively reshaped. All too often, when the bulldozers had moved on and the concrete had dried, what was left was nothing more than disparate groups of people in new housing. Over the years, however, bonds would eventually reform and community cohesion would re-establish itself - as long as the estates were left standing long enough.

Not in Front of the Children

Undeniably, there was an urgent need for better housing, but as factions like the New Brutalists or the New Empiricists argued the toss in the pages of *The Architectural Review*, the voices of those being rehoused were often lost in the noise. The debates were understandable, given that these were professionals seeking to define the direction of travel for their chosen field - even if they didn't have manifestos to wave or flags to march under. Of course communities were consulted, but all too often those slated to live in these places, whether they took the form of bold visions or practical solutions, found their requirements met in the most sterile of ways. In addition to this a combination of bad design, cheap materials and shoddy workmanship often undermined what were essentially good ideas. Damp and condensation issues became a particular problem in many of the new low-rise and high-rise concrete system built estates, as well as failures in essential services like lifts or waste disposal.

The most numerous, visible and perhaps most controversial of all the post war housing solutions were the local authority prefabricated high-rise (and low-rise) estates. With a less flamboyant lineage than the concrete offerings of the Smithsons, or Brutalist towers of Balfron and Trellick by modernist master Erno Goldfinger, these prefabricated, system built solutions were a kind of bastard sibling of the modernist architecture. Sitting on the intersection of scarce resources, the pressing need to solve the housing problem and the apparently limitless possibilities of off-site factory produced prefabricated system building, the council high-rise appeared to offer a perfect solution. Co-opting parts of Le Corbusier's vision for uniform sentinel towers and merging it with elements of the new picturesque that provided for open landscaped spaces, these blocks present a striking visual spectacle, even today. Modular in construction and made out of panels of precast concrete that could be put together quickly and conveniently, these multi-storey blocks offered homes that boasted all the latest modern conveniences such as central heating and modern kitchens and bathrooms. All of this could be put together, using a crane, by an unskilled workforce which, alongside the factory produced components, kept costs down. A generous subsidy, devised by the MacMillan Government in 1956, that rewarded those construction companies who built higher and higher, more and more handsomely, sealed the fate of the nation's city skylines. Upwards became the answer. High-rise building of this kind was new to Britain but, although initially expensive, by 1965 high and medium-rise solutions were seen as being on average slightly cheaper than traditional approaches. (Unfortunately, this perception was based on incorrect figures: the true costs across the board were actually some twenty per cent dearer.)

In a climate that still valued green spaces in the urban landscape, and also sought to save the edges of cities and towns from the creeping development that had worried so many during the 1920s and 1930s, the appeal was obvious. Back in the 1930s Quarry Hill flats filled a void left by the slum clearances in the Mabgate and surrounding area in Leeds; now the emerging variants of what was a rapidly evolving building system would squeeze every last ounce of value out of newly cleared slum sites across the country. However, where Quarry Hill was a locally tailored answer, born out of Christian Socialism, this new generation of social housing stemmed almost entirely from the needs of the corporate construction sector and its shareholders.

The preeminent system for building these towers was known as the Large Panel System, which was designed and developed by Larsen Nielsen in Denmark in the years immediately after World War Two. Out of this root came a large number of proprietary systems, also developed on the continent, for which UK construction firms either bought the rights or purchased lock, stock and barrel. By 1965 this simple and, on the face of it, highly cost effective solution had been adapted and modified to create some 138 different kinds of system, which were used by over 160 developers. Taylor Woodrow licensed and rebranded the Larsen Nielsen system as Taylor Woodrow Anglian (following a merger with the concrete component manufacturer Anglia Building Products). Other firms, such as Wates, developed their own solutions. The Wates system differed from most others in that they set up a "factory" to produce the component panels on site.

Guided by the prerequisite of uniformity LPS was part of the European development of new industrialised techniques for mass housing and the UK's building industry embraced it. The 'Bison Wall-Frame' system, developed by Concrete Ltd and launched in 1963, was produced in a string of factories situated throughout the UK and facilitated the rapid construction of blocks of over twelve storeys high. There was also the French developed Tracoba system, which was imported by the firm Gilbert Ash, though towers built using this system tended to suffer from problems with damp, and the Balency system used by Cubitts. Other examples are Shepherd's Spacemaker system and Cruden's Skarne which, like the Wates system, utilised on site casting.

These were "complete" systems, wherein all elements were included to create an entire building and were, by their nature, "closed", which meant that one system would be incompatible with another. Brand A Large Panel system could not be combined with Brand X Large Panel system. Local authorities often reused the same designs of multiple blocks of both high and low rises. Rolled out across an area this created a kind of grinding visual monotony, a new kind of poverty that reinforced the sense of hopelessness and alienation many residents felt. Added to this the landscaping the designs called for tended to be an afterthought, with a thin smattering of hastily planted (and often quickly vandalised) trees failing to make an impact on the vast green spaces of the flat grassy desert.

In essence these systems, and in particular that of Larsen Nielsen, resembled a carefully balanced stack of cards, held together by a few strategically placed bolts. As demand grew the construction firms operated at the edge of what was possible at the time, often pushing the designs beyond what was expected of them. A good example of this occurred with Taylor Woodrow Anglia, who took the Larsen Nielsen system, which was initially designed to be used in buildings of no more than six storeys, and upscaled it to twenty storeys and beyond.

Large concrete panels were swung upwards and stacked by cranes and manoeuvred into place by inexperienced and unskilled workers who were paid by results. This was a boom time for the construction firms and the returns were high. A climate of economies of scale, reinforced by an emerging trend for companies to create conglomerates, led to a loss of oversight at a time when there was desire to reduce costs. With gaps between panels down which coins could be lost and smoke and noise leaking between the flats, these buildings often appeared to be held together with nothing more than spit, newspaper and a prayer.

Concerns were expressed about the Taylor Woodrow Anglia Larsen Nielson system built towers. However it took a collapse at the Ronan Point block in the East London borough of Newham to bring the problems with this system into sharp focus.

The trigger for this catastrophic failure, the making of a cup of tea, was something so mundane and common to every UK household that it seemed to add an extra dimension to the shock felt across the land. In the early hours on the 16th of May 1968 Mrs Ivy Hodge, the occupant of flat 90 up on the 18th floor of the two hundred feet high, twenty two storey Ronan Point tower block, turned on her gas stove and lit a match. In an instant a relatively small explosion knocked Ivy unconscious but also blew out the concrete panels which formed the external walls of her flat. This was quickly followed by a progressive collapse down one side of the building that killed four and injured seventeen. The only reason there were not more casualties was because most of the residents were asleep in bed. High-rises and system built solutions never really recovered from the bad press this disaster created.

An investigation found that the explosion occurred because a substandard brass nut, which had also been overtightened, had been used to connect the gas hose to the stove. When this connection failed gas had leaked into the flat, rising up and collecting above head height at the ceiling, where it was undetectable. The explosion itself was quite small, but poor workmanship (each of the wall panels were only held together by pairs of slowly rusting bolts) and a design pushed beyond its limits meant that the building failed. Successive work by a whistleblower, the architect Sam Webb, and the investigatory committee found that strong winds and fire could be enough to cause a progressive collapse in buildings of this kind. Indeed, following his extensive investigations Webb concluded that in "high winds it (the part of Ronan Point still standing) was beginning to break up," and was "moving on its lifting bolts.... held up by the 'blast angles' fitted after the public inquiry." What was left of Ronan Point was demolished in 1986.

System building had, according to some critics, come about due to a hasty response to the long term and seemingly insoluble housing crisis. This problem was further exacerbated when underlying economic factors, which culminated in the devaluation of sterling in 1967, meant that spending had to be cut. The sterling crisis has been rather unfairly laid at the door of Harold Wilson's Labour government, but its genesis can be traced back to decisions taken in the 1950s by MacMillan's Conservative administration that stalled the economy. A significant problem was the £800 million deficit Labour inherited from the Conservatives when it was elected in 1964. This deficit was turned into a surplus by the time Labour lost the 1970 election to Heath's Tories. However, the 14% cut in the value of the pound in relation to other major currencies added to a host of gathering problems. Price and wage inflation and union militancy related to the rising cost of living and the resultant wage demands all created an atmosphere of instability as the 1960s drew to a close. The need to cut costs fed into a growing public belief that the tower blocks were a rather dodgy, cheap solution that had nothing to do with good housing. Faced with a style of architecture and way of building that was wholly foreign, the population of Britain felt suspicious. The Ronan Point collapse confirmed these suspicions.

Over time, as new problems with the brave new world of concrete emerged, such as weakening caused by crystallisation in High Alumini Cement amongst others, public perception grew that those at the top were lining their pockets. Warnings about High Alumini Cement, or HAC as it was known, had been made as early as 1963 by Professor Adam Neville of Leeds University, but were ignored. Despite these red flags, several instances of "rotting" in significant structural parts of buildings led to catastrophic failures: the roof beam collapse at John Cass School, Stepney in 1974 led eventually to questions being asked in the House of Commons. On December the 9th Neil Macfarlane the MP for Sutton and Cheam highlighted the problem with HAC when he said that it was "rapidly becoming a combination of misery, apprehension, worry and fear for thousands of people in the United Kingdom."

The public's perception appears to have had a ring of truth. An investigation by Patrick Dunleavy would eventually uncover a complex picture of links connecting ministers, civil servants and the sprawling construction conglomerates who fed at the trough of the concrete construction boom. The number of MPs and ministers with connections to construction firms was astounding. But what Dunleavy uncovered was more than your everyday links to industry lobbyists. The Conservative Party was a major beneficiary of funds from the sector, receiving donations from Taylor Woodrow and McAlpine. Sir Keith Joseph MP, the aggressive proponent of free market economics who would provide much of the intellectual heft behind the Thatcherite project of the 1980s, was the Minister of Housing in MacMillan's government between 1962 and 1964. This was right at the moment the more extreme high rise solutions were being rolled out across the country. Curiously enough Joseph was also the son and heir to Samuel Joseph, the head of the family owned Bovis construction and project management empire. Evelyn Sharp, the senior civil servant at the Ministry for Housing and Local Government during the years 1952 and 1964, when so many of the important decisions on system building were taken, was connected to Neil Wates of the construction firm Wates. Also, in an example of a poacher telling a gamekeeper on how best he'd like his snares setting, the Ministry for Housing and Local Government was advised by the Chairman of Concrete Ltd, Kenneth Wood. Of course, given the number of concrete buildings being built at the taxpayer expense, it would be surprising if they had not taken advice from industry specialists. Geoffrey Rippon MP, who was Minister for Public Building and Works in 1962, was a director of Cubitts, a construction firm that would be acquired by Tarmac in 1976. During his tenure as Minister for Public Building and Works Rippon attempted to push through the replacement of the Sir George Gilbert Scott Italianate style Foreign and Commonwealth Office, which was built between 1861 and 1868, with a modernist concrete block. Was this done purely in the service of what politicians of today like to call "the national interest"? Who knows? Mercifully for our national heritage the Foreign and Commonwealth Office did not go the way of Philip Hardwick's 1837 Euston Arch and was saved by a campaign by the Victorian Society.

Whatever the truth behind these connections between politicians and business, the atmosphere it created fed into a longterm belief amongst Britain's working class communities that those in authority were only interested in helping themselves.

In his 1968 book *Working Class Community* Brian Jackson explored the roots of the rising tide of violence and rioting in working class communities. Highlighting the "frustration which is part of the common texture of working class life" Jackson painted a picture of disaffected and angry youths with little respect for or fear of an established order that was symbolised by the police and the press. Directionless and volatile, the riots in Huddersfield that he describes began accidentally, formed and motivated by a "latent hostility" that needed an outlet. Simple phrases like "you can't stop me copper" and "you're all the same you coppers", shouted by members of a jeering crowd of four or five hundred captured what was the prevailing mood amongst young working class adults. Some local observers, like Frank Thewlis, feared that it might be the beginning of a race war; others, from the town's temperance organisations, laid the blame at the door of alcohol and "the old battle in the working class - drinkers versus the dry." *The Yorkshire Post*, Jackson noted, suggested a new angle, fear of the Bomb.

The popular national press simply put it down to a collective madness hitting the town.

Disaffection was not a new thing in working class communities and the relationship between them and the authorities manifested itself most clearly in the way they were treated by the law and the police. As Jackson points out, the hatred of the police that lay just beneath the surface was no surprise when, as a force, they tended not to serve society as a whole but instead "acted as agents of the controlling middle class."

One important aspect of these riots was that, although they were mainly the work of young apprentices, they were always "verbally backed by older people." These feelings ran deep within working class communities and were not reserved to a small section of hotheaded youngsters letting off steam or venting anxieties over issues relating to nuclear disarmament. This ignorance of the causes was, according to Jackson, not born of a desire for a cover up, but came about due a malaise that ran much deeper: the middle classes were sealed off, prevented from seeing the real reasons for the trouble, by a wall of attitudes and values. A wall of attitudes and values that, when the local Chief Constable said "people simply went mad", meant he was "speaking *his* truth."

Jackson was by no means alone in his theory of an unscalable wall between the middle and the working classes. In his 1961 book *The Stagnant Society* Michael Shanks placed the inability of these two groups to communicate, characterising them as being more foreign to one another than people from different nations, as being at the root of at least some of the UK's economic problems. The disjuncture, explored by Shanks, between the hypothetical "Economic Man, whose actions can be determined by subtle manipulations of Government policy," and the realities "a good deal lower down the social scale" and "the rest of that vast grey army of older working class" was a conundrum still unsolved even as the 1970s got underway.

Having played its part in the dilution of the aims of and solutions to the housing crisis, these unresolved issues would, in many ways, inflame the industrial disputes and union militancy of the late 1960s and 1970s. This was particularly so as localised and shop steward led militancy fragmented any hopes of a coherent, national solution to the problems at hand. The belief, explored by Shanks, but held by much of the middle class at that time, that when the economy needed it, workers should take a pay cut or accept a shorter working week, is given short and humorous shrift by the writer. However, its highly visible presence in the discourse of the nation shows how distorted paternalistic attitudes towards the working class remained even at the start of the 1960s. These attitudes played a part both in the decisions made by the country's political masters and in the way that those decisions were received.

Whatever the complex mix of causes, few could have forecast the range of problems that would unfold in the system built homes that rose up in the sky. Slum clearances, rehousing, social reform and even consumerism were part of a series of interacting experiments, the results of which could not be forecast. Rigid, entrenched and longstanding systems of living and working were under attack, intervened in and interfered with, sometimes at the behest of higher authority, sometimes on the whim of the market. The age old call of "we know what's best" received the equally old response of "we don't give a fuck".

The violence Jackson saw in the working class communities of Huddersfield was not a new phenomenon, though it tended to occur in less visible forms, directed against outsiders. As Richard Hoggart wrote in *A Local Habitation* "...any newcomer not born rough Hunslet working class was an outsider to be labelled and abused, verbally and physically." His experience of the deprived working class area of Hunslet in Leeds, which he moved to as a child in the years before World War Two, could have been replicated anywhere in the country, even into the 1970s. This was a place of gangs and territories, where invisible geographical lines could not be easily crossed without some form of painful tariff being extracted. In these circumstances recourse to a higher authority for protection, even from parents, was not done as it would create further mistrust and result in much worse punishment. For his part Hoggart worked out that he had to establish himself "in some way so that there would be an invisible ring round" him, so that he could "operate in the playground and the streets." Using the thing that separated him, his verbal skills, as his currency, Hoggart "gained at least some identity" and was to make his peers laugh. By doing this he was able gain their trust and acceptance.

This is a simple enough story of childhood bullying, but in many ways it goes to the heart of how finely balanced those communities that were erased in the name of slum clearances were. Everyday life, even that of a school boy, was subject to a complex set of negotiations and rules that had grown up over many decades as a means of creating order from within whilst allaying suspicions and fears. Although as valid as the social mores found in any other part of society Britain's entrenched attitudes about class meant that their importance was all too easily disregarded. Viewed from afar by the middle class and the nation's political masters the subtle interactions of history and place, of longstanding family relationships and friendships, were at best invisible and at worst feared. But these patterns, which had grown up over the years, were the glue that held these communities together. The street, the pub, the shop, the front step, all these familiar things anchored people in ways that were simply not understood.

Not in Front of the Children

Richard Hoggart elucidated this in his 1957 book *The Uses of Literacy* when he wrote: "Home may be private, but the front door opens out of the living-room on to the street, and when you go down the one step or use it as a seat on a warm evening you become part of the life of a neighbourhood. To a visitor they are understandably depressing, these massed proletarian areas; street after street of shoddily uniform houses intersected by a dark pattern of ginnels and snickets (alley-ways) and courts; mean, squalid and in a permanent half fog..." Hoggart describes a place of poorly maintained properties where work and home life exist in the same space, with houses "fitted into the dark and lowering canyons between the giant factories and the services which attend them." However, despite the grimy buildings, the high embankments and networks of railway lines and canals, "to the insider, these are small worlds, each as homogeneous as a village.... they know it as a group of tribal areas."

Places like Hoggart's Hunslet existed up and down the country, each one a tribal enclave, a village. Surrounded and assailed by a hostile wider world of broad main roads and "bosses' cars", better clothes, unaffordable shops and big houses, it was natural for these communities to hunker down and look inwards. Conversely, it was equally natural for "the haves" to fear and misunderstand these dirty, "improperly fed and inappropriately clothed" strangers and the dark, forbidding places in which they lived. The misunderstanding and neglect that had consigned these communities to a fate of poverty wages, bad housing, disease and poor sanitation for over 150 years meant they and their roots could be casually swept away.

Despite perceptions, these were not the lawless and disorderly hell holes that much of the middle class feared they were. Within these small worlds there was law and there was order - maintained by the organic contracts of family, kinship and neighbourhood, by an intimate knowledge of each other that had grown up naturally and out of circumstances. Powerful and all pervasive, and operating in a way beyond the ken of the mainstream world of magistrates and the courts of law, it ran deeper than the punishments of an untrusted and fickle police. It took its form in many ways, from community and cooperation, to the clip round the ear or the shout of "I know your mam". Within this contract was the "abundant mutual help" that Brian Jackson wrote of in *Working Class Community*. This was available for everything from "looking after children, cooking meals and sharing shopping" to the "great personal crises of death, accident and illness" - along with a "constant flow of advice and encouragement." Family, the extended family, friends and neighbours helped with all manner of arrangements that were there to fill any need.

Hunslet would have its own modern redevelopment and rehousing scheme - one that swept away the ginnels and snickets of Richard Hoggart's youth. This was the medium-rise, system built Hunslet Grange (or Leek Street flats as they were known locally) that featured the 'streets in the sky' walkways that were fashionable in 1968 when construction began. Initially it was popular with the new residents, due to the spacious well-lit interiors and a variety of modern conveniences like rubbish chutes. Community and convenience were catered for with a pub and shops located within the bowels of the development. Unfortunately, in a familiar story, poor design and construction, particularly the inadequate heating and insulation that led to huge problems with condensation and black mould, meant it was destined to fail. By 1983, beset by the spiralling cost of maintenance and remedial work, social problems and a rabbit-warren layout that meant the place acted as a magnet for trouble makers, demolition work began on the flats. By the end of the decade the nearly 1250 family flats had gone, leaving the city with a burdensome legacy of debt and a severe housing crisis.

Between 1964 and the end of industrialised and semi-industrialised house building nearly 500,000 houses and flats were built across the land. Not all were failures, but many proved to be expensive experiments both in financial and social terms. Damp and condensation could lead to problems with black mould in flats, there might be problems with standing water in communal areas and underpasses, furniture could move as towers tilted in the wind and lights might go on and off without warning. Alongside these practical problems, the collapse of the delicate community balance that came with the uprooting and relocating of whole neighbourhoods manifested itself in anti-social behaviour and crime. Without the woman at the end of the street who knows your mother, or the man in the corner shop to keep a watchful eye, these estates, with their hidden corners and characterless walkways and corridors, soon seemed beset by problems. Vandalism, graffiti, drunks urinating in lifts that were inadequate or seldom worked, no go areas, all this and more quickly saw many of the clean lined concrete utopias quickly transformed into bleak dystopias. The absent and careless private landlords, who ignored peeling paint and crumbling plaster, had been replaced by local authorities which often struggled beneath the weight of problems these multi-storey estates presented. In the worst cases, whether it was the spiralling maintenance costs, due to the never ending round of remedial works, or the constant interventions needed as social cohesion evaporated in the face of rising unemployment and drug use, these developments acted as running sores, draining resources from local councils. In a further betrayal, press reports fed into a narrative that cast those who lived in these communities as spongers and wasters, condemning whole generations to a scrapheap that was said to be of their own making.

Attempts to police communities who were historically used to looking out for their own and in their own ways led to a harsh and alienating management style and, in particular, a plethora of notices coldly warning against all kinds of activities, from ball games to loitering. For the rehoused children and teenagers the transition from the rough and ready world of derelict, scrubland playgrounds, where the only limitation was the turf of your gang, must have been a difficult one. Boundaries had been erased and new demarcations and alliances would have had to be formed.

The collision between long established but rapidly disappearing patterns of living, made up of matriarchies, families and neighbourhood, and the framework imposed by a new place with its new rules was just one part of the problem. The old industries that, hitherto, had provided employment down the generations were disappearing, even as early as 1961. The certainty a young man previously had that he would follow his father's path of employment was going or gone, replaced by jobs in emerging industries or no jobs at all. The issues thrown up by the emerging freedoms of the permissive and consumer society also created problems. Barriers were breaking down as an apparently egalitarian world of unbounded pleasures, in the form of nightclubs and music, brought people together in ways unimaginable just a generation before. Tensions between what went before and the expectation inherent in this land of plenty had grown as change accelerated, so it is no surprise that problems with rebelliousness and disrespect were seen in these communities.

Local gangs and their battles had always existed, but now their activities were often writ large, as parts and places that were once ignored or invisible came to the attention of the country at large. Why did this happen? Perhaps it was because the money that had been spent on the housing projects demanded accountability. Perhaps it was because there were new kinds of newspapers, television and radio news that sought out these stories and blew them up into more than they were. Perhaps it was because young working class boys and girls were out there, visible as never before, enjoying the fruits of their labours at the seaside, in town and down the local club. Whatever the reasons and whatever the outcomes, soon a combination of rapidly decaying buildings, often badly built, poorly designed and poorly managed, and residents who quickly came to resent the false promises of their new homes, would lead to an ever quickening decline. When the economy began to falter in the last few years of the 1960s, before collapsing as the 1970s got underway, many of the new high and medium-rise estates became nothing better than grim traps of longterm unemployment, drug addiction and despair.

By the time *Mary, Mungo and Midge* hit our TV screens in 1969, our national love affair with modernist system built housing was over. A combination of public mood in the aftermath of Ronan Point and the end of government subsidies for tower-blocks meant that the flow reached its peak in 1968, declining until 1974 when the last was built. Mary's latchkey existence of self-reliant autonomy may have been portrayed amidst the still lustrous glow of modernist idealism, but that particular vision was already damaged beyond repair. The show ran for one season of thirteen episodes, which was not unusual for the time. With its beautiful animation and happy, simple stories that imparted a sense of solid social order, it ostensibly offered a vision of the modern world as it could be.

Viewed from the top floor of Mary's tower-block the townscape below teemed with possibilities. Old buildings and the rows of houses with pitched roofs stood in the lee of the tall, sleek concrete boxes. Cars passed along the roads in an orderly fashion, busy but with no hint of congestion. People went about their lives with the reassuring regularity of a well-practised routine as they did their shopping and went to work. Everything buzzed with community life, from the well-kept parks to the shops with their dressed windows and happy customers. Unfortunately, for many, this was as much a fantasy as the bucolic idylls of traditional children's television.

As beautiful as *Mary, Mungo and Midge* is its core message speaks of loneliness in a busy world. Mary is neglected by her parents and has to find companionship and love in her pet dog and a mouse. Her existence is exemplified by remoteness and she views the world as if through a telescope. It speaks of how a much needed change in our urban environment brought about dislocation by separating family life, work life and community life. Into the gaps fell the the young, the old and the vulnerable, those who previously relied on a fragile but effective social contract that was underwritten by memory and a sense of place.

A decade after *Mary, Mungo and Midge* first aired Jeremy Seabrook wrote in his book *What Went Wrong?:* "Parts of Bradford look as though they had been abandoned; as though people had deserted the worn out housing and exhausted landscape and gone elsewhere." Recording the "mixture of discipline and charity" that once formed the heart of this and other communities he also recognised the consequences of its demise. Across the land people had more money and better working conditions than ever before, but they also felt alienated, resentful and betrayed. It seemed that, despite its many successes, one of the nation's most important social quests had somehow got out of control and damaged the very people it was supposed to help.

Not in Front of the Children

It is, of course, wrong to characterise all system built housing as bad. Many estates were excellent and continue to provide good homes and sound communities for those who live in them. They are places that flourish and are loved. But for each of these successes a price was paid elsewhere, in the many, many failures and the bad decisions that were made. Working class culture, the communities and the people, the warp and weft of history and values that made them who they were was, all too often, carelessly swept aside. It important not to fall into the trap that reimagines life in these communities before the slum clearances in an idealised way. Life was hard. People lived in poverty and change was essential. Unfortunately these changes were often implemented in haste and at a cut price and much of what should have been achieved was undermined.

Chapter Three

Mr Benn and the Five Stages of Grief

When David McKee's Mr Benn walked his peculiar walk down Festive Road for the first time in 1971 Britain was a nation struggling to acclimatise to the changes, economic, sociological and cultural, that had been wrought over the preceding decade and a half. The miracle of full employment and the promise of material plenty was, by this time, a dream greatly tarnished, and strains brought about by societal shifts that placed individualism over collective responsibility and community were beginning to tell. The quest by successive governments to find a happy balance between economic prosperity, growth and inflation, whilst at the same time tackling long term problems with low productivity, was now complicated by seemingly insoluble factors, both at home and abroad. The consumer escapism of the 1950s and the pop culture escapism of the 1960s had lost some of their gloss. Ted Heath was in power, elected in a surprise victory over Harold Wilson in the June of 1970, and a multiplicity of long building pressures had already begun to take their toll as his administration sought to marry an instinct for consensus with an emerging philosophy that called for harsh economic and political medicine.

The story of *Mr Benn* begins back in 1967, the year of the summer of love, when media stories and popular histories would have us believe that everyone was wandering around naked with flowers in their hair. Whatever the realities of everyday life for the majority the UK's population, change was in the air.

McKee, who was born in 1935, published his first book for children in 1964, having worked as a freelance painter and illustrator following his graduation from Hornsey College of Art in 1959. Called *Bronto's Wings*, this first book was about about a dinosaur who wishes he could fly so that he could migrate south with the birds for the winter. This theme of a deep yearning for change and escape from the chains of common experience is one that surfaces again and again in McKee's work. It is also one that would form the core of the *Mr Benn* books and television shows. And it seems that his debut received a positive reception. In her magazine *Growing Point* Margery Fisher described the illustrations in *Bronto's Wings* as being "most impressive" and hailed McKee's inclusion of lots of "the tiny details children like to search for in picture books." Although only two years into its eventual thirty year run *Growing Point* was, by that time, already regarded by guardians, teachers and readers as a definitive guide to the best of what was new in children's literature. McKee also had the book *Two Can Toucan* published in 1964. This story had been written earlier, during a stint at Plymouth College of Art, prior to Hornsey, during which time he acquired his first degree.

The first Mr Benn book was *Mr Benn, Red Knight*. Having established a reputation for an idiosyncratic and creative approach to story-telling and illustration from his very first book, McKee developed this further in the television series. It is easy to see why these stories appealed to BBC Television, with their folding together the humdrum and the everyday with an anything-can-happen spirit of adventure. Following the publication of the *Mr Benn, Red Knight* book the BBC, who had already used some of David McKee's work as the basis for children's shows, asked him to develop the Mr Benn concept as a series. There were thirteen episodes produced across two series in the original run of *Mr Benn*. The first series of six episodes was broadcast from the 25th February to the 1st of April 1971 and the second series was broadcast from the 21st of January to the 1st of

April 1972. According to this source both series were aired at 1:30pm on BBC One in the Watch with Mother slot. McKee animated the series with the help of Ian Lawless under the direction of Pat Kirby. As with much of the animation produced for British television at the time, *Mr Benn* was made under the wing of one the country's many boutique outside production companies that sprang up after the war. It was to be the first project of Zephyr Films, a company that would re-emerge in 1990 and which continues to produce a host of successful film dramas into the twenty first century.

McKee opted for a narrator, rather than have the characters speaking. He choose Ray Brooks, an actor whose CV included a variety of parts from playing Terry Mills in *Coronation Street* to a starring role in the award winning 1965 British comedy *The Knack ... and How to Get It.*

Music played an important part in children's television of this era and the jazz musician, big band leader and composer Duncan Lamont, writing under the pseudonym Don Warren, provided a suitably imaginative score. The theme tune, again by Warren, is particularly interesting, resembling as it does the music that might introduce a full blown grown up sitcom with a slightly unhinged edge to its jaunty, upbeat mood. Warren's score was ably interpreted and perhaps extemporised on by the jazz bassist Ken Baldock, the keyboard player and composer Harry Stoneham, the jazz trumpeter Kenny Wheeler, Art Morgan on drums, Peter Hughes on sax and woodwind, Terry Emery on percussion and Ray Swinfield on sax, flutes and other woodwind. All these musicians were, however, highly accomplished and versatile so its anybody's guess what they actually played at any given time during the recording sessions. Lamont's work is described by Stephen Graham on the website marlbank.net as as being jazzier than that of fellow 1970s television composer Ronnie Hazelhurst. Graham also describes Lamont's skill in arranging as being based on an ability to "strip away the glare without making it at all bland". Graham also notes Lamont's use of "natural textures such as that of the woody resources of the marimba again swinging it a little more..." As David McKee wrote in the notes for *As If By Magic,* a CD collection of Lamont and Wheeler's music: "From the very beginning the music was always an important part of the films..."

Dressed in his bowler hat and pinstriped suit, the character of Mr Benn represents an archetype of ordinariness and respectable citizenry. He is wearing the traditional uniform of the civil servant, the lawyer, the banker and the insurance worker; a commuter outfit found only on the streets of London. The Beatles used a man dressed in this outfit on a train in their film *A Hard Days Night* to stand for the old ways that they, as representatives of youthful rebellion and exuberance, were pushing back against. A man dressed in this way stands for the old order of war veterans who shook their heads at the emerging freedoms in British society in the 1960s. Such is the disapproval and shock of the man on the train in *A Hard Days Night* that Lennon is moved to shout "I bet you're sorry you won." Someone bowler hatted and in a pinstriped suit was stable and reliable and could be trusted with important things like your money or the administration of government. This very staid image and what it represented was perfect for the irreverent lampooning of the establishment that was popular with comedians at the time. Monty Python made perfect use of the juxtaposition of the bowler hatted Whitehall civil servant and the absurd in their Ministry of Silly Walks sketch from 1970.

One thing is missing from Mr Benn's outfit of officialdom - his umbrella and briefcase. That was the part of the uniform McKee dispensed with, probably for ease of animation and so as not to clutter up the image. But this omission, set against the parts of the uniform that are still intact, leaves Mr Benn looking oddly naked, incomplete and maybe even a little flighty.

The bowler hat did not arrive fully formed as an item of clothing that symbolised a particular section of British society. Its history is quite colourful and surprising. It was commissioned by Edward Coke in 1849 from the hatters Lock & Co of St James's, London. Coke wanted a hat, a replacement for the impractical top hats they usually wore, that would protect his gamekeepers' heads when they were on horseback. Coke is said to have checked the robustness of the design by stamping on the crown twice before accepting delivery. The hat was designed and manufactured for Lock & Co by fellow London hat makers Thomas and William Bowlers of Southwark. It became an indispensable piece of headgear for working class men in Victorian England because of the protection it offered. In the early years of the twentieth century its popularity spread and it was worn by people from many different walks of life and classes, including railway workers, taxi drivers, porters and landowners and, in the shape of Stanley Baldwin, even a Conservative Prime Minister.

The pinstripe suit is said to have originated as a uniform that was used by banks in London to differentiate between different employees. Originally the trousers were the only item to have the stripe but when the style came into fashion in the USA in the years after World War One both the jacket and trousers were striped. Unfortunately the story of the pinstripe is not so straightforward and some commentators see the pinstripe as originating either on the margins of society, as a way of distinguishing prisoners and prostitutes, or as a nineteenth century bourgeois boating fashion.

Whatever the origins of the suit and the hat, by 1967 what they represented was clear and David McKee's decision to clothe his main protagonist in this armour of the establishment creates an interesting tension between the storylines that follow.

Mr Benn lives alone in an ordinary house, number 52, on Festive Road. The street, being a Victorian or Edwardian terrace of red brick, offers something familiar, reassuring even, to all viewers, both young and old. Indeed, the ordinariness of the street is always restated in Ray Brook's opening narration. In the first episode Mr Benn receives an invite to a fancy dress party. We are told he does not like parties but that he likes dressing up. Over the course of the series, as we get to know him and his bustling street, where cool dudes with trendy clothes and fashionable facial hair chat at each other's gates, we come to understand that he is actually a solitary figure, an introvert. In many ways as a person Mr Benn, in his old fashioned, sober suit and hat, is at odds with the modern world; he is a person who, despite his adventures, really prefers not to be in the limelight and who welcomes the opportunity to slip away through a discreet doorway and avoid any fuss or praise. These traits connect him with a certain image of Britishness - one of restraint and humility - that is, in itself, at odds with the gaudy look-at-me consumerist-pop-culture world of the late 1960s and early 1970s.

In order to go to the party Mr Benn must find a suitable costume and he sets out to look for one. He tries "the big shops", modernist structures that are depicted as a characterless rectangular rack of oblong windows through which Mr Benn is viewed moving, from outside. He tries "the not so big" and the small shops on the side street, where more interest and detail is found, until, at last, he discovers a hidden back lane. This is an example of one of those old, rambling places, where history was found, which were being so efficiently erased from the city and townscapes across the country. On this lane Mr Benn discovers the fancy dress shop that provides him with the costume and all his coming adventures.

Our protagonist is guided to and from these adventures, though never accompanied, by the bespectacled, fez wearing shopkeeper. His mild, patient and understated manner acts as a parallel to Mr Benn's own understated persona. It also acts as a contrast with the thrilling happenings that occur on the other side of the green door - that ordinary looking portal to adventure and self-discovery that is found within the changing room. In each episode Mr Benn chooses a costume and is ushered into the changing room where he dons the outfit, beginning a transformation which is completed by his interaction with the world beyond. Transformation is an incorrect description because, no matter what occurs through that doorway, Mr Benn's innate character remains unchanged. Indeed it is his personality, his belief system, his way of approaching the various problems and puzzles he encounters, that always offers the key, the solution.

He does not grow large nor does he shrink small, but in his costumes, the adventures he finds himself on and the way these are approached there are parallels with Lewis Carol's *Alice in Wonderland*. Like *Alice in Wonderland*, *Mr Benn* is often said to have druggy undertones. However, although the fez wearing shopkeeper suggests a line that connects to exotic hookahs, the smoking of hasheesh or opium and the vivid yet inexplicable adventures of a tripped out state, McKee denies the possibility that everything was just a dream by rooting *Mr Benn* in the real world. He does this by the use of mementos: Mr Benn brings back something - a box of matches, a medal, a photograph of a herd of elephants - to remind him of where he's been and what has transpired. This concrete proof, taken back to Festive Road, the ordinary street and the ordinary house, anchors the stories firmly in Mr Benn's everyday reality.

By 1971, when the show was first aired, British confidence in itself, its institutions and its way of life had been shaken by a number of factors. The conservative establishment, the thing symbolised by Mr Benn's outfit, had been rocked by a number of scandals and events that undermined the state's illusion of surefooted competence.

Perhaps the most famous of these was the Profumo Affair of 1963. John Profumo appeared to be the quintessential old school Conservative. Elected to the House of Commons in 1940, during the dying days of Chamberlain's wartime government, he was also serving as an officer in the British Army. He attained the rank of Brigadier and his war record was good, with service in North Africa, where he was mentioned in dispatches, and the D-Day landings in Normandy, France. He left the army in 1950. The youngest MP in the House at the time of his election, he was well regarded by his fellow MPs and rose quickly through the Conservative party, notwithstanding a brief blip when he lost his seat to Labour's Dick Mitchison in the Labour landslide of 1945. He returned to parliament in 1951, when the Conservatives regained power, and in 1952 he was appointed Parliamentary Secretary to the Ministry of Civil Aviation - a department of particular importance as Britain sought to retain its global influence and deploy its own nascent arsenal of nuclear weapons. A year later he was made Joint Parliamentary Secretary of the Ministry of Transport and Civil Aviation. As his career progressed he built on his not inconsiderable talents and contacts moving to become Parliamentary Under-Secretary of State for the Colonies in 1957, Parliamentary Under-Secretary at the Foreign Office in November 1958 and Minister of State for Foreign Affairs in early 1959. In the summer of 1960 he was appointed Secretary of State for War. At this time he was also sworn of the Privy Council, joining the body of senior politicians that, amongst other things, advises the sovereign on the exercising of the Royal Prerogative. Educated at Harrow and Oxford, Profumo capped an apparently charmed life with his marriage to the film star Valerie Hobson in 1954.

The drama of the Cambridge Four (later Five), a Soviet spy ring involving high ranking members of British intelligence, had begun to unfold, in the public eye at least, in 1951 when Donald Maclean and Guy Burgess fled to the Soviet Union.

Both men were said to have drinking problems and Maclean reportedly had a nervous breakdown. In the January of 1951 Maclean is said to have bragged about being a communist saying, "of course you know I am a Party Member, have been for years!" The Foreign Office appears to have been patient, even nurturing, with these men over a number of years prior to 1951. It allowed numerous second chances and periods of "recuperation" after various incidents involving heavy drinking and bouts of what can only be termed undiplomatic behaviour - such as Maclean breaking into the flat of a female member of the US Embassy in Cairo in 1949/50. Burgess's 'indiscretions in Tangier', or his 'unnatural proclivities' as official records have it, were also a concern at a time when homosexuality was still illegal in the UK. His treatment was more severe than Maclean's and he was demoted and sent to be Second Secretary at the British Embassy in Washington. In the April of 1951 a decrypted Soviet signal transmission, collected as part of the Verona project intercepts, unmasked Maclean.

The story took a further twist when Kim Philby, a man who, since 1949, had been First Secretary to the British Embassy in the USA, the senior representative of British Intelligence in Washington, warned Maclean. Both Maclean and Burgess then fled to the Soviet Union. Philby had been aware that Maclean was an agent for some time before but had protected him. Despite the suspicions of a leading CIA figure, James Angleton, Philby continued his own activities as a double agent for a further twelve years, until he defected to the Soviet Union in 1963.

The suspicion that Burgess and Maclean had defected to the Soviet Union was of course confirmed by British intelligence very early on but kept out of the public domain, even though there was a huge amount of press speculation. The truth emerged in 1956 when both men were paraded at a press conference which was held, no doubt for symbolic effect, in a hotel overlooking Moscow's Red Square. During this press conference both men denied being spies, saying that their defection was undertaken in order to "work for the aim of a better understanding between the Soviet Union and the West".

Other members of the Cambridge Five spy ring were Antony Blunt and John Cairncross. Philby, who was made an Officer of the Order of the British Empire, is regarded as the most prolific and effective of the five spies. His work for the USSR was rewarded in 1965 with the Order of Lenin - the same year his OBE was withdrawn.

Although the most famous of the spy scandals, it was not the only one. In 1961 the former diplomat George Blake was handed a 42-year prison sentence for spying for the Soviet Union. In 1962 the junior civil servant John Vassal was arrested after being blackmailed into spying for the Soviet Union. Vassal, a homosexual, had been photographed by the KGB in compromising positions with numerous men after getting drunk at a party. Rumours also abounded across the land about the existence of a mysterious "third man" involved in the Burgess and Maclean story. Philby was confirmed as that "third man" in 1963.

Profumo stumbled into a scandal of his own making in 1961 when he embarked on a brief sexual relationship with Christine Keeler. Keeler has been variously described as an aspiring model, a showgirl and a call girl. This was the height of the cold war, only a few months before the Cuban Missile Crisis of October 1962 that brought the world to the brink of nuclear war.

What Harold Wilson called the "ceaseless interweaving of innuendo and rumours" about Profumo's private life was rife, fuelled by a newly irreverent atmosphere in which the media were keen to push the boundaries. The explosion of the tabloid press and the rise of television played a significant part in this change in attitudes. The BBC's satirical television show *That Was The Week That Was* was a particular thorn in the side of the establishment, dishing out weekly doses of searing and witty observation on the nation's ruling elites. Previously, genteel attitudes and deference to those perceived as betters had dictated that any impropriety would be delicately "swept under the carpet". In the early 1960s this changed and anything and anyone became a target for journalists and satirists. *That Was The Week That Was* lampooned the hypocrisy and double standards in British life, tackling class, sex and pregnancy outside marriage, sacred national institutions like the BBC and the monarchy, people in positions of power like the Prime Minister Harold Macmillan and Britain's diminishing status as a global power. With its audience of 12 million viewers the role of this kind of satire in changing the face of Britain is easily as important as the pop music revolution spearheaded by the Beatles. John Profumo, the Harrow and Oxford educated former military man, socialite and high flying Conservative party star, was a perfect target for them and they duly obliged with their clever reworking of the music hall song 'She Was Poor But She Was Honest'.

On the 22nd of March 1963 the Secretary of State for War John Profumo got to his feet to respond to an earlier speech by Barbara Castle, the MP for Blackburn, made under Parliamentary Privilege, that had raised the issue of rumours connecting Profumo with both Christine Keeler and allegations of witness disappearance and perverting the course of justice. After a short statement, in which Profumo told the House that he and his wife had met Keeler in the July of 1961 at a house party and that he had not seen Miss Keeler for some time, he said: "Miss Keeler and I were on friendly terms. There was no impropriety whatsoever in my acquaintanceship with Miss Keeler." He then went on to attack the use of Parliamentary Privilege to slander his name and threatened to issue writs if any "scandalous allegations" were "made or repeated outside the House."

He was lying to the House. This was an unacceptable transgression - even for one so well connected as he - even at the dawn of the pop culture explosion when all totems and shibboleths seemed to be under assault. Within ten weeks Profumo would get to his feet in the House once more, this time filled "with deep remorse", to admit that he had misled the house with his statement and was resigning.

Among those mentioned as being at the house party in Profumo's original statement were Mr Eugene Ivanov, an attache at the Soviet Embassy, and Dr. Stephen Ward, an osteopath and a portrait painter. These two would play their own part in the escalating drama that unfolded around Profumo and also, taken with what Peter Wright called "a succession of scandals" that stretched back to Maclean and Burgess, help end the Prime Ministership of Harold Macmillan. The whole nation would be titillated to learn that, as well as Profumo, both Ward and Ivanov had had sexual relationships with Keeler and Ivanov's status as an official at the Soviet embassy did more than raise a few eyebrows. The FBI were particularly concerned about the leaking of nuclear secrets and launched an investigation into Profumo under the name *Bowtie*.

A victim of the moral panic that ensued as the conservative establishment rocked on its heels, Ward was prosecuted for living on immoral earnings. These charges were, according to Geoffrey Robertson QC writing in the Independent in 2014, made with no evidential basis. Despite this lack evidence Ward was dubbed a "thoroughly filthy fellow" by the prosecution and found guilty by a judge who, as Robertson says, "manipulated legal rules to ensure a conviction." Shunned by his society friends and disgraced Ward committed suicide by taking an overdose of sleeping tablets.

Another actor in this tragic play was Mandy Rice-Ward who, in a sign of how high and how deep attempts to cover up the scandal went, was briefly "imprisoned on a trumped up charge" by the "corrupt Scotland Yard officer, Inspector Herbert", and coerced into giving evidence against Ward. Christine Keeler was tried and imprisoned on charges related to Ward's.

This was the British Establishment, the old guard that was so mercilessly and effectively mocked by *That Was The Week That Was*, engaged in an unseemly and highly visible struggle to preserve reputations and the status quo. Under the full glare of the press, and in particular a tabloid press keen for salacious details that would sell newspapers, the meltdown of the government played out in public. This demise, which would see the Tories in opposition from 1964 until Heath's shock victory in 1970, was a slow unravelling rather than sudden and explosive end.

Macmillan had taken over as Prime Minister when Sir Anthony Eden resigned the leadership of the Conservative Party in the January of 1957 and, despite Macmillan's "never had it so good" rhetoric, problems had been mounting for a long time for the Conservatives. Dogged by health problems, Eden had struggled as Prime Minister. His mishandling of the Suez crisis in 1956 all but sealed his fate as his already low approval ratings in the country plummeted. His decision to invade Egypt, with France and

Israel, in an attempt to take back the Suez canal following its nationalisation by the Egyptian President Colonel Nasser, ended in disaster.

The Suez crisis did not just happen out of the blue but was rather part of a long line of what were, at the time, setbacks and humiliations for Britain as an imperial power. The British presence in Egypt and in particular around the Suez canal was underwritten by the 1936 Anglo-Egypt Treaty. However, in October of 1951, the recently elected nationalist Wafd government of Nahas Pasha abrogated the treaty, insisting that the British meet the long stated demands of the Egyptian government that the British military presence in the country end. In 1954, with a new government in place under Nasser, who had seized power in a coup d'etat, the British agreed to withdraw, completing the process by the June of 1956. Egypt, which had ostensibly become an independent state in 1922, was finally free of British influence. On the 26th of July 1956 Nasser announced the nationalisation of the Suez canal, a key asset for the independent Egyptian state, but also a key strategic asset for Britain. The canal was, until Nasser's nationalisation, owned and operated by the joint British and French Suez Canal Company and had been since its construction in 1869.

Israeli forces launched an attack on the 29th of October 1956. This was done to provide the pretext for Britain and France to intervene. Anglo-French forces launched their assault on Suez on the 5th of November. Lies over Israeli involvement would come back to haunt the Prime Minister.

In the light of an American post war foreign policy agenda that was committed to bringing an end to old style European colonialism, the military action by Britain, France and Israel to retake the canal was bound to cause problems. President Eisenhower is said to have been incensed. There was also the potential response of the Soviet Union to consider. The Soviets, who launched a bloody suppression of the Hungarian Revolution on the 4th of November, were rumoured to be considering an invasion of Egypt to support Nasser. Led by the USA, the international community condemned Britain and France. At home too the backlash was significant.

Suez marked a turning point for Britain as an imperial power. Any illusions about economic and military influence evaporated. East of Suez, those British spheres of influence and power beyond Europe, from the Middle East to South East Asia, in Malaysia, Singapore, the Persian Gulf and the Maldives would, in a few short years, be lost.

The Eton and Oxford educated Macmillan took over from his Eton and Oxford educated predecessor, the 1st Earl of Avon, Sir Anthony Eden, in the January of 1957. Eden's resignation in the aftermath of Suez was described by his official biographer, D R Thorpe, as "a truly tragic end to his premiership". With the humiliation of the Suez crisis, the spy scandals of Burgess and Maclean, and an economy which was not performing well in the face of international competition from Germany and Japan, SuperMac as he would soon be dubbed had his work cut out. Problems with inflation raised the spectre of mass unemployment, of the kind that had stalked the 1930s, once again. With his party and the government he led in a state of demoralisation and a sense of unrest in the country Macmillan told the Queen that he did not expect his government to last more than six weeks.

Adopting an approach that was, in some ways, similar to that adopted by the French government after World War Two, Macmillan tackled the task at hand through economic planning, investment and modernisation initiatives in key sectors of the British economy. Defence, electronics, the aircraft industry, the railways and roads all benefited. A rapprochement was sought and found with the United

States, first with Eisenhower and then Kennedy, where good personal relationships were built. Britain's international status was rebuilt through his work on the 1963 Nuclear Test Ban Treaty. Macmillan also came to see that the country's long term problems with productivity and efficiency needed new thinking and new solutions and set about the difficult task of reorienting Britain as part of the European family of nations.

Macmillan's interventionist approach is unsurprising given his history. In the 1930s he was a keen advocate of the role that government could and should play in the economic life of the nation, writing and speaking with what Anthony Sampson called "missionary zeal, about planning." In 1932 he published *The State and Industry* a pamphlet that called for the establishment of an Industrial Council that would be tasked with planning and strategy. This was followed soon after by another pamphlet, *The Next Step,* that advocated a form of selective protectionism for the home market as well as the establishment of a range of panels and boards to oversee and coordinate finance and industry with government. However, this was no prescription for socialism. As Anthony Sampson notes in *Macmillan: A Study in Ambiguity*, his proposals were attacked from the left. The Marxist thinker John Strachey complained in his book *The Coming Struggle for Power* that Macmillan's advocacy of a certain degree of centralised control would be achieved by each industry being "consolidated by the great banks and trusts, the independent producers are to be squeezed out; trade-union officials are to be 'associated' with the councils controlling these increasingly monopolistic industries; and finally the apparatus of the State is to meet and fuse with the apparatus of consolidated industry at the designated point, at the point of the imposition of tariffs by which external competition is to be progressively eliminated."

Obviously this was not Strachey's flavour of centralised planning.

As mentioned in the previous chapter Macmillan's government adopted a stop start approach to the economy, suppressing demand when the economy looked like overheating and inflationary pressures became unsustainable. This made it difficult for ordinary people, workers who had jumped into the consumer revolution of the 1950s and bought the newly available products for house, home and family on hire purchase. This, coupled to his government's attempts to resuscitate the City of London, reestablishing its international preeminence as a trading and financial centre, and save sterling's status as a reserve currency, would lead to economic problems in the medium term, particularly for Wilson's Labour administration. In the longer term Macmillan's activities, particularly in terms of the City, can be seen as a forerunner to the process completed by Thatcher in the 1980s - a policy that would eventually see London's old private banks and financial institutions succumb to American takeovers. Thatcher's big bang (and her selling off of the "family silver" through privatisations) was, however, far beyond anything Macmillan and his fellow One Nation Tories would have countenanced.

The domestic problems would persist, however, and so would interdepartmental tensions over how best to handle them. At the heart of Macmillan's government, in number eleven Downing Street, was the Chancellor of the Exchequer Peter Thorneycroft. He proposed a series of cuts to public spending across all departments that were met with concerted resistance from ministers. In the face of such divisions Macmillan's response was to prevaricate. This lack of leadership meant that positions across his cabinet solidified. In the end Thorneycroft, who had lost support in the wider party due to his dogmatic approach to spending cuts, would resign in the January of 1958. He was joined in resigning by his colleagues in the treasury Enoch Powell and Nigel Birch. Despite his dismissal of these events as a "little local difficulty" the loss of his Chancellor and junior ministers from his treasury team was a significant blow to Macmillan's leadership.

A consummate showman, Macmillan's attempts to downplay this crisis at the heart of his administration, as he set off on yet another overseas tour, make sense in the context of his own agenda. Even though the evidence to the contrary was overwhelming he wanted to give the impression that everything was tip top, both at home and abroad. A good deal of his energies were devoted to this feint even as he embarked on his mission to rebuild Britain's international prestige and influence. Pictures of the nation's Prime Minister getting off a plane in a far flung corner of the globe or rubbing shoulders with Eisenhower or Kennedy helped promote the idea to the electorate that Britain was once again important and strong. It was also designed to help bolster Britannia's bargaining power. This dovetailed nicely with the rather illusory image that the country was still the preeminent industrial power, and that through a combination of inventiveness, expertise and investment new opportunities would be Britain's for the taking.

Unfortunately the reality, like the modernisation of the nation's industrial base and infrastructure, was rather more flimsy than the media coverage and propaganda of the day showed. Whether responsibility for the failures of the modernisation programme lie with Thorneycroft, Powell and those ideologically committed to spending restraint, or with Macmillan's tendency to dally when it came to big decisions, fail it did. Macmillan's premiership of "warm opium and treacle", as historian Correlli Barnett has it, proved to be a time big on rhetoric but short on concrete and effective policy. Cosy illusions may have been comforting for an establishment unable to come to terms with the loss of Empire, but time and time again opportunities to set the country on the right track seem to have been missed. These opportunities were missed by every post war government of every political hue because of a foolish attempt to retain Britain's status as an independent big hitter on the global stage.

This exercise in folly was not the sole preserve of the Conservative party. Despite the British economy being in danger of becoming what Correlli Barnett describes as an 'imminent national shipwreck', huge and unaffordable defence spending commitments were made by the outgoing Labour administration in 1949. Big defence cheques were signed by governments of both hues and, although it is tempting to imagine what our industrial base would have looked like now if the vast sums spent had been diverted into other sectors, at the time prestige, security and political influence were paramount. This was not motivated by deluded hubris but by a genuine fear of what might happen if Britain lost its seat at the top table of nations. The responsibilities, though growing fewer with every passing month, to the former colonies, the Commonwealth and even the sterling area weighed heavily on those in power. Alongside this was a weight of history and a desire to preserve sovereign independence. From the moment peace was declared significant energies would be expended and all manner of tricks and contortions would be pulled in the country's quest to look bigger and more important than it really was.

There was also the fact that spending on developing and building the paraphernalia that goes with military expansion acted as its own kind of economic boost. This was especially the case in the 1950s when all defence procurement was made from firms who were still British owned and did their

Research and Development and manufacturing on these islands. Jobs growth and skills retention and development was more than a small incentive. Unfortunately the energies required to service the ongoing demands of rearmament had a deleterious effect on the ability of certain sectors to service the demands of the burgeoning consumer market. As Barnett notes on the specific though not unique issue of providing the military with new wireless apparatus: "In that same year of 1953 those demands were sucking 32.6 per cent of the radio industry's work force, just at a time when a vast new world market for domestic radios and televisions was about to tune in."

Again this situation is wrapped up in the national obsession with status. Barnett describes this as the Britain's "nostalgic belief" that "as a first-class world power" and an equal with its partner America, it should be able to service all the most advanced requirements of its armed forces.

In the fast evolving hi-tech world of the Cold War this blind and obsessive pursuit would lead to an over stretching of R&D and manufacturing capability. In time it would also lead to a costly chain of events that would damage Macmillan's government as well as our country's much coveted international prestige.

The ideological struggle at the heart of the Conservative Party, between the Powellites and the One Nation Tories, would resurface again and again over the years. When the Conservatives scraped back into office in 1970 with Macmillan's protege Ted Heath, after six years of Wilson's Labour government, the fault lines were still there. From the mid-1950s onwards, Enoch Powell and others had played a prominent role in promoting an agenda that envisaged a greatly diminished role for the state alongside an untrammelled free market and lighter regulation. They and their allies in industry also advocated a more aggressive stance towards the unions. Some, such as construction industry supremo Sir John Laing, dreamt of a return to the strictures imposed on unions during the war years.

During Heath's time at the Ministry of Labour, between October 1959 and July 1960, he came under pressure from the right to implement sweeping and radical changes to Trade Union law. Demands were made for the ending of the closed shop, an imposition of secret ballots for strikes, and the abolition of political levy, a key source of funding for the Labour Party. Although strikes were becoming more common they were still well below the level of anything that could be considered damaging to the economy. Heath's approach was consensual, typified by a desire to avoid unnecessary and needless provocation. His biographer, Philip Zeigler, describes the future Prime Minister as being 'well disposed towards the unions,' and an adherent of the *One Nation* view that 'a strong and independent Trade Union movement is essential to the structure of a free society'. Heath's close and often informal relationship with Trade Union leaders at this time set the scene for the future difficulties he would face from those who rejected the ideals of One Nation Conservatism.

Over the course of the 1960s and then, with a gathering pace throughout the 1970s, those Powellite MPs who wished to leave behind the even handed paternalism of Benjamin Disraeli would gain in confidence. As industry and the economy suffered and shop steward led militancy grew, their prescription of fewer rights and protections for workers and a reduction in regulation in the name of "cutting red tape" seemed, to some at least, the way to go.

In the end Macmillan's plans to maintain sterling's position as a reserve currency amounted to nothing more than a managed decline that, under different policies by subsequent governments, lasted until the late 1970s. As Catherine R. Schenk showed in her paper, *The Retirement of Sterling as a Reserve Currency after 1945: Lessons for the US Dollar,* the status that sterling continued to enjoy between 1945 and 1977 had little to do with policies pursued by either by Macmillan or succeeding governments.

Instead sterling's prolonged role as a reserve currency was the result of a broad coalition of national self interests and, in particular, preexisting structures within the international monetary system. Many economists had predicted a rapid switch to the US dollar after World War Two, but even with the help of economic models and systems specifically designed to favour the US dollar, this did not occur as planned. In the years immediately after the war it appears that old habits really did die hard with Britain's historic role helping the home currency account for nearly 90% of global foreign exchange reserves. Even though this level fell, by the 1950s the pound's position was still strong. Indeed, as that decade began half of the world's foreign exchange reserves were still held in sterling; the sterling area, which consisted of thirty five nations, accounted for half of the world's trade. In terms of distribution of foreign exchange reserves the fall of sterling would be gradual at first, before accelerating more steeply after 1967 and Harold Wilson's devaluation of the pound. The long hangover of the pound finally came to a whimpering end around 1977. It seems that sensible attempts to decouple sterling from the reserve market, which were undertaken by the governments of Churchill and Eden, were abandoned due to difficulties they created both in economic and political terms.

A host of factors plagued Macmillan's government and led to the perception that this was an administration and a political party in trouble. In addition to the Suez crisis and the subsequent military drawdown, economic problems, the spy scandals and the Profumo affair, which all played a part in the unfolding narrative, there was another factor. Linked more than anything else in the minds of the country's leaders to the nation's ongoing status and security was the idea of an independent nuclear deterrent. This was the future of warfare in the big boys club that Britain still desperately sought to remain a member of. Unfortunately exertion required in terms of resources to develop both a nuclear device and a practical delivery mechanism would prove to be too much.

Undoubtedly Britain had the brains and the technological expertise to develop whatever it wanted. In 1956 it was the first country in the world to develop, design and open a large-scale nuclear power station. This plant at Calder Hall in Northumberland was the first of a string of home grown nuclear power stations. Unfortunately the British design was expensive to both build and run and, because of this, the Magnox and its successor design the Advanced Gas Cooled Reactor was unable to find a market beyond these shores. Other nations opted instead for the American Pressurised Water Reactor. Whatever the commercial failings of Magnox it satisfied its primary design requirement by providing the country's emerging nuclear weapons programme with Plutonium-239.

In October 1952 Britain had become only the third nation ever to develop and test an atomic bomb when a fission device was detonated on the Western Australian Monte Bello Islands, in a programme under the code umbrella of *High Explosive Research* but known specifically as *Operation Hurricane*. The device was detonated onboard HMS Plym, a River class frigate that was in service between 1942 and 1952. This feat, begun under Attlee's Labour government and completed under the Conservative administration of Sir Winston Churchill was a tremendous achievement. The country was labouring under the great financial constraints and near bankruptcy of the post war era and only had a relatively small pool of expertise to draw upon. But despite this, Britain's history of being the first place to effectively study the feasibility of the bomb helped tremendously.

Again the purpose of this exercise was to establish a sovereign and independent Britain as an equal with its ally the United States of America and a global power. The McMahon Act of 1946, which had effectively welched on an earlier agreement that both nations would share technological advances, had forced Britain to go it alone. One month later, in November 1952, the United States rubbed a bit more salt into the still smarting wounds left by the McMahon Act when it effectively saw and raised the British device by testing a thermonuclear or hydrogen bomb. Britain had enjoyed the brief illusion of parity and now it was gone. Keeping up with the Joneses was going to prove difficult and expensive. At the time Britain knew next to nothing about how to make a thermonuclear fusion bomb; however, in a fine example of the plucky, make do and mend spirit that had seen the country through the war and would characterise much of what happened over the next fifty years of peace, the nation's top scientists got to work in 1954. The project was led Sir William Penney, the former head of the British delegation at the Manhattan Project and father of the Bomb detonated on the Monte Bello Islands.

It wasn't all no, no, no from the Americans. They very kindly allowed the British to fly aircraft through the highly radioactive mushroom clouds to take readings.

By 1957, an incredibly short timescale considering the handicaps the scientists worked with, *Operation Grapple*, which was the name given to the series of tests, got underway. The first fusion test, on Malden Island and known as Green Granite, detonated but failed to produced anywhere near the expected yield and fell well short of those achieved by the USA and the USSR. The second test, a modified fission design that was developed with an eye to a failure in the race to develop a fusion device, produced the largest fission explosion ever recorded. Prime Minister Anthony Eden had stipulated that, should fusion prove to be impossible, then the scientists should produce the largest fission device possible. Although not exactly a case of "if you can't fight wear a big hat", any future involving this solution would have failed in the programme's primary goal of placing Britain on a par with America.

America's first thermonuclear device, 'Ivy Mike', was recorded at 10.4 mega tons. Although this bomb was actually more of a small industrial complex and totally impractical as a weapon (unless you had several months, an army of contractors and an obliging enemy) its yield dwarfed the first two British efforts of 300 kilotons and 720 kilotons respectively. The third test, another fusion bomb, had a yield of only 150 kilotons.

A second round of tests, in late 1957, produced Britain's first real thermonuclear bomb and the country joined the megaton club with a yield of 1.8 megatons. The mysteries of H-bomb design had been mastered and America duly extended the hand of cooperation once again in 1958, although it is important to note that this rapprochement was more influenced by the shock experienced in Washington when the Soviets launched Sputnik than any innate sense of fraternal generosity. Relations between the US and Britain improved to such an extent that Macmillan began to dream of an interdependent relationship in tackling the threat from the Soviet Union.

Over the course of the next year various devices would be tested at Malden and Christmas Islands with yields climbing to 2.5 and 3 megatons. Testing then ceased until 1961. By the time they resumed circumstances had changed once again and Britain was relying on American designs of nuclear weapons.

Not in Front of the Children

A range of exotic and sometimes weirdly alarming names such as Blue Danube, Red Beard, Violet Club, Yellow Sun, Red Snow and Blue Steel mark a nuclear weapons programme that encompassed free fall bombs to rocket powered stand off missiles to ballistic and anti-ballistic missiles. Parallel to this the Ministry of Defence also developed jet aircraft suitable for the purpose, culminating in the expensive excellence of the three V bomber designs. The plethora of designs and solutions, described by Matthew Jones as a "very expansive programme" in *The Official History of UK Strategic Nuclear Deterrent,* is perhaps indicative of the desperate struggle facing Britain as it strove to retrieve and retain its status as a global power. So many types of bomb, so many types of aircraft: the cost was projected to be significant, perhaps even unsustainable.

Macmillan's commitment to Britain's strategic deterrent was such that he was almost prepared to sacrifice all else in its pursuit. In the July of 1957, as deep cuts loomed, Macmillan told the Defence Committee that the strategic deterrent, "must have first call on our resources." Other areas, such as "maintaining adequate forces to carry-out our world-wide commitments" came lower down a pecking order which would, in time, see vast sums spent on the unfolding story of the strategic deterrent. In the mind of the government this deterrent would enable Britain to maintain its influence in the world. This became the mantra for Macmillan whenever he was called on to justify the planned spending on these weapons. Implicit in the government's policy of this time was an acceptance that it was nuclear deterrence or bust. As Air Chief Marshall Sir William Dickson put it: "if a war began between the major powers, even if it started with conventional weapons only.... how could it be prevented from turning into a global nuclear conflict." However, the doctrine of deterrence was, by this time, almost fully established and nuclear weapons were regarded by the country's leader as the decisive factor in preventing major war.

Despite all the energies expired in the pursuit of sovereignty and status through nuclear weapons, in July of 1958 the British Minister at the Washington Embassy, Lord Hood, sat down with John Foster Dulles to sign the 'Agreement on the Uses of Atomic Energy for Mutual Defence Purposes'. An old stager, who was appointed by Woodrow Wilson in 1918 as American legal counsel for the Versailles Peach Conference, Dulles was a ferocious opponent of the "Godless terrorism" of communism. Although undoubtedly shaped by his experience of the destruction of the two world wars he, perhaps more than any other person, was responsible for the game of chicken that the West and the Soviet Union engaged in right up until the middle of the 1980s. An active proponent of the twin policies of 'massive retaliation' and 'brinksmanship', he believed that the geopolitics of the modern world demanded a new set of solutions. Under his response there would be no space for American isolationism, describing neutrality as both "immoral and shortsighted".

Within the 'Agreement on the Uses of Atomic Energy for Mutual Defence Purposes' was the explicit mention of the transfer (sale) of "one complete submarine nuclear propulsion plant with such spare parts therefor as may be agreed.." along with enriched uranium for the propulsion plant. However, perhaps the most crucial part was the agreement to resume the exchange of information. This area covered the development of defence plans, the joint training of personnel in the fields of military and nuclear energy, sharing of information about enemy capabilities, research and development and, more specifically, the development of compatible delivery systems.

Meanwhile a cornerstone of Britain's defence policy, the de Havilland medium-range ballistic Blue Streak missile, had passed the design stage and was in development. This process, carried out in 1957, 1958 and 1959 revealed problems with its complex, lightweight design and the missile was in danger of being obsolete before it entered service. Costs began to rocket and the silo based system's vulnerability to a pre-emptive strike counted against it.

An alternative was quickly sought. In the face of the rapid strides being made by the Soviet Union in the field of surface to air missiles (SAMs) the RAF's V bomber fleet, deployed with free fall weapons, looked like an even more vulnerable proposition. Even the Avro designed Blue Steel stand-off missile, also in development at the time and the most obvious solution, appeared to be vulnerable to SAMs. Other issues around Blue Steel were reliability problems, accuracy issues, and safety problems around fuelling. Avro proposed the faster and longer ranged Blue Steel II, but as it was still on the drawing board it was a long way off entering service. Blue Steel II was cancelled in late 1959 and Blue Streak was cancelled in early 1960. In the March of that year the new caring sharing relationship paid dividends when President Eisenhower agreed to sell Macmillan 144 Skybolt missiles. As was the way of things at the time, Britain, which was still pretty cash strapped, negotiated an agreement whereby its own contribution to the funding of the development of Skybolt would be limited. Homegrown British warheads were also specified for the British missiles. Also, Britain would make available bases on the west coast of Scotland to the American Polaris missile submarines.

Given recent history, with the 1946 McMahon Bill and America's sudden and surprising refusal to share nuclear secrets with Britain, perhaps a trap should have been sensed. Certainly American policy had, before the change of heart in 1958, thus far been aimed at preventing Britain from acquiring second generation independent nuclear deterrence.

Despite its deficiencies the Blue Steel missiles still came into service in 1963. However, with the longer range Skybolt there was the prospect, design limitations permitting, of the V-force's 70 Vulcans, 50 Valiants and 39 Victors operating as they were initially conceived, as an effective part of the nuclear deterrent.

Everything looked promising, barring a few minor hiccoughs, from this side of the pond. Despite the other remaining aspects of Britain's nuclear deterrence Macmillan appears to have pinned all his hopes on Skybolt and cancelled development funding for other projects. Unfortunately, technological developments had continued apace on the other side of the pond and Skybolt was superseded by 1962.

With a new man, Kennedy, in the White House, and a US secretary of defence, Robert McNamara, vehemently opposed to "limited nuclear capabilities, operating independently," the programme was cancelled. A ruthless climate of brutal honesty was capped off when Dean Acheson, President Truman's former secretary of state and Kennedy's advisor on NATO affairs, attacked Great Britain as a country that "has lost an empire and has not yet found a role." Continuing, he mercilessly outlined Britain's stark geopolitical truth in the cold war world: "The attempt to play a separate power role - that is, a role apart from Europe, a role based on a 'special relationship' with the United States, a role based on being the head of a Commonwealth which has no political structure or unity or strength and enjoys a fragile and precarious economic relationship - that role is about played out." For Acheson the only viable future for Britain lay as a member of the European Common Market; an organisation the country unsuccessfully applied to join in 1961, in what was a further humiliation.

In the end face and prestige were salvaged when, in the December of 1962, Macmillan persuaded Kennedy to sell the hugely expensive Polaris submarine based nuclear weapons system to Britain. The cost of this solution was significant in both monetary and political terms. Kennedy's Secretary of State for Defence had wanted to implement a 'dual key' system, fearing that the UK might drag the USA into an unwanted nuclear conflict. After coming under pressure from Macmillan, who let it be known at a conference in Nassau in the Caribbean that if 'dual key' was insisted upon Britain would go it alone, Kennedy pulled back and agreed to autonomous UK control of the weapons. In the end the solution provided for British subs, carrying American missiles, topped with British warheads.

Unfortunately, although face was saved, by whatever indicators used, Britain was greatly a diminished power. The Empire was gone, traditional heavy manufacturing was struggling to adjust to the new market competition and sterling resembled a ghost of its previous self. A poor balance of payments and disquiet amongst the general population about the domestic economy merged with the seemingly unending series of scandals. By the October of 1963 Macmillan had gone. He left behind him what Douglas Hurd called "a government becalmed in a sea of satire and scandal", but took with him his undoubted ability to shape the news agenda and the national narrative.

Alec Douglas Home, the man described by Harold Wilson as "an elegant anachronism", became leader. Meanwhile, Heath continued his steady climb up the greasy pole, equipping himself ably in the simultaneous positions of Secretary of State for Industry, Trade and Regional Development and President of the Board of Trade. Once in this role he burnished his credentials not only as a traditional One Nation Conservative but also as someone of an interventionist and reforming bent.

One year later, in the October of 1964, Alec Douglas Home suffered defeat in a General Election at the hands of

Harold Wilson's mildly resurgent Labour. He resigned as leader of the party on the 22nd of July 1965 opening the way for a leadership contest that would see Ted Heath emerge as favourite. The national Tory press were quick endorse someone they saw as being a "man of action". The *Daily Mail* saw him as being "aggressive in thought and speech" and the *Daily Express* described him as tough and ruthless. Away from Fleet Street the influential Conservative think tank, the Bow Group, described Heath as "aggressive and dynamic". Others, meanwhile, lauded him as being professional, classless and abrasive.

It seems clear that, after a succession of aristocrats and upper-class leaders, and the success of the grammar school educated Wilson, Conservative Britain wanted a no nonsense, dynamic technocrat and man of the people. In the grammar school educated Heath, a man from a relatively humble background, they thought they had found their answer. Heath and his youthful team seemed to offer the right blend of modernising drive, enthusiasm and efficiency that would be needed to deal with challenges of the coming decade and put the "traditional party of government" back in power.

Heath took over the reins to great fanfare on the 28th of July 1965; however, by the autumn his good press had turned bad as his reinvention of the party, dubbed the 'long policy rethink' by some, turned out to be no more than a reworking of old, stale ideas dressed up in buzz words. Within a few short months many on the Conservative benches were beginning to wonder if they had not picked a lame duck leader who had, according to Alan Watkins writing in the *Spectator*, been oversold.

After a decade during which the Conservative party had indulged in numerous grandiloquent claims about the country's international power, prestige and the economy and the lives of the general population, they had fallen for the deception of their own sales patter.

Heath was, however, no stranger to mockery or bad press. As Lord Privy Seal, with responsibility for the UK's failed first application to join the European Economic Community in 1961, he was dubbed Grocer Heath by *Private Eye* magazine when it became clear that each item, including the humble contents of the weekly shop, would have to be given forensic attention during the negotiations. However, this was a complex task, made all the more difficult by the hostility of the French President, Charles De Gaulle, and his government, and a hand, given to him by London, that saw Heath driven towards an opening negotiating position that he described as "unrealistic". It is likely that this sprang as much Heath's own approach as from the negotiating position he was given or, indeed, any shortcomings on the side of the members of the EEC.

The gentle ribbing of Britain's premier political satire magazine was nothing compared to the attacks that would come from a significant part of his own party when he ascended to the position of Leader of the Opposition. The long held suspicions on the right of the Conservative Party about Heath's consensus minded inclinations and interventionist attitudes were magnified when he put in a series of poor performances against Wilson in the Commons. Heath's approach, which had been so recently lauded as one of his great strengths, that called for reams of factual information and carefully worked out dossiers, led his old enemy, Enoch Powell, to describe the House as being "almost dead" after one of his long and detailed speeches. On the opposite side of the House Tony Benn described Heath as "dull and statistical". Set against this was Harold Wilson, a man whose quick wit, intellectual flexibility and tremendous grasp of detail made Heath look sullen and inferior. The Conservative Party began to wonder if they had, as the MP Alan Watkins put it, "made a terrible mistake".

Despite his experience Heath appeared nervous at the dispatch box, his delivery led to him being dismissed as "a second class orator" by Labour's Dick Crossman, and he was taunted by Wilson for failing to "transform the political scene and electrify the Conservative Party" as had been expected. The rebirth of the Tory Party, at the hands of a new kind of classless Conservative, the son of a builder come businessman and a maid, had failed. They wanted to capture the zeitgeist with a man of the time, someone who was hard professional, abrasive, scientific even, but also personable, but what they got was an illusion. Heath had succeeded thus far by being who he was, a detail obsessed technocrat. The mistake was that in constructing the image that won him the leadership Heath and his team forgot his strengths. In time he would find an uneasy compromise between the real Heath and the fictional Heath and almost find his feet in the Commons, across the dispatch box from Wilson.

In some ways the elevation of Heath to the role of leader of the Conservative Party was another manifestation of the self-deception that plagued the Tories during the three decades after World War Two. Unable to accept the loss of the Empire and the diminished status of Britain on the world stage, the party found themselves caught between multiple positions. There was a hope and a belief, at least in some sections of the party, that by co-opting the language and imagery of the modern they could short circuit the long climb back to international influence and prestige. But in doing this they sought to resurrect an old and defunct image of Britain, instead of embracing a new and realistic concept of what the country could be. Science, new technology, techniques and buzzwords had been corralled and coerced in pursuit of aims that, given the country's economic situation, even after the end of austerity, were fanciful.

The truth was that no amount of effort would see this small island reach its previously attained heights ever again. In some respects the Conservative Party were attempting to use the energies present in the newly emerging cultural mood of the late 1950s and early 1960s to reanimate the cobbled together corpse of a romantic fantasy of British power that had been dying a slow death since 1870. On the other side of the political divide the Labour Party were slowly waking up to the forces for change beginning to move through society. Very soon they would take the image of Britain as a modern and technologically advanced nation and add to it the vitality of popular culture and youth. Within two years of their victory by four seats, in 1964, Wilson and his government would perfect a message that chimed perfectly with the people of Britain to deliver a resounding majority that would help push through transformative social legislation.

In 1960 Macmillan had given his 'wind of change' speech to the South African Parliament that signalled that the days of Empire and colonies were over; in 1961 Britain applied to join the EEC, in what was a sign that it had finally been accepted that the country needed a new place in the world. But in spite of this, and even though the Conservative party spoke the language of modernisation, it would be nearly twenty years before they set out with confidence in a genuinely new direction. Even then, the long hangover of Empire and paternalism would linger in the language, attitudes and global aspirations of successive Tory leaders and members of parliament right up until today.

Heath, for his part, was a moderniser, in the truest sense of the word, but he was neither modern nor hep, groovy or cool. And he never would be. He lacked the skills that allowed Macmillan to sustain the seemingly contradictory messages of traditionalism and modernity simultaneously, and his classless, dry administrator's style proved to be an anathema to a party that, despite its protestations, was still in thrall to the past.

Labour's margin of victory in the General Election of 1964 was slim but this offered little comfort to an establishment, particularly in the shape of MI5, that perceived Wilson as a threat to the British way of life. In their file on him MI5 described him as a "dangerous socialist who has ties to an East/West trading organisation," with "a number of East European emigre businessmen among his closest associates." There may have been an openness in the way Heath and his ilk dealt with the union movement and the left, but for many others there existed a deep seated paranoia about the Labour party and the union movement in general.

According to Peter Wright, the senior British Intelligence officer who wrote the infamous *Spycatcher* book, the disquiet felt about Wilson by MI5 began after the premature death of Hugh Gaitskell. Wilson's predecessor as leader of the Labour Party died in the January of 1963 and following his death Gaitskell's doctor contacted MI5 to express his suspicions about the manner of his passing. Gaitskell had died of a rare disease called lupus disseminata and, according to the doctor, there was no possible explanation for how he had contracted it. The story, which unfolded over the year between Wilson's election as Labour leader and his becoming Prime Minister, revolved around MI5 investigations and covertly acquired information involving secret Russian KGB experiments in developing and delivering poisons. These suspicions and fears would stalk Wilson's entire time as Prime Minister.

Whatever was happening in the world of politics, in wider cultural terms, the pressure had been building on

Britain's traditional establishment for some time. The long existing fractures that had divided British society, since well before the dawn of the industrial age, appeared to be on the verge of disappearing as the promise of a classless, egalitarian society beckoned. These fractures, the battle lines of the class war, had been drawn up over the demand for political rights and recognition from the new social groups in British society that emerged out of the industrial revolution. The new bourgeoisie, the lower middle and the new working class, had emerged from this rapidly changing Britain and, over the years through their experiences and travails organically developed seemingly coherent identities and goals based on their different needs. These groups, the bourgeois, the lower middle class and the working class, were not separate entities - they were nuanced, with blurred lines of demarcation that were dictated by subtle gradations of skills and income.

The labourers, working men, intelligent artisans and educated working men (and all manner of subdivisions within) of the working class represented a class structure within a class structure and also a kind of conduit to aspiration and achievement within that group. Equally, within the middle class the levels were many, though the nomenclature was more specifically rooted in the specific jobs they did, stretching from the clerks and domestic servants to the shopkeepers, merchants and small business owners of the lower middle class, to the clergymen, lawyers and doctors and, at the very top, the factory owners and large scale business owners of the upper middle class. Within this middle class group existed the petit bourgeoisie, that favourite of Marxist thinking. For the philosopher and cultural critic Walter Benjamin this group was characterised, in England at least, by a shop culture that set the personal and family space of the sitting room as the centre for a game of relative and hierarchical prestige through conspicuous consumption.

This model of living, of keeping up with the Joneses consumerism, would spread rapidly in the years after post war austerity, as full employment, rising wages and easy credit gave the population access to a way of living that made the home the new centre of life. Alongside this the formation of the Welfare State and R A Butler's Education Act of 1944 changed the daily lives of millions of people.

The Butler Act was conceived in the grand and paternalistic tradition of One Nation Conservatism and its prescriptions, although genuinely revolutionary in many respects, were built on what had been almost infinitesimally slow progress in the years since 1870. For many years education was defined purely in terms of literacy and, in some circumstances, numeracy - though for the most part the basic guide of whether a person was literate was whether they could sign their name.

In *Education and economic decline in Britain 1870 to the 1990s* Michael Sanderson points to literacy rates, as measured by this most basic of standards, as being around eighty per cent in 1870. However, the picture, even by this meagre benchmark, was patchy across the different sections of society, with miners and metalworkers out performing their working class brethren in terms of growth in levels of literacy between 1870 and 1914, and those in the upper and upper middle class sections of society being "almost totally literate by the 1870s." According to Sanderson the growth in literacy that occurred in all social classes between 1870 and 1914 was due to the creation of School Boards, as "units of local government," under the auspices of the 1870 Forster Act. These School Boards had the power to compel children between the ages of five and ten years old to attend school.

Not in Front of the Children

The Forster Act, and those that followed, aimed at curtailing the employment of children, placing a duty on parents to ensure that their offspring were educated to an "efficient elementary" level in "reading writing and arithmetic". The school leaving age was raised incrementally over the course of a few short years at the end of the nineteenth century but it was not until the Fisher Act of 1918 that a uniform national school leaving age of fourteen came into force. This Act also expanded tertiary education provision, such as technical training institutes and colleges, and implemented medical inspections and nursery schools and finally abolished those fees that remained in a system that had been all but free since 1891.

In *Education and economic decline in Britain 1870 to the 1990s* Sanderson dispels the myth that schooling during this period was a "soulless affair of drudgery enforced by harsh discipline" by pointing to Jonathan Rose's study of 1993 which posited that around seventy per cent of children enjoyed their schooling. Despite this rosy picture, and notwithstanding a massively expanded school building programme under the auspices of the School Boards, Britain spent less, as a proportion of its GDP, than its competitor economies. This may have been a factor in the country's declining productivity and competitiveness in the years after 1870.

Just as the First World War focussed minds on the need for improved housing and health for the common man so it was with education. Sanderson points to the "remarkable increase in the number of children going to grammar school" from 187,000 in 1914 to 337,000 by 1920. Added to this, the conflict brought a relative affluence to members of a working class who enjoyed rising wages and high levels of employment and this meant that they could "now afford to let children stay on into secondary." Similarly, at the top end of education, in the university sphere, the requirements of fighting a modern total war, in which machines and all manner of new technologies were needed if victory was to be achieved, meant that a hitherto dry and rather moribund sector was called upon to interface with British industry in a new and vital way.

Unfortunately the impetus and vitality the conflict gave to improvements in education and its access tailed off after the armistice, even though the need for a literate and numerate population had been brutally underscored by the experiences of war. Plans for continuing technical education for sixteen and eighteen year olds, known as Continuation Schools, that were drawn up under the Fisher Act of 1918, either never got off the ground or were derailed by funding cuts in the early 1920s. This provision would have provided a valuable link between industry and schooling and its failure to materialise, alongside the withering of a prewar technical schools initiative due to financial constraints and a lack of support from employers, represented missed opportunities for British society and and British industry.

A variety of factors combined in the years after 1918 to stymie the various education initiatives that had been proposed. The great depression reduced the money available for education schemes, with defence spending taking priority by a factor of two or three, and high levels of unemployment, and the surplus of skilled labour it created, removed the apparent need for greater training. Also, on a domestic level, the straitened circumstances that much of the working class found themselves in meant finding work, in whatever form, took priority over learning. Without the pressures of war focussing the minds of policy makers and industry, short term thinking dominated once again. Another generation of talent, and the economic boost it could have provided, was thus lost to the nation through poor education provision.

Not in Front of the Children

During the 1930s, however, reorganisations in primary and secondary education were undertaken - although these were piecemeal when compared to the breadth of vision to be found in the debates of the time. Of particular note was the figure of Sir Henry Hadow, the educationalist and Vice Chancellor of Sheffield University. His thoroughgoing Board of Education reports *The Education of the Adolescent* (1926) and *The Primary School* (1931) had some impact in the prewar years, before 1939, and prefigured much of what was to be found in Butler's 1944 reforms. Within the long established elementary area Hadow recognised, and perhaps helped enshrine, the concept of primary education finishing at the age of eleven and that this stage must "have a character of its own".

Within the primary sector he acknowledged that this education fell into two well marked sectors, up to seven plus and up to eleven plus, and that, "where possible there should be separate schools for children under the age of seven." The growth of understanding of the physical (and psychological) changes that occur in children as they grow, and the changes that occur between the ages of seven and eleven, is marked out by a recognition of this being "a stage of vital importance" that should be given "appropriate educational treatment." In particular Hadow highlights this stage as "affording the best opportunity.... for making good past defects in the development of young children, and preparing them for the heavy demands entailed by rapid growth during puberty." Signalling the ever growing awareness of the importance of good health in children, and in particular "defects in vision or hearing, or any nervous peculiarities", and its impact on learning, the report calls for a concerted approach to be taken involving both teachers and school medical officers in tackling the "defects...responsible for much of the so-called backwardness in young children."

Not in Front of the Children

The 1931 *The Primary School* report and the 1926 *The Education of the Adolescent* report were part of a series of six influential parliamentary Consultative Committee reports made between 1923 and 1933 that placed a host of ideas, such as the applicability of different types of psychological testing such as intelligence, vocational and scholastic, at the heart of government thinking in the years after the war. Tellingly Hadow acknowledged the importance of the role played by make-believe - a factor that would come to play an increasingly important part in children's early years learning come the late 1960s.

In the report Hadow also signals the logic that would give rise to the eleven plus exam and the separation and streaming of children in secondary education in the years after the 1944 Butler Act. He writes: "Older children differ far more widely in intellectual capacity than younger children. It would, therefore, seem that while at the infant stage children may be grouped together without much regard to varying degrees of mental endowment, by the age of ten pupils in a single age group should be classified in several sections..." For Hadow, as was laid out in his 1926 report into secondary education, a good and successful national education system entailed all children receiving an education after eleven years of age in either a grammar or technical school. At this time the Local Education Authorities, which had been established more than twenty years before in 1902, were given increased funding as part of moves to facilitate what Lord Eustace of Percy, the President of the Board of Education described to parliament in December of 1926 as, "an expanding service and must be an expanding service." Indeed, Local Education Authorities, the guardians of local education provision since 1902, were encouraged to build new secondary schools at this time. Unfortunately, the provision of secondary education places for eleven to sixteen year olds was woefully small; rising from a meagre 7.2 per cent in 1922 to a paltry 9.9 per cent by 1937 according to Sanderson. However these weak figures should be seen in the light of just how enormous the task at hand was.

The country's school estate was patchy and many of those buildings that there were were crumbling and this acted as a drag on any progress. Such was the scale of the job at hand, just in terms of the elementary provision, that many MPs expressed concerns that even a survey of the work required would "have a depressing effect on a number of authorities". This survey of the "defective elementary school premises in urban areas", just one part of Lord Eustace of Percy's remit, would highlight the plethora of obstacles faced, many of which appeared to be statutory, by those wishing to reform the nation's education provision. The attitudes and requirements of previous times were woven into the administrative fabric of the school system. For his part Lord Eustace set about revising the regulations for "elementary, secondary and technical education, and the training of teachers in such way as would wipe out, as far as possible, unnecessary distinctions and unnecessary detailed requirements". In doing this it was hoped that a clear view would be attainable of the "educational needs according to the actual facts."

Unfortunately, neither One Nation Conservative paternalism nor the reforming zeal of the minority Labour governments of 1924 and 1931 could contend with the derailing effects of the Great Depression. A particular failure of this time was the inability to extend the benefits of grammar school education into working class communities. The National Governments of the 1930s and the Second World War would, however, do much to foster a climate of cooperation and, in 1944, R A Butler's Education Act cemented the ideal of educational progress in legislation. This much feted Act achieved many of the oft frustrated aims of those reformers who worked tirelessly to modernise the schooling of children in England and Wales. Amongst its achievements was the raising of the school leaving age to fifteen, a long held ambition amongst campaigners that had been thwarted again and again, and reforms to the grammar school sector, such as the abolition of fees, that ostensibly opened the way for greater access for children from poorer backgrounds.

Nowadays the Butler Act is often credited with establishing the grammar, secondary and technical school model; however, although the Education Act of 1944 placed a requirement on local authorities to provide appropriate secondary education for all, the nature of the provision was left up to each individual Local Education Authority. What was there already would dictate what would come after. This would be the case until the 1965, when Labour's Secretary of State for Education implemented the comprehensive school policy, not through an Act of Parliament but by means of an instruction mechanism to local authorities that was known as Circular 10/65. Comprehensives were not new. The first few examples had appeared as experiments in the years after the Second World War.

Passed in the months leading up to the D Day landings in June the government had to balance the passage of the Bill against the need to avoid a vote against the government at such a crucial time. One such issue of difficulty was the issue of equal pay for male and female teachers. In this particular instance War Cabinet meeting minutes of 28th of March 1944 show all members of Cabinet, right up to the Prime Minister Winston Churchill, being exercised by the possibility of defeat in a vote and what this would mean in terms of "opinion abroad" at a time when the "Government were committed to formidable military operations in the near future." In typical Churchillian fashion the Prime Minister proposed making the issue a "major one of confidence". In a very British way the issue of non-interference by the President of the Board of Education in the decisions of the independent wage tribunals was decided as something that would "form a feature of the post-war Civil Service."

Between 1944 and 1947 a succession of Acts radically altered the education systems of England, Wales, Northern Ireland and Scotland, building on the work of Hadow, Fisher and earlier administrative reformers such as Sir Robert Morant. A previously patchy and inconsistent provision became more uniform, at least outwardly. In tandem with the introduction of the Welfare State and the formation of the National Health Service by the Labour government, which again built on a wartime report written by Lord Beveridge in 1942, the health of the child was central to these reforms. Medical treatment, and milk and school meals for those who required them, were part of a package designed to ensure that children were fit and healthy enough to learn to the best of their abilities.

Despite the not insignificant change wholesale and uniform prescription was avoided. Private schools, which had been the focus of persistent campaigning by the Trades Union Congress during the war years, remained. As Ken Jones points out in his book *Education in Britain 1944 to the Present*, the continued presence of this system of fee paying schools would serve to re-entrench the dominance of the elite in university access and, subsequently, "positions of social and political power." Butler's much vaunted universal education provision, and those of the 1945 Labour government, eschewed homogeneity in the sector. In some ways this bequeathed a somewhat distorted system that, it could be said, failed to reshape the country for the needs of the modern world. All kinds of bastions of old privilege remained. In addition to the public schools a number of fee paying state supported schools offered a limited number of local authority scholarships to those children deemed educationally adept enough to join the ranks of those whose parents could pay - what Ken Jones calls the "top players of the state secondary sector". The comments of Labour's Secretary of State for Education, George Tomlinson, indicate a recognition that, no matter how far reaching the 1944 - 1947 reforms were, the system still had a long way to go: "My party... looks forward to the day when the schools in the state system will be so good that nobody will want their children to go to independent schools."

Just as Churchill and the War Cabinet had to balance change against public opinion so the post war governments had to accept that any developments had to be evolutionary. Labour were, after all, democratic socialists and anything that removed choice or the freedom to choose would have been contrary to the core beliefs of the party. Notwithstanding the inequalities that remained, the refashioning of education was a step change in the education millions of children would receive. Just as the National Health Service found a workable combination of public and private, as in General Practice provision, within the scope of local factors, so did education. For those who had long sought reform, only to see it flounder and fall short due to lack of political will or a shortage of money, the universal provision of secondary education suited to each child's needs was a significant victory.

Naturally, the debate did not end there. Calls would come (and still do come) from left and right to make education either more egalitarian or less expensive. In the context of the nation's perilous post war financial situation the changes could easily have been watered down to a point where they became meaningless or were swept away altogether. Demands from some on the right to end or reverse what had been agreed would continue even as the economy picked up in the early years of the 1950s, but for the most part there was agreement. The belief that Britain was a modern country that was fit for the modern world helped fuel a consensus that both national economic and personal growth depended on a continued commitment to good secondary education for all.

Between 1964 and 1970 Harold Wilson's Labour government built upon these changes as Britain underwent a process of unprecedented cultural and social revolution. Many sacred cows were slaughtered as traditions were upended and moral values challenged by the storm of opportunity created as the country groped toward egalitarianism through a universal provision of education, health and housing.

As with health and housing, education saw a rise in spending in the years after 1945, rising from an inter war level of around 3 to 3.5 percent to 4.1 percent on previous levels in 1965. From here it climbed steadily throughout the 1960s and early 1970s, before peaking at over 6 per cent in the mid to late 1970s. During the 1960s this level of spending was, however, lower than in all other advanced western economies, but in spite of this, and the game of catch up it would force the British economy to play, the level of spending would be more than twice the amount spent in the years before World War One. The rapid expansion of provision of secondary years education in the years after the Butler Act was added to by a growth in higher education as access to colleges, universities and new polytechnics further opened up education for the working classes.

But it was not simply about getting numbers through the door. In 1965 the Labour Secretary of State for Education and Science, Anthony Crosland, moved to tackle not only a long looming teacher shortage, caused by the boom in child numbers as well as the expanded access, but set about addressing teacher-pupil ratios as well. At the time complaints about what William Hamling, the Labour MP and teacher, referred to as the "illiterate louts...turned out from our schools" were commonplace in the press. However, Hamling bemoaned not the loutish behaviour of these products of the education system but instead the wasted talents of the majority of students. He spoke of the many young people (he actually spoke only of men but such were the times) with "brains, independence, and self-reliance," who would be a benefit to the teaching profession. In some ways Hamling's words highlight the enormity of the shift that had taken place in the years since the 1945 Butler Act.

In 1965 the preoccupation was with anxieties over a wasting of the talents of educated young people; eighteen years earlier, when the school leaving age was raised to fifteen, politicians and business leaders were more concerned with what impact losing three hundred and fifty thousand juvenile workers would have on traditional sectors like the cotton industry. That particular sector suffered an immediate shortfall in recruitment of eleven thousand. Indeed the hit to the economy due to the removal of this band of labour was not insignificant wage inflation between 1947 and 1948. Although the impact of this change was dramatic the distortion it caused was, however, only temporary - perhaps ameliorated by the beginning of postwar immigration in 1948. This much needed boost to the country's working population came from across Europe, Ireland and, mainly due to the British Nationality Act of 1948 that gave Commonwealth citizens free entry to Britain, from the Caribbean and the newly independent India and the new state of Pakistan.

The anxieties over wasted human capital that preoccupied politicians in the 1960s would, in time, provide impetus for the move towards non selective, comprehensive education. The growth in sociological studies, driven to an extent by the influx of people from working class backgrounds into university education and then university teaching, as access was extended, provided more and more evidence of the impact of a range of hitherto unconsidered factors on educational attainment.

In 1964, as the number of grammar schools in the country peaked at nearly thirteen hundred, there also came a growing understanding of the range of issues, from background, levels of poverty, family life, expectation of achievement, and any number of other sociological and psychological considerations, that the eleven plus based system ignored. A combination of longitudinal studies and in depth field reports by sociologist/educationalists like Brian Jackson, Dennis Marsden and James William Bruce Douglas uncovered the realities behind the assumptions law makers and educationalists had made about the lives of working class children. In particular these works shone a light on the myths surrounding background, intelligence and educational aptitude.

The importance of this work and its impact on the mindset of policy makers, both locally and nationally, cannot be under estimated. Variations in access to grammar school were stark due to regional variations in coverage and competition for limited places. Alongside this was the inherent bias of the 11 plus towards children from middle class backgrounds due to what Sanderson calls the middle class child's naturally "acquired range of vocabulary and fluency in grammar" from the home rather than school.

Alongside the rising understanding of the iniquities of the selective grammar school system researchers like Marsden and Jackson also sought a more radical rethinking of the national approach to education. According to Ken Jones in *Education in Britain* what they called for was not simply a way of "compensating for working class deficiency" but instead a "rethinking of what constituted education itself." In doing this Jackson and Marsden sought a system that avoided the "vastly simplified" readings of people's circumstances.

For the first time the multiplicity of subtle and complex interactions that could be found in any given street, neighbourhood or broader locality was recognised. Jackson and Marsden called for an education system that was responsive to this huge variety of circumstances. They were not alone. As Jones points out, Jackson and Marsden's prescription replicated attempts already being made by teachers, in the nation's new secondary moderns, to devise methods that were "based on dialogue rather than on cultural imposition." A host of educators and campaigners, many with what were described as 'sobering' experiences teaching in secondary moderns in urban areas, added their voices to the call for "a programme of curriculum reworking" that reflected the changing nature of post-war society. These calls also recognised the emergence of new dynamics within society that were driven by television, consumerism and free time and spawned the arrival of the teenager. Although some writers say that Labour's position remained focussed primarily around expansion of fair access rather than any revolutionary reshaping of education, the interventions of Wilson's government were groundbreaking.

Comprehensive schools may have existed before 1965, as part of a variety of local solutions, but taken in the context of the slow pace of reforms thus far Circular 10/65 was a paradigmatic shift in the approach of central government. In spite of this, however, the overarching approach still suffered from many of the same drawbacks found in the old system and it was left to individual teachers to try new methods, such as exploring the cultural realms of students, access to the arts, or an informality of approach in the classroom. Mainstream teaching opinion and government policy remained resistant. From 1965 onwards the number of comprehensive schools in the education mix expanded rapidly.

However, as Derek Gillard points out in *Education in England: a brief history* the Circular lacked any form of compunction, relying instead on wording that "made it clear that the government expects LEAs to go comprehensive". The document, in being an invitation to reform rather than an edict for change, reflected Labour Party policy that went back to George Tomlinson's time at the Ministry of Education between 1945 - 1951 that sought consensual change. This approach would not change after the snap 1966 general election when Wilson turned a barely workable majority of only four into a majority of ninety six. Despite this incremental approach the comprehensive reforms triggered a series of extensive, if rather unevenly applied, changes to the curriculum and teaching methods that would have an impact on schooling across the years.

Just as academics and politicians began to wake up to the rich diversity in working class culture, it was about change beyond recognition. However, the high handed paternalism that marked the elementary system of the years before Butler's reforms remained at the heart of the attitudes of the teaching profession for many years to come. The influx of new forms of popular culture, such as pop music or American comics, were regarded as obstructions to learning and it could be said that their presence was seen as a further manifestation of a working class culture that was scorned by much of the teaching profession as low brow. The job of the education service, it seems, was to elevate the student by inculcating values and attitudes that were essentially alien.

Change was occurring - even if it proved to be somewhat truncated in the end. In the Primary sector, although the 11 plus was the most visible casualty of the introduction of the comprehensive reforms, this exam, or variations of it, and the selection it represented, remained in many areas. This was for the most part due to an ideological commitment of the Conservative party to selection. As Derek Gillard notes in his comprehensive study of England's education system on his website educationengland.org.uk "the Conservatives seemed determined not to notice" that elsewhere "selective education systems were being replaced with comprehensive ones." Most of Europe, the Scandinavian countries, Canada, New Zealand and Japan had all "begun the process immediately after the war." Indeed, in some quarters of the Tory establishment doubts went further than a suspicion of comprehensive schooling to "doubts about the benefits of mass education" altogether.

Labour's pre-election rhetoric in 1964 envisaged a Britain where a reformed education system would sit at the heart of a bold phase of economic regeneration. All sectors, both private and public, would be marshalled together in a coordinated effort to modernise the country and turn around an already decades old slow decline. The stop go economic policies deployed by the Conservative government over the previous decade would come to an end and be replaced by an incomes policy, to control wages and prices, and interventionism. To facilitate a change in approach, attitudes and abilities that was deemed necessary to meet the challenges the nation faced Wilson's government proposed that the twin motors of investment and reform would be directed towards all aspects of the education system from Primary through to University level. The full power of the state would be brought to bear to promote innovation in industry, science, education, the economy. A new dynamic class of citizen would emerge, emancipated by a paradigmatic shift in social and cultural attitudes, to take advantage of the opportunities presented by this change. This was to be a democratic socialist revolution.

Unfortunately, the glint in Harold Wilson's eye was quickly dulled by the cold realities of life in office. For some the chain of events that followed is seen as the work of powerful forces of opposition, whose remit extended beyond the the ballot box, the niceties of domestic or even international politics and into the realm of international finance, manoeuvring to defend their own entrenched interests. Within weeks of Labour taking office in the October 1964 sterling began to come under pressure on the foreign exchange markets. Following this turn of events the pound remained weak. Longstanding economic problems, inherited from the previous administration, were suddenly viewed as needing urgent attention. It is worth noting, however, that although the Labour government were adopting a different economic orthodoxy to their Conservative predecessors, their intended approach was commonplace in the west at the time, and particularly so in Europe. By July of 1965 a second sterling crisis was underway. Under these pressures public spending was reduced and credit tightened.

Wilson called a snap general election in the March of 1966 and, despite his currency induced travails since coming to office, he greatly increased his majority from seventeen to ninety six. By the summer of '66 a third sterling crisis was underway and confidence in the pound collapsed. The government responded with a range of measures, including a raising of the Bank Rate to 7 per cent, wage and price freezes, curbs on the availability of Hire Purchase, cuts in public spending and restrictions on foreign travel.

The crisis abated and the pound recovered by the spring of 1967, allowing the more optimistic in the government to foresee a balance of payments surplus by the end of the year. Unfortunately, international tensions, including the closure of the Suez Canal, and a slew of poor trade and employment figures and industrial tensions, coupled with the end of restrictions on Hire Purchase and a boost in public spending, led to renewed pressure on sterling. At this time the government also announced that it intended to apply for membership of the European Economic Community.

On the 18th of November 1967 Harold Wilson announced a devaluation of the pound against the dollar, from $2.80 to $2.40. Over the preceding three years the pound had received extensive support from the IMF and the central banks of allies.

Despite these problems Wilson's government succeeded in implementing a series of important and significant reforms post 1966 that went a long way to realising the revolutionary ideas developed during the years in opposition. By harnessing the work of what Ken Jones calls "sympathetic academics and journalists" from the "new educational establishment" that had grown up following the post war reforms, the social and cultural make up of the nation was reimagined and then radically rebalanced.

This was not a sudden moment that came out of nowhere, but instead an evolution that can be traced back to the beginning of the twentieth century. However, the shifts created by Wilson's government, which were built on more overt changes that had been well underway since the 1950s, gave previously invisible and disenfranchised groups a voice in the national discourse for the first time. Women, ethnic minorities, homosexuals, young adults, teenagers and even children would all be viewed differently by the time Labour left office in 1970.

There was strong opposition to this from a variety of disparate sources that ranged from small c conservatives to the British Establishment, sectors of industry and even the security services. The difficult balancing act required to achieve his and his cabinet's stated aims meant that Wilson's government often had to rely on more circuitous methods so that the delicate coalition of voter interests that gave him his majority would not be blown apart. This has led some biographers and commentators to view Wilson's role as being more passive, but in truth this does him and his government a great disservice.

Much of the impetus for the changes came from a range of drivers that touched all classes and all kinds. In *Neophiliacs* Christopher Booker argues that the disintegration of the "traditional framework and attitudes of the lower classes" occurred due to the opening up of the minds of the "young urban lower class" during the 1950s through their experience of National Service, and by their access to "arts and drama schools, technical colleges and universities". Alongside these opportunities for personal growth and education Booker also points to the impact of "the new prosperity" that gave rise to a "sense of being on an ever-rising escalator." The Labour government of the 1960s recognised this and built upon it. It chose to see the change already underway not as a dangerous threat to the established order but as a dynamic and positive force that would unleash the untapped potential of the country's greatest asset: its people. More significantly policy began to reflect new attitudes towards the education and development of the youngest in society.

The work of the Population Investigation Committee began in 1945, under the direction of Dr JWB Douglas. Originally investigations were undertaken to examine the provision and effectiveness of ante-natal and maternity services. These investigations grew out of concerns over trends in infant mortality and fertility and the likely impact these factors would have on "national intelligence". Due to the success of the work the scope of the committee's investigations was extended to look at a variety of factors that could affect the life chances of children and in particular their intelligence and educational attainment. Funded by grants from foundations from its inception it was not until the early 1960s that the work of the Committee received government funding. This move coincided with a greater understanding of the importance of early years learning as a foundation for future achievements.

Maternal care, housing conditions and other general environmental factors were all examined and it was established that these factors had a deleterious effect on the IQ or measured intelligence of young children and thus their eventual success in the 11 plus exam. JWB Douglas's study *The Home and The School*, published in 1964, built upon this work, eschewing the prevailing emphasis other studies had placed on secondary and university education and instead choosing to focus on primary years. The work of the Population Investigation Committee ran parallel to and fed into the work of the government's Central Advisory Council for Education, which was established under section 4 of the 1944 Butler Education Act. The CACE's remit tended to focus on children of secondary school age, dealing with aspects such as a broadening of education to include extra-curricula activities and the role of exams.

In 1963 the CACE's chairman John Newsome published *Half our Future* (known as the Newsome Report) that acknowledged the essential importance, long understood by educationalists, that with specific measures and tailoring the educational attainment of those children previously deemed as being of lower ability could be vastly improved. This chimed with the slowly dawning realisation, which was perhaps the newly emerging spirit of the times that Wilson sought to capitalise on, that recognised that "human capital" could not be squandered if Britain was to succeed in the modern world. In other words, throwing people on the scrap heap at any age was neither good for the individual or the country. The CACE's remit ran only to England but other reports were written for other parts of the UK.

The Plowden Report, also known as *Children and their Primary Schools,* of 1967 was commissioned immediately after the Newsome Report and its findings signalled a long overdue shift in attitudes and methods in primary education. Alongside the Gittens report in Wales and *Primary Education in Scotland* it recognised that, freed from the yoke of selection and examination at eleven, children could and should enjoy a very different kind of education. Academic surveys, the work of social scientists, played a central role in the education reforms of the 1960s and the results of their work was regularly deployed by the various government commissions that sought to solve the evolving problem of how to make education work for the times. Reports like the Robbins Report, the Crowther Report, the Newsome and the Plowden Report were often supported by volumes of field research evidence and detailed interpretations. Echoing similar moves across whole sectors of British life, with moves that began in the closing years of the war, there was a belief in the power of empirical and scientific studies, coupled with analysis and theory, to solve any problem at hand. During the 1960s these reports were not simply treated as documents to debate but played a key role in government decision making and policy formulation.

With an essentially redistributive ethos at its core the Plowden report called for a targeting of resources in poor and deprived areas as way of offsetting the host of newly recognised disadvantages caused by poverty. It envisaged a proper engagement with problems caused by what Ken Jones refers to as "poor mother-child relationships and insufficient language stimulation". Instead of writing a child off as difficult, stupid or lazy, a range of active processes would tackle those issues that meant working class kids began life behind their middle class peers.

Not in Front of the Children

Influenced by the progressive atmosphere of the times Plowden draws extensively on the work of the Swiss psychologist Jean Piaget, whose work on child development, which began before the war, had done much to undermine the idea that individual intelligence was fixed. The sequence of intellectual development represented a more refined understanding of the processes at work in education, learning and development and Piaget's four stages, delineated as sensori-motor, intuitive thought, concrete operations and formal operations underpin much of Plowden. Central to this was the understanding that children think and reason differently, passing through these four invariant stages. For the first time the child was placed at "the heart of the educational process" and that process was seen as being experiential.

The rigid approach that thus far had seen children introduced to educational tasks without any regard for whether the child was ready was to be replaced by methods that recognised the huge range of "individual differences between children of the same age". For Piaget knowledge was not something handed down by the teacher but instead was something constructed through a child acting on objects - in this way, knowledge of the object would be gained. The passive learner, the dumb vessel for rote learning, was transformed into the active learner. An altogether more kindly and nurturing approach, Plowden emphasised learning through play, activity and experience, along with an awareness of the importance of the role of the internal and emotional life of a child in the learning process.

The world of painting and making models from egg cartons, dressing up boxes and imaginary play so familiar to anyone educated in the 1970s had arrived.

Condemned by its critics as being overly touchy feely, where every child was a winner so winning meant nothing at all, and lacking the necessary meat to prepare the individual for the world of work, Plowden sought to unlock the imaginative, creative and educational potential of every child in ways that, for many, were too revolutionary. It was also criticised, perhaps unfairly as it was part of an evolutionary process, for not dealing with the issues caused by racial diversity. For those who suffered from a difficult start in life, and who, under the old system, would have been written off, it sought to make redundant any need for streaming by tailoring the education they received to their specific circumstances.

Despite the criticisms and fears, Plowden's influences remained strong, if often diluted and undermined through a lack of resources, well into the twenty-first century. Like the permissive society, Plowden would come to be seen by some, who choose to ignore the already long entrenched decline that Plowden, Newsome et al were tasked with addressing, as symptomatic of a malaise that has afflicted British society since the 1960s.

The escapism that sits at the heart of *Mr Benn* was an escapism from an adult world of crowded streets and traffic jams, fading international prestige, seismic political and social change and the collapse of the old order and the certainties that went with it. Symbols of economic, civic and institutional continuity, such as the civil service and the government, along with other long venerated institutions of privilege like public schools and universities were being assailed from all angles. The long feared masses, the great unwashed, the lumpen proletariat were on the move, with access to education and opportunity at a level unthinkable even twenty years before. There was optimism but it was also a time of fear and insecurity with many, even those whose lives had benefitted immeasurably from the changes being wrought, asking where it would all end.

Not in Front of the Children

And then, with the streets teeming with the visible signs of this change, in the shape of new styles, booming pop and consumer culture and societal shift that saw sex and drugs and all manner of disruptive and disrespectful behaviour, the innocents, in the shape of the country's children, were also offered a chance to join in. Through Plowden even children from the most impoverished of backgrounds were invited to take flight and join with this world of possibilities, where their horizons were only limited by the scope of their newly released imaginations. Dressing up, make believe, game playing, creative expression and emotional literacy would, henceforth, be part of the daily life of millions of children. No longer seen as something worthless and unnecessary, play was understood as being a fundamental part of how a child learns. This built on the work of the psychologist and educationalist Susan Isaacs and her assessment that play was "the child's means of living and understanding life". In particular, in the early years of school children were encouraged to play dressing up games and imagine themselves as train drivers, doctors, nurses, chefs, cowboys, anything.

That world, where imagination and freedom of thought beckoned, was the one that Mr Benn escaped to every time he stepped through the green door at the back of the fancy dress shop.

However, and this is perhaps one of the most important aspects of Mr Benn, his experiences were not just fantasy or dreams that come to an end when, beckoned by the shopkeeper, he steps back into the changing room. No: through the mementos he gets to keep, like the box of matches in the *Red Knight*, the photograph in *Hunter* or the clown's red nose in *Clown,* Mr Benn's adventures are signalled as being real. For any child watching, this simple act validates their play, connecting their own internal world of make believe with the world of the grown ups.

Not in Front of the Children

Programmes like *Mr Benn* (and the books it came from) brought an end to a self satisfied world of children's entertainment, where the key message was one of preservation of the status quo, and captured the spirit of the times. From the mid 1950s onwards wave upon wave of changes had crashed against the citadel of patronage and established privilege. And with each of those changes the chances of unrest increased as long standing problems merged with issues created by a society built increasingly on possessions and credit.

The brief economic prosperity of the post austerity years ended in the late 1950s due to the stop start interventions of a Conservative government struggling to manage rising inflation. The good years of job and wage security, and the concomitant expansion of consumer spending, did not quite come to a crashing end, but the quid pro quo of the consumer boom, and the debt that fuelled it, was an increased sensitivity to the slightest change in the economic outlook. Alongside those who did well, in the regions of the country well placed to seize the opportunities presented by the new economy, were others who did not.

Growth, which was always relative anyway, was affected by a host of complicating local factors and was anything but uniform across the country. In particular, those areas of the economy that had long suffered from under investment and outdated practices, where systemic uncompetitiveness and low productivity had been hidden by the war and the economic Indian summer that the old empire provided as one last parting gift, were hit hardest. The traditional manufacturing sectors and those who worked in them, by their very nature often rooted in specific geographical regions, would finally pay the price for decades of neglect and under investment. The north east of England, Scotland, Northern Ireland and South Wales all struggled to adapt to

162

the multiplicity of factors that would, in time, make their core economic activities unsustainable. Germany and Japan in particular would benefit from a judicious use of post war aid and planning to leapfrog and leave behind the old lady Britannia in industries she once considered unassailably her own.

Parts of Britain would continue to struggle for many years, their plight exacerbated by inconsistent government policies that would see interventions curtailed on a whim or improperly delivered as the political climate or economic priorities changed.

This blight would affect even those sectors, like the aircraft industry or electronics, that were hailed as representing the best of British in the New Elizabethan Era. Inflated with unrealistic demands for all manner of projects these sectors would see unsustainable and damaging demands made on both manpower and capital, before ballooning costs or a shift in requirements saw their investments written off without a single order being placed.

However, the range and availability of new professional, semi-professional and service sector jobs grew. The hi-tech sectors flourished and the new education system provided the workforce of skilled and able labour needed. The shifting patterns of employment, away from old heavy industries towards new jobs in the service sector and hi-tech industries like electronics went hand in hand with the expanding abilities of the nation's workforce.

Unfortunately, the structural weaknesses within the British economy remained and in the late 1950s and the early 1960s a lot of political energy was devoted to the idea of modernisation. 'Human capital', the educated worker whose importance to the new skilled economy replaced the raw material of old like coal and iron, emerged in the 1960s as the benchmark that had to be monitored and nurtured by means of improved education. However, for all the investment in new schools and colleges, Britain's performance, in terms of growth, was roughly half to two thirds of that of her major competitors between 1960 and 1973. The list of causes for this malaise is long. Some of them were external, but many were self inflicted: oil price shocks, incomes policies, demand management, bloated defence spending in pursuit of sovereign pride and global influence, short term-ism and under investment, obsolete equipment, sluggish management in industry, outdated regulations and working practices, disappearing markets in the old empire, the dragging effects of the sterling area, low productivity, poor or inadequate training and education, and uneven growth - all of these contributed to the true picture of decline that lay behind the myth of plenty that grew up around the 1950s and 1960s.

For many in the blossoming suburban centres where new prefabricated school buildings, brimming with equipment and ambition, sprang up alongside the estates and shopping areas, life was markedly different to anything that had been experienced before. As we saw in the previous chapter, some were left behind as Britain's old Victorian cities witnessed a flight of talent, either out of their urban centres to their suburban fringes or, in the worst cases, to different cities altogether, where the new kind of highly skilled jobs could be found. A not insignificant group of low and under skilled workers, often immigrants from the Caribbean and Ireland and the traditional British working class, who did the low skilled, low paid jobs that remained, continued to suffer from poor social infrastructures such as slum housing and dilapidated and underperforming schools. This group, locked in a cycle of poverty, prejudice and disenfranchisement, would remain an insoluble problem for decades to come.

More sensitive to the ebb and flow of the country's economic life, their experiences of and interactions with the cradle-to-grave ministrations of the welfare state were illustrated perfectly in the 1972 BBC documentary *The Block*. Unemployed and unemployable, poorly educated and poorly fed, shunted from slum home to slum home and never able or allowed to put down roots, in many ways the lives of these families resemble those of the poor from one hundred years before. The collision of attitudes, between the highhanded and patronising officials and the struggling and bewildered residents of the block is as fascinating as it is bleakly sad. The recipients of this bottom layer of safety net provision are variously awkward and belligerent or subservient and obsequious in their dealings with the besuited officials as they are channelled through the system by agents who are suspicious of their motives and weary of the problems they cause.

On the whole though, the post war education reforms meant access to a better quality of education for longer. A better curriculum and an engagement with new educational ideas meant that, as well as developing young people fit for the needs of a modern economy, the system created a force for change in society. Youth, the teenager, and the emergence of a popular culture that was aimed specifically at them, meant change.

There was a belief, at the beginning of the 1950s, as prosperity grew and the benefits of the welfare state made themselves felt, that the class war was finally over. As the 1960s got under way, however, the new pressures in people's lives, from the things they wanted and the payments due, from the freedoms gained and the questions that those freedoms raised, merged together. By the latter part of the decade the result of all of these pressures would be growing civil and industrial strife.

By 1971, when Mr Benn first hit the nation's TV screens, the optimistic, experimental exoticism of the late 1960s had given way to a very different reality, as the economy faltered, inflation took hold and union militancy increased. In 1970 Ted Heath's Conservative party had won a shock election victory over Harold Wilson's reforming Labour party, bringing an end to six years of unprecedented progressive political change that included the abolition of the death penalty, the decriminalisation of homosexuality, the legalisation of abortion, divorce law reform, the Equal Pay Act, the expansion of the voting franchise to 18 year olds and the introduction of comprehensive schools. What had occurred in that election of 1970 was a backlash by significant numbers of terrified small 'c' conservatives. These were the people that Barbara Castle referred to as the "silent majority sitting behind its lace curtains", people who believed that traditional values were in mortal danger, threatened by the evils of immigration, promiscuity, drugs, rock and roll and homosexuality. The post war years had seen unprecedented levels of change, as family, community and society were altered beyond all recognition, in part due to a rapid expansion of consumerism and a concomitant increase in permissiveness in all spheres of life. The reforms of Wilson's government represented not a leading edge after all, but instead a trailing wake, as national institutions caught up. Society is, however, not homogenous and as the British people struggled to adapt to the plethora of changes wrought on them in the 1950s and 1960s there would be many who wished to turn the clock back to what they saw as a simpler time.

Chapter Four

Scooby Doo and Our American Monsters

The term "permissive society" was coined in 1968 and very quickly passed into the lexicon of overused phrases deployed as a catch all for the perceived decline in morality and standards. Labour were in power, Churchill was dead and the Conservative Party were in disarray. The establishment feared the left and a breakdown in the social order, of the deference to authority that was the long term source of their power. Staid certainties that had underwritten British society for decades seemed to be under assault as citizens embraced a new found confidence and patterns of living and life shifted. Wilson's Labour government presided over unprecedented progressive political change that included the abolition of the death penalty, the decriminalisation of homosexuality, the legalisation of abortion, divorce law reform, the Equal Pay Act, the expansion of the voting franchise to 18 year olds and the introduction of comprehensive schools.

The phenomenon of mass popular culture gripped the country and through it sex, it seemed, was everywhere: in the cinema, on the television, in the pages of literary fiction and the grinding, pounding beat of rock music. For many it was all too alien and strange. The contraceptive pill had removed the fear of pregnancy and because of this church teachings, which said sex was wrong, no longer seemed to matter anymore. London swung and, if the hysterical tone of the British press was to believed, the whole nation was engaged in what the *People* newspaper called "decadent moral behaviour".

167

Not in Front of the Children

British and American society and culture were in lockstep as never before, with a rapid and fruitful cross fertilisation of ideas and concepts creating a juggernaut of potent ideas and attitudes. Film, television and music all benefitted from this process in a time of unprecedented creativity that would give momentum to the changes and a voice to those upon whose lives they were wrought.

American movies had exerted their own influence over British audiences for decades but with the increasing uptake of television this influence would be extended further still. For British children the American cartoon show offered a very different alternative to the kind of thing being produced by homegrown animators. These shows were faster paced and more exciting than their British counterparts and their hand drawn stars were generally cooler and more with it. Usually the product of lucrative sponsorship hook ups the US cartoons mimicked the pacing and style of the emerging world of mass television marketing.

By the mid-1960s pop music itself, that signifier of rebellion for much of the 1950s and 60s, had been dragooned into the service of the big sales push. Hollywood had recognised the potency of the pop music revolution when they commissioned the *Monkees'* TV show - constructing a mock Beatles band that was, for the American NBC network at least, designed to sell Kelloggs breakfast cereals.

The decision by Kelloggs to harness the power of pop made perfect commercial sense. If you were eight years old in America in 1968 the chances are you'd start your day with a nice bowl of sugary cereal. The most important meal of the day was big business and, with children being the most lucrative part of that business, 90 per cent of all cereals advertising was directed at the youngest in society. Post Cereals, General Mills, Nabisco, Quakers Oats, Ralstons and Kelloggs fought it out on the gingham battlefield with brands like Hunny Munch, Corneroos, Clackers, Rice Cream Flakes, Sugar Cones, Cocoa Krispies, Apple Jacks, OKs and Sugar Smacks. Kelloggs dominated the sector, holding 43 per cent of the market, driven largely by their pioneering of pre-sweetened cereals and an aggressive use of television ad campaigns from the mid-1950s onwards. Where adults had to settle for soberly packaged regular products like Raisin Bran and 40% Bran, kids were lured by an array of brightly coloured "cartoon pitchmen" such as Tony the Tiger and Yogi Bear.

Never one to miss a sales opportunity, Kelloggs identified the burgeoning pop music phenomenon of the 1960s as an efficient route into the homes and minds of America's young. Taking up the sponsorship of NBC's new rock 'n' roll band based TV show, *The Monkees*, from its inception in 1966, Kelloggs enjoyed considerable penetration through its association with the Prefab Four.

Hit records, Emmy Awards and a mainlining of the cuter aspects of the pop culture zeitgeist made this relationship a fruitful one. Where serious bands like the Byrds or Jefferson Airplane sought to explore difficult questions in their music, The Monkees offered an extreme form of escapism. At a time when the airwaves were full of bad news stories about Vietnam this was just what was needed, even for many older teens. By 1968, however, with Micky Dolenz, Michael Nesmith, Peter Tork and Davy Jones of the Monkees looking to seize creative control over their music, doubts would emerge over the compatibility of the show with the Kelloggs corporate vision. Alongside exercising their artistic muscles in the recording studio the band wanted to change the format of their television programme from one that followed their madcap adventures into a more variety based offering. The upshot of this newfound expressive confidence was that NBC cancelled the show and Kelloggs, perhaps uneasy about the potential for real rock 'n' roll behaviour from the band as they continued with their careers, withdrew their sponsorship of reruns. NBC were left with a gap in their primetime schedule and Kelloggs needed a new pop group to appeal to eight year olds - preferably one that would not succumb to the lure of the counterculture.

Kelloggs discovered a new vehicle for their product in the costume clad figures of *The Banana Splits Adventure Hour*. But the band format was appealing and other channels sought to develop their own pop music based shows in the form of cartoons.

Scooby Doo, Where Are You!, the cartoon show about the crime fighting adventures of four young adults and their dog, was produced as a response to the changing tastes and attitudes of the late 1960s and represented a shift from the superhero orientated action cartoons that dominated the kids' TV schedules of the mid-sixties. Made at a time when TV studios and advertisers found themselves looking for total control over their fake pop charges, animation offered the perfect solution. *The Archies, Josie and the Pussie Cats* and their puppet cousins the Banana Splits were just some of the more successful formats that studio bosses came up with. Scooby Doo and the gang also came out of that push - though in the end they never really played any gigs at all.

A small group of animation studios had fulfilled the seemingly unquenchable appetite of the kids of America for superhero cartoon action. Shows like Hanna-Barbera's *Space Ghost* (1966-1968), *Frankenstein Jr.* and *The Impossibles* (1966) and Gantry-Lawrence Animation's *The Marvel Super Heroes* (1966), offered an exciting blend of fast moving, colourful and violent action to the Saturday morning TV audience of boys and girls. However, although attitudes to what was permissible on television were pretty open, in comparison to the UK, there were a number of active and vocal parent watch groups in the USA that found the content of these shows unacceptable. Accordingly, *Scooby-Doo Where Are You!* was planned by CBS and Hanna-Barbera as an uncontentious alternative for the Saturday morning slot in the schedule.

In his blog *TV Legends Revealed* Brian Cronin pinpoints the inspiration behind the show as being a combination of the early sixties live action TV show *The Many Loves of Dobie Gillis* and the 1968 animated series *The Archie Show*. More directly, Cronin reveals that Fred Silverman, the head of daytime programming at CBS, asked Hanna-Barbera for a series that combined the "gang playing in their band" element of Archie with a mystery solving element.

Silverman was a fan of the Universal Monster and Horror film series that began in 1923 and ran until 1960 and he wanted his new cartoon show to have some of those spooky elements. These seminal horror films, featuring the acting talents of such greats as Boris Karloff, Bela Lugosi, Vincent Price, Claude Rains, Lon Chaney and Basil Rathbone, bequeathed to the world a host of classics including *Son of Frankenstein*, *The Invisible Man* and *House of Dracula* and, by the end of the sixties, had inspired a new generation of imitators.

Hanna-Barbera asked writers Joe Ruby and Ken Spears to produce the show alongside artist Iwao Takamoto. The first incarnation of the idea, dubbed *Mysteries Five*, featured five teenage members of a band called the Mysteries Five who, along with their bongo playing dog, Too Much, solved mysteries. The idea was reject by Silverman, but after several reworkings, including the ditching of the band idea, making it less scary and more funny, plus a couple of title changes, the show was pitched to the executives upstairs at CBS. It was accepted. A remnant of the original concept did survive in the name of the Scooby gang's van, the Mystery Machine.

Not in Front of the Children

The show first aired in September 1969 and ran for 25 episodes over two seasons. A light psychedelic theme tune was composed by David Mook and Ben Raleigh and performed by Larry Marks. Mook, a composer, arranger and producer for Hanna-Barbera, also wrote the music for *The Banana Splits Adventure Hour*. Raleigh was a notable lyricist whose songs were recorded by Nat King Cole, Aretha Franklin, The Monkees and many more. Larry Marks is better known for his work as a producer at Colombia and A&M Records, where he worked with artists such as The Flying Burrito Brothers, Gene Clark, Liza Minnelli and Helen Reddy. After the first season the Marks version was replaced by a more punchy recording of the song from Arkade frontman Austin Roberts.

Despite the apparently supernatural pretext of *Scooby Doo Where Are You!* rationalism and deductive reasoning always wins the day and proves there are no such things as monsters - although this success is always helped along by a large dollop of chance and accident. It could be said that the pretext and plots of *Scooby-Doo Where Are You!* have the gang engaged in a microcosmic version of the philosophical struggle that engulfed the USA in the late 1960s. As Tribbe explores in his book *No Requiem for the Space Age*, this was a struggle that saw the preeminent idea of American postwar rationalism pitted against the new consciousness of the countercultural revolution: one that elevated the status of the spiritual, mysterious and utopian. In 1969 the USA was, according to Tribbe, faced with a stark choice between "the rationalist trajectory that had guided the nation through the post war years and ultimately took them to the moon," and new cultural priorities. Referring to Reich's 1970 book *The Greening of America*, Tribbe explores the challenge the young made to the established order and the arrival of "an entirely new consciousness". Reich called this "Consciousness III" and described it as being "deeply suspicious of logic, rationality, analysis and of principles." Each mystery solved in *Scooby-Doo Where Are You!*, each unmasking of a spook or ghoul as another dodgy museum curator peddling fakes, may be seen as operating as a victory for the attitudes of the establishment. Technology is represented by Fred and his contraptions, rational thought by Velma and the rule of law by the arrival of the Sheriff. However, these victories are only ever achieved with the accidental assistance of Shaggy and Scooby in the form of chaotic and ill-disciplined interventions.

Their status as a gang is dubious. The constituent parts operate in contradiction of the accepted youth conventions, with each member coming from a different teen tribe: Fred is a brave and muscular surf-jock, with a love of contraptions and machinery, who seeks to take charge and to tackle problems head on; Velma is an intelligent, sharp witted and independent feminist woman who, suffering neither fools nor foolish superstitious ideas, adopts a positivist approach to any mysteries; Shaggy is cowardly, an embodiment of selfish fulfilment and personal gratification - an embodiment of the counterculture as viewed by the establishment - while Scooby is Shaggy's Id, a physical manifestation of his pleasure principle; Daphne, in her mini dress and Alice band hairstyle, a style that was already three years out of date in 1969, bobs along like a mass culture cork, an outdated old guy's view of what the kids are into today. Daphne and Scooby also act as a kind neutral glue for a group that is, socially at least, worlds apart.

Just as Velma's withering put downs of the blithering Shaggy assert the icy preeminence of the intellectual self over the unthinkingly superstitious and gullible, so Shaggy's constant desire to leave the job at hand to gratify himself with ridiculously over indulgent confections, like chocolate covered hot dogs, debases him. So unable is he to control his desires that he will even eat Scooby snacks: a dog treat.

Lacking either self-respect or self-control the unkempt Shaggy is thus placed at the level of a dog.

Fred's contraptions, representing what Reich calls Consciousness II and the world view of liberal post war rationalism, are often interfered with by the chaotic and slapstick behaviour of Shaggy and Scooby. These accidents occur as they pursue their own selfish desires. In this way Shaggy is the embodiment of the establishment view of Consciousness III and of Marcusian ideas of the New Left. Scooby on the other hand is a dog and can't help himself.

One member of the cast of *Scooby-Doo Where Are You!* is worth a particular mention. Shaggy was voiced by Casey Kasem, an actor, voiceover artist and DJ who, just prior to working on *SDWAY!*, appeared in three Biker films. *The Glory Stompers*, which starred Dennis Hopper, *The Cycle Savages* which starred Bruce Dern (and was co-produced by Kasem) and *Wild Wheels* all explore the violent and misogynistic world of the youth gangs that represented part of the threat to the stability and order of American society. Don Messick (Scooby), Frank Welker (Fred), Nicole Jaffe (Velma) and Stefanianna Christopherson (Daphne in season 1) had altogether more respectable and mundane CVs.

But what of the Britain that *Scooby-Doo Where Are You!* was parachuted into in 1969? Despite appearances and the cultural cross pollination, Britain and America were radically different places. Formed by different experiences and governed by the interaction of wildly different social forces and conventions the porting of this, and other cartoons like it, into the local cultural nexus throws those peculiarly British aspects into sharp relief.

It can appear as if British popular culture of the Sixties arrived fully formed, delivered from another planet, in 1962, through the combined actions of a group of mysterious creative wizards and magic gurus. Of course this is untrue: ordinary working class people had always enjoyed entertainment of one kind or another, often to the dismay of their self-appointed guardians in the bourgeois and upper classes. The difference in the 1960s was that, with an increasingly open society, and driven by the expansion of television and the availability of recorded music, this grass roots, popular entertainment appeared to have a wider impact. The commercial possibilities of exploiting both working class culture and the market that was the working class were, indeed, significant. However, in opening this Pandora's box, and unleashing the monsters within, fears, long held by the establishment, on both the left and right, were ignored.

Stretching as far back as the 1930s Britain's elites had expressed concerns about the effect leisure activities would have on the attitudes and outlook of the working class. At that time many in those elites feared the negative consequences of the boom in cinema-going and, as Robert James notes in his book *Popular Culture and Working-class taste in Britain, 1930-39*, many investigations found that "much of what was wrong in society could be blamed on the type of leisure activity in which people partook." And it wasn't just cinema that was considered dangerous. The BBC was noted for its active attempts to diminish the impact of American jazz music during the 1920s and 1930s. Incidentally, faced with the increasing inroads made by continental radio stations, such as Radio Luxembourg, during the 1930s, Auntie's efforts to kill jazz proved futile - a mistake it would repeat during the 1960s.

As James notes, during the 1930s middle class left-wing observers had concerns over popular culture that revolved around a "dissatisfaction with the working classes' apparent lack of interest in politics." Eminent writers such as George Orwell and J B Priestley felt that leisure, and in particular cinema, prevented the working classes from engaging in political activity by distracting them and causing them to be apathetic. Popular culture was viewed as debased and debasing, signalling a race to the bottom. This dissatisfaction led those observers of working class life and leisure to imagine a time when they would and should approach the lives of their selected targets in the proletariat with the spirit of missionaries. They saw themselves as agents for change in what James calls a "crusade for cultural renewal." The quarterly journal *Scrutiny* and the *Left Review* offered different approaches - with *Scrutiny's* own avowed organised ideology free stance, as stated in its 'manifesto', standing in contrast to the *Left Review's* communist credentials, as backed by the Comintern and the International Union of Revolutionary Writers.

Concerns over the corrosive effect of mass culture would continue throughout the 1940s and 1950s. During the 1950s, as the opposition Labour Party floundered, even in the face of a torpid and increasingly moribund Conservative government, the voices of young intellectuals on the left grew louder, more urgent and more divisive. On the one hand, there were those who were loosely focussed around the Partisan Coffee House in Soho. John Berger, Stuart Hall and Raymond Williams, the social and cultural theorists, Karel Reisz and Lindsay Anderson the film makers, Doris Lessing the novelist and the folk singer Peggy Seeger were all to be found within the cramped confines of the Partisan, enjoying the Carlisle Street cafe's fevered intellectual atmosphere. This non-aligned vision, as espoused by Frank Leavis's *Left Review*, lay at the heart of what would become known as the New Left. This was a rejection of all establishment power - in whatever form it took. American capitalism and consumerism and Soviet control of the communist party were rejected, as were the mainstream prescriptions of Labour's democratic socialism.

Incidentally, there also emerged an alternative path for the Labour Party when Antony Crossland (the future reforming education secretary under Wilson) published his own revisionist text *The Future of Socialism* in 1956. This painted a new social democratic vision for Labour, "revising Marxism," as Crossland claimed, and placing some form of accommodation with capitalism front and centre. Repudiating a dogmatic adherence to nationalisation he dismissed ownership of the means of production as irrelevant, stating: "it would be more significant to define societies in terms of equality, or class relationships, or their political systems." Crossland's ideas called for a perpetual state of scrutiny of the means of achieving the aims of socialism that took account of changing conditions and circumstances. This, Crossland argued, would see "a redistribution of rewards, status, and privileges egalitarian enough to minimise social resentment, to secure justice between individuals and to equalise opportunities".

The New Left, as it developed beyond the cosy confines of Soho's coffee shops, emerged in part due to the collision between a hitherto idealistic ideological commitment to the authoritarian worldview propagated by the Communist Party of the Soviet Union and the hard realities of that system's response to the Hungarian Revolution of 1956. Many members of the Communist Party of Great Britain and the Communist Party of the USA struggled to come to terms with the brutal repression of a revolt that began as a loose and leaderless student demonstration and progressed to a popular uprising. Alternatives needed to be found.

Trotsky had long held an appeal for those on the left who sought to distinguish themselves from the bureaucratic Soviet Communism of Stalin and co, but by the late 1950s and early 1960s a new generation of believers required something other than this other. To this end these fresh young idealists sought out forgotten leaders and thinkers whose programmes had been snuffed out, it seemed, all too soon. There, in the writings of György Lukács, Antonio

177

Gramsci and Rosa Luxemburg, in the untested, virgin terrain of philosophies and ideas unsullied by the corrupting forces of history and real world events, they discovered potential, reinvention and, perhaps most importantly of all, a future not bloodied by associations with the brutal authoritarianism of the Soviet regime. In an age where the individual story was increasingly preeminent, the romantic appeal of these figures was a potent factor: Luxemburg, the Polish-Jewish Marxist theorist who was murdered by government mercenaries during the German Spartacist uprising of 1919; Gramsci, the Italian Marxist philosopher and politician, co-founder of the Italian Communist Party who was imprisoned by the Fascists and died after nine years behind bars, aged only 46; György Lukács, the Hungarian Marxist philosopher, politician and commissar who was forced to abjure his writings and narrowly survived Stalin's Great Terror and also the purges that followed his involvement in the 1956 Hungarian Revolution - each of these figures offered a possible future path for the left. More importantly, however, their writings also offered intellectual renewal and, along with writers like Theodore Adorno, Max Horkheimer and Herbert Marcuse, the means by which the left could engage with the world as it had become under post war capitalism.

Gramsci's work on the coercive use of cultural hegemony by the ruling class - Adorno's writings on the subjugation of mass society through popular culture - Marcuse's discussion of history as a fight against the repression of our instincts - each of these gave the New Left an answer to the overwhelming appeal of capitalist consumer culture.

The intellectual father of the New Left is widely regarded as being Herbert Marcuse, the German Jewish critical and political theorist and leading light in the Frankfurt School of Critical Theory who emigrated to the USA in 1934. His critiques of capitalism and entertainment culture argued that these aspects of modern society represented a new and insidious form of social control, what he described as "bubblegum for the eyes". Another slightly less catchy term that Marcuse coined was "repressive desublimation" which speaks to the process by which an individual unwittingly adopts a degraded humanity through an engagement with an alienating culture. Glibly speaking, Marcuse's postulation in *Eros and Civilization* (first published in 1955 but republished in 1966 with a "political preface") that sex is the preserve of those in power, the betters in society, and that the worker may only indulge when it does not interfere with production and economic performance, gave an intellectual framework around which the sexual freedoms made possible by the new contraceptive pill could be hung - sex became a form of legitimised rebellion. In some respects a rejection of the heavy hand of Freud, nineteenth century morality, protestant guilt and all manner of outmoded and controlling social mores, *Eros and Civilization* helped define the subcultures of the 1960s. The time for repression, it seemed, was over and those unwritten rules that governed the lives of ordinary people could now be challenged. Whether it was through challenging perceived totalitarian aspects in capitalist democracies, as in his 1965 essay *Repressive Tolerance*, or speaking at and in support of the student protests, Marcuse was as much part of the dissenting politics of the time as he was its intellectual father. His influence on a generation of thinkers and activists cannot be underestimated. Kathy Acker, Abbie Hoffman, Angela Davis, Robert M Young and Norman O Brown, to name but a few, would all exert their own long felt influences on the political, sociological and countercultural movements that would emerge in the 1960s and 1970s.

With all this talk about sex and repression it is perhaps unsurprising that there were those in the fields of psychiatry and psychoanalysis ready to embrace this new paradigm. R D Laing's radical approach, contained both within the pages of his book *The Divided Self* and the walls of his experimental asylum Kingsley Hall, co-opted a range of ideas from the philosophers of the left. Aside from his administering of LSD, the it drug of the time, Laing's practices were based around a framework that saw nervous breakdowns as being brought about by the conflict experienced when an individual's false mask of the self is suddenly removed. Appositely, for a time when sections of society were discovering a conflict between their own outlooks and desires and those of their mothers and fathers, Laing suggested that the "family's function is to repress Eros" and separate the individual from real experience. Many newly opened young minds in Britain's institutions of higher education were receptive to his call to shake off the "false consciousness of security" induced by family and reject their status as respectful, one dimensional people - at least until the year of their university finals.

Perhaps alive to this new fashion for psychiatric illness and its capacity to provide release, a point raised by Jon Savage in his book *1966*, the Rolling Stones put out their tenth UK single '19th Nervous Breakdown' on the fourth of February 1966. A sneering attack on spoilt rich kids, the song targets the children of the wealthy elites who lay claim to a host of mental health problems despite their cosseted lives. There is even a possible reference to the vogue for LSD as a therapeutic treatment with the line: "On our first trip I tried so hard to rearrange your mind."

The hunger for new approaches and fresh paradigms also led those on the New Left to explore the metaphysical essays of a young Karl Marx dating from the early 1840s. Naturally, as this work had been completed whilst he was only just in his twenties, Marx had published very few of these junior texts. Interest in them rose in the early 1960s, mainly because they chimed with the spirit of an age where the discourse was preoccupied with a transformation of mankind's alienated consciousness instead of control of the means of production.

For the old guard of the left, the academics, and the leadership of the established Communist and Trotskyist parties, this rummaging around in Marx's laundry basket was deeply troubling. It threatened their carefully constructed and policed authority and hierarchies with its glib and devil-may-care interpretations of the great man's private works. Added to this all they wanted to do was talk about sex - a subject that would never sit easily with the Old Left's hidden roots in Methodism and Protestantism.

Worst of all, a desire for collectivism had, it seemed, given way to reactionary individualism. Rejecting the 'repressive tolerance' of Western capitalist consumer society was one thing, but accepting that that consumer society no longer functioned, as capitalism once had, through the straightforward economic exploitation of the proletariat turned things upside down. Added to this, Marcuse's idea that capitalism now deployed a range of subtle and not so subtle devices to subvert and divert a nebulous form of human energy away from its real sexual, civic and social needs must've seemed alien, strange, even laughable, to the old guard. Unfortunately for that old guard, Marcuse's epistemology resonated so effectively with the broader changes that were occurring in society that it vaulted the walled confines of university campuses and became part of a broader popular consciousness. Capturing the minds and imaginations of a significant part of a whole generation of young people, if only in terms of a third hand and diluted influence on fashions and attitudes, it would form the foundation of much of the countercultural lifestyles that swept the West in the 1960s and beyond.

For the vast majority of the Great British general public this would mean being confronted, if only in the news, by men with long hair and sexually precocious young women in shockingly short skirts. A seemingly unruly rabble, these young men and women protested against the H Bomb or in support of civil rights, challenging the sage and hitherto unchallenged wisdom of their elders and betters.

London was the focal point for this rapid change, its influence resonating not just throughout the British Isles but around the world. Driven by media interest from both home and abroad the capital would come to be seen as a symbol of a 'social revolution'. Music, art, fashion, photography and design vibrated with a popular energy never known before. Exciting new materials and styles dazzled a nation still waking up from the long grim years of austerity. Sooty brick and stone, dark wool and worsted, the daily visual appetite for so long in dear old Blighty, was suddenly and shockingly juxtaposed against shiny, brightly coloured plastics and PVC. Elsewhere in the country things would happen more slowly, if not at all, as families and communities, dismayed by the fanciful dreams of their own local Billy Liars, resisted and mocked the insidious cult of the teenager. As nice as it is to think that the world of Carnaby Street and the Kings Road flooded out and over the murky skylines of Britain's declining industrial cities, lighting people's lives with the 'Op Art Look' and the mood of Swinging London, little changed, in the material sense, for the vast majority of working class people. Life went on, as it always had, with bills to pay and jobs to be done.

London and in particular Soho's role in all of this didn't come about due to a convoluted design or a sophisticated marketing plan. It grew up organically, through complex interactions between different cultures, classes and ways of living that, as Frank Mort explores in his book *Capital Affairs*, revolved around sex and sexuality, crime and the criminal underworld. In particular the establishment's evolving responses to these issues, through the press and government enquiries, would help shape the national climate in the 1950s and 1960s. What Mort describes as the "moral anxiety" and the "escalating concern about transgressive sex" placed London in a "paradigmatic role in national debates" about pubic probity. The "successive moral panics" that were driven by salacious and sensationalist coverage in a newspaper industry seeking to respond to the challenge, "thrown down" by television, to "revamp its language", in turn fed into calls for action from purity campaigners and then through into government responses.

Perhaps the most famous of these, by dint of its unexpected consequences on the Victorian, even medieval, moral and ethical underpinnings of British society, was the Report of the Departmental Committee on Homosexual Offences and Prostitution - more commonly known as the Wolfenden Report. Male homosexuality had been illegal in England since 1553 through the Buggery Act; this law had been made more punitive with the introduction of the 1885 Criminal Law Amendment Act - which made all homosexual acts, even those conducted in private, illegal. However, in the changing climate of the late 1950s, and following a string of high profile convictions for homosexual offences, the decision to look at the law's response to both homosexuality and prostitution was pressing.

The report's committee, which was chaired by John Wolfenden, was constituted of three women and twelve men and included representatives from political, religious, medical and judicial backgrounds. Aside from the medical component of the committee, Dr Joseph Whitby and Dr

Desmond Curran, whose professional experience was particularly focussed around the field of psychiatry, its make up resembled the British establishment in miniature: Mrs Mary G. Cohen the vice-president of the City of Glasgow Girl Guides; Reverend Canon V A Demant the Catholic-Anglican Regius Professor of Moral and Pastoral Theology at Oxford University; Mr Justice Diplock the High Court Judge; Sir Hugh Linstead OBE the pharmaceutical chemist, barrister and Conservative MP for Putney; Peter Francis Walter Kerr the 12th Marquess of Lothian, peer, landowner and Foreign Office minister; Mrs Kathleen Lovibond CBE, chair of the Uxebridge Juvenile Magistrates' Court and active member of the Conservative women's organisation; Victor Mishcon Labour Party member of London County Council; William T Wells the Labour MP and Barrister; Lady Stopford, a doctor and magistrate; Goronwy Rees, Principle of University College Wales; Reverand R F V Scott, Presbyterian Minister.

Rees would resign from the committee in 1956, around the time drafting of the report began, when he was outed as the anonymous author of a series of sensationalist Guy Burgess focussed articles in the *People* newspaper. This scandal would have a significant impact on the work of the Wolfenden inquiry, potentially undermining its carefully calibrated and rigorous work.

The committee, appointed in 1954 by the Conservative Home Secretary David Maxwell-Fyfe, was charged with looking into "the law and practice relating to homosexual offences and the treatment of persons convicted of such offences by the courts; and the law and practice relating to offences against the criminal law in connexion with prostitution and solicitation for immoral purposes." Parliamentarians of the day were acutely aware that public opinion and attitudes towards homosexual sex and prostitution had moved on and that the law had ceased to function in step with what the Home Secretary Maxwell Fyfe called "modern knowledge and ideas". As early as 1927 the Street Offences Committee, under the Chairmanship of Mr Hugh Macmillan, had stated that: "As a general proposition it will be universally accepted that the law is not concerned with private morals or with ethical sanction." This proved to be the Wolfenden Committee's guiding principle as reflected in their processes and the final report. However, Wolfenden also accepted the 1927 Street Offences Committee's further stipulation that: "On the other hand, the law is plainly concerned with the outward conduct of citizens in so far as the conduct injuriously affects the rights of other citizens." This starting point would, in many ways, lead to the division of opinions on the final report that saw its recommendations, with regard to the decriminalisation of homosexuality, being viewed by many as unacceptable. Conversely its recommendations on prostitution were widely welcomed.

On homosexuality the committee made a distinction between "homosexual offences" and "homosexuality" - which "as such does not, and cannot, come within the purview of the law." But areas considered by the committee, their starting positions, shed light on the attitudes, beliefs and prejudices of the times and give an indication of how far opinion moved because of its work: the question of whether homosexuality should be regarded as a disease was examined exhaustively because it was felt that, if such a conclusion was established, homosexuality would be primarily a medical concern and that their responsibility, in the legal sense, would be diminished. Their conclusion was that "evidence put before us has not established to our satisfaction the proposition that homosexuality is a disease." Amongst a range of other questions the committee also discounted a link between homosexuality and the possibility of an increase in paedophilia, describing them as being "recognisably distinct". The age of consent was chosen to be twenty one years old - describing this as an age when a person could be regarded as an adult, whilst also protecting the young and immature.

Myths, as they existed in the society of the time, were many about homosexuality, and the committee sought to debunk at least some of them. A general belief that homosexuality was more prevalent amongst members of particular professions or classes was laid to rest through a forensic study of medical and police statistics and expert witnesses.

For prostitution the committee recommended a calibrated approach: measures, ranging from cautions through higher initial fines upwards to more punitive tariffs, were suggested to facilitate the removal of sources of affront to public decency caused by the presence of prostitutes looking for customers on the streets. Although the committee stopped short of sanctioning either licensed prostitutes or brothels it recognised the need, when weighed against the effect the committee's measures would have on street prostitution, for prostitutes to be permitted to operate in private.

Described as "shockingly pragmatic" the proposals simply aligned British law with many European cousins and were rooted in the utilitarianism of Jeremy Bentham and, more specifically, his premise that homosexuality was an offence dictated only by fugitive conventions of taste and morality. Wolfenden's separation of private consent and morality from public regulation and legality would have an impact far beyond its terms of reference, triggering an avalanche of progressive legislation, from governments of both stripes, throughout the 1960s.

Wolfenden, which saw medical professionals, church men and police officers giving evidence in support of a change in the law to a cross party committee of experts, drawn from a variety of fields, was a result of the post war era of consensus politics. Forensic research, careful examination of evidence and a spirit of collaboration were viewed as having the potential to find solutions to society's ills. This reflected a wider public debate.

The Council of the British Medical Association offered its own comprehensive evidence, under the chairmanship of Dr. Ronald Gibson. Wide ranging and described as covering "ground more sociological than medical" by the British Medical Journal, Gibson's BMA's special committee concerned itself with "problems of which even the factual basis for a solution is unknown." In terms of prostitution the emphasis was on the vulnerability of women drawn into it. Citing reports from as far afield as Denmark, issues highlighted included "mental deficiency", "mental sub-normality", "psychopathy" alongside "bad training and bad example at home" and "faults of character or in attitude to life." Drafted by the Medical Women's Federation, the BMA's committee's proposals emphasised early intervention, through social education, in the lives of children and increased efforts reclaiming the lives of young prostitutes through residential treatment and prolonged aftercare.

London-centric in its focus, due to what Mort identifies as the capital's "potentially paradigmatic status" and the escalating number of sexual offences being reported there, the committee avoided the statistical and analytical pitfalls of an overly diffuse study. Its combination of old world propriety, which saw the euphemism Huntley and Palmers (named for a nearby famous biscuit factory) used for homosexuals and prostitutes, expert scientific and sociological knowledge and evidence taken from committee member interviews with prostitutes and homosexuals from across the capital, was peculiarly British and of its time.

Not in Front of the Children

In time its careful though by no means perfect work would see the end of the lurid high profile trials, which often seemed devised to serve the needs of an aggressively negative and salacious press, and society and its laws would shift in a more enlightened direction.

Conducted in a complex climate in which long established conservative social mores clashed with Christian and progressive agendas there would be, both during the evidence gathering stage and after the report had been published, various forms of backlash and resistance. Old fashioned strict paternalism and morality were projected as long tried and tested remedies, as witnesses such as Sir Lawrence Dunne, the Chief Metropolitan Magistrate, sought to preserve and strengthen the status quo and their own sentencing powers. The committee's legal recommendations, made in its report of August 12th 1957, were widely covered in the nation's press and reflect a debate that was carried on at all levels of British society. The *Daily Herald*, a newspaper that would be relaunched as the *Sun* under Rupert Murdoch's ownership in 1964, led with the headline "Prostitutes... The threat of JAIL will drive them off the streets - BUT WHAT HAPPENS THEN" on 24th November 1958 - bemoaning the lack of progress made since the publication of the report fourteen months before. Citing the lack of action in dealing with "the greatest evils of our day" this vivid piece of journalism warned of the growing menace of prostitution on London's "vice-ridden" streets and claimed that MPs who debated the report knew nothing about the "wicked and the weak; the brazen courtesans-and the baby-harlots" who plied their trade on the streets.

On a provincial level interest was equally high. The *Bognor Regis Observer* of Friday 13th of December 1957 carried a story on the Bognor Regis Christian Council's response to Wolfenden. According to the *Observer* the

Christian Council saw Wolfenden as running "contrary to the mind of Christ." The BRCC's prescription for dealing with prostitution and homosexuality boiled down to "Christian education in our homes and schools." On Saturday 14th of September 1957 The *Hastings and St Leonards Observer* carried a report, from the unusual location of St Helen's Fete, which said the local Conservative Association saw the issues raised as "a new social challenge".

Whatever the tone of the responses the overwhelming attitude was that the Wolfenden Report represented a wake up call. A succession of high profile court cases had created an atmosphere of degradation. The upper classes seemed to be mired in an endless cycle of sex scandals with members of the lower orders. An explosion in violent crimes, robbery, gang warfare, sex crimes, prostitution, pimping, drug trafficking, back street abortions, unmarried mothers, juvenile delinquency and violent working class youth tribes seemed to threaten the fabric of society. Across the western world the black economy of World War Two had provided a fertile soil from which all manner of criminal activities had grown. On the streets of London, politicians, campaigners and the police reported a rise in sex crimes, homosexual activity and prostitution in Piccadilly, Soho and beyond.

Despite giving the appearance of being in terminal decline the establishment, or at least the heirs to the establishment, thrived through their ability to respond to the cultural shifts underway. The old and venerated institutions, that mesh of self reinforcing and self perpetuating privilege, did indeed wilt beneath the onslaught of social and economic changes wrought during and after World War Two. The monarchy, the aristocracy, peers and the political class, the Anglican church and the landed gentry, all suffered to varying degrees in the postwar years as the symbolic trappings of their status were made anachronistic and irrelevant. However, even in light of the thinning of the herd that occurred through the impact of death duties and taxation on the country's landed class, by the end of the 1950s the old networks of power, and in particular those of the new generation, had reestablished most of the control lost. Ironically, the challenges to the social order that came about due to the stripping away of the ruling elite's symbolic power may have ushered in the necessary realism that allowed the ruling classes to adapt their power to the new age. Freed from the constraints of 'Society' and social display, as well as from the class within a class demarcations between 'old' upper class, upper class and other divisions, a new generation of elites were able to redraft the terms by which prestige and influence were judged. The backward looking differentiation of "polite people" and "rude people", as defined by Harold Nicolson in *Good Behaviour*, was there to be challenged. Those who embraced it found an exciting rush came with the earthier, uncultivated folks from below stairs. Instead of retreating to the gentlemen's clubs of the West End, manning the broken gilded barricades as many die-hard Tories did, they embraced the new popular culture and all it meant.

Phrases like "Classless", "New Aristocracy" and "New Class" peppered the press in 1965 as the men and women from working class backgrounds who drove the new revolution in music and art rubbed shoulders with the upper class and upper middle class. This group of "twenty or so young people", with their "youth, vitality, creativity, originality, life and excitement" sat at the heart of Swinging London. Pop singers, models, photographers, pop artists, writers, magazine editors and interior designers, they represented the newly projected image of Britain's international fame or, at the very least, its supporting cast. A long building press obsession with this group reached its apogee upon the publication of John Crosby's *Weekend*

Not in Front of the Children

Telegraph article that offered a who's who of London's swinging scene. The artists David Hockney and Peter Blake, the photographer David Bailey and the designer Mary Quant were named alongside the boutique owner Barbara Hulanicki and Gerald Scarfe, *Private Eye's* satirical cartoonist.

Classlessness may have been the watchword but the social roots of these individuals mattered completely. Maybe this served as a way of emphasising the egalitarian nature of a country where East End working class lads, like Terence Donovan or Terence Stamp, or provincial boys like the Beatles, could mingle freely and equally with the public school educated Lord Snowdon and David Hicks.

As Christopher Booker points out in *Neophiliacs*, another crucial ingredient in the atmosphere of the time was that of "revolt against the stuffy" and the "old fashioned". A rejection of "bourgeois" social convention, of the hidebound prescriptions found in Harold Nicolson's *Good Behaviour*, and an iconoclastic embracing of "rude" behaviour would see sections of the nation's press "delighted" by everything from inappropriately casual clothing to smoking where one shouldn't.

The Beatles were perhaps the most obvious trailblazers of these kind of carefully calibrated slights against the old, with their cheeky chappie, naughty boy behaviour and impudent language perfectly pitched to shock. When the Fab Four received their M.B.E.s from the Queen, Paul McCartney's remark that Buckingham Palace was a "cool pad", or that George Harrison found the Queen to be "sort of motherly", carefully enhanced the appeal of the group, whilst neutralising any possibility that the award and its associations would make the Beatles part of the old establishment. The disrespect was playful enough to be charming whilst also irritating small 'c' conservatives. Already global superstars, having spearheaded the British Invasion on a wave of Beatlemania, the band's brand represented a national achievement of a Britain once again holding its own in the world. Previous sources of pride, the old industries whose exports gained Britain the title the "workshop of the world", were all but gone. As a columnist at the *Daily Worker*, the newspaper for the Communist Party of Great Britain, put it in December 1963: "The Mersey Sound is the voice of 80,000 crumbling houses and 30,000 people on the dole."

For a good many in the ruling elites the Beatles and the British Invasion was an opportunity not to be passed up. After years of humiliation on the international stage at the hands of the Yanks, forced to endure the indignities of Skybolt, Elvis and American Rock 'n' Roll, not to mention the home grown miseries of Profumo, even Conservative ministers such as William Deedes found something to celebrate. At the fag end of Sir Alex Douglas-Home's government Deedes would, in keeping with a Conservative Party edict to mention the mop topped ones at every possible turn, give a speech praising the "something important and heartening" that was happening. Heralding "a cultural movement of the young which may become part of the history of our time" Deedes saw the rise of their kind as being a necessary antidote to the march of automation and the decline in old industries. It offered, he said, a chance "to restore the human instinct to excel at something", equating their work with a "declining craftmanship" of old.

Many may have embraced the new trends, seeking in them, perhaps cynically in some quarters, reinvention and renewal, but for others the music, the hair, the lack of manners and decorum spoke only of decline. Deedes' rather contorted attempt to ameliorate the effects of the new cultural paradigm received a characteristically withering response from Paul Johnson of the *New Statesman*. No fan of the Beatles and seeing no merit in the "indispensable" and "delinquent" teenager and their "bottomless chasm of vacuity", Johnson described the Beatles' music as being the "the monotonous braying of savage instruments" and warned of "the growing public approval of anti-culture". Johnson's rejection came from a particular kind of ingrained prejudice that, despite all noise about classlessness, continued to course through the veins of British upper middle class society. Writing with relish about the "huge faces, bloated with cheap confectionary and smeared with chain-store make-up, the open, sagging mouths and glazed eyes, the hands mindlessly drumming in time to the music," Johnson leavened his critique with acerbic concern for this "fodder for exploitation". However, no matter how unpleasant or condescending his observations were, they shed a cold light on the gulf that existed between the carefully constructed images of the Beatles and their ilk and their fans. Those "young girls, hardly more than sixteen, dressed as adults," who struggled to imitate the look of Jean Shrimpton or Mary Quant, did so with the meagre contents of a weekly wage packet which, although unprecedented in many ways, left them a million miles short of the luxurious lifestyles they sought to imitate.

On the other side of the supposedly rapidly disappearing class divide, the *Daily Mirror's* William Connor, who penned an opinion column for over thirty years under the pseudonym Cassandra, appealed to the prejudices of his working class readers in hard hitting language when he wrote of the Beatles "as unskilled as a quartet of chimps tarring a back fence". Designed to appeal to fathers and mothers, offering ammunition against the home invasion of transistor radios and records, his pejorative description was part of an age old compact of disapproval that had forestalled any kind of individuality in previous generations of working class young people. However, now that their heads had been turned by young men with collar length hair, the clothes of their fathers and mothers no longer suited.

They wanted their own distinct futures, away from the past and all it represented. The traditional way, which said boys and girls would dress in the clothes of their parents and live the lives they did, was over.

The British teenager, the new invention at whom a plethora of new fashions were aimed, was working class in warp and weft, connected to social conventions and cultural associations which, though influenced by America and its own youth revolution, were very particular and specific to Britain's industrial cities. The forces at play in the 1960s, of youthful rebellion and its desire for change, would prove to be both a perfect market and product for those with the wealth and imagination to produce, develop and exploit them. This was driven by a genuine fascination and excitement, by a desire to participate and shape, and it led to unprecedented and unexpected collaborations, in music in particular.

The British teen of the 1960s, defined by marketing experts as being between 16 and 21 years old, was best placed to benefit from and enjoy the new financial and social freedoms that came with increased economic prosperity. The new individualism, exemplified, at least in the early to mid 1960s, by those disposable incomes rather than any political philosophy, demanded individually pertinent, honest responses that resonated with their experiences - this was found in the self-penned songs and cocky working class demeanour of the Beatles, the Rolling Stones and their ilk.

Individualism, allied to the aspirational instincts that consumerism and materialism cultivated, sat perfectly with the shifting nature of employment in the UK. The introduction of new technology and the dissolution of traditional heavy industry, and the break up of working class communities through slum clearances and rehousing programmes, all added momentum to the changes underway. The possibility was presented that anyone, no matter from what or where they hailed, could join the new 'classless' society and, perhaps rather paradoxically, join the 'New Aristocracy'. You could be John Lennon, Paul McCartney, Mick Jagger, David Bailey, Terence Stamp, Michael Caine, Marianne Faithful or Mary Quant and appear in the pages of the *Weekend Telegraph* or meet the Queen. Alongside these calls to dream sat a world of things - of records, clothes, furniture, and even food and drink, all advertised with skilful aplomb, that worked in concert to make the illusion real.

The boom in the birth rate at the end of the war meant that a generation of young people, who entered their teenage years in the 1960s, were a powerful social and economic force. As Tony Judt points out in *Post War*, "Most young people in history have entered a world full of older people, where it is their seniors who occupy positions of influence and example." This was not the case for the generation of the mid 1960s. Increased access to education of a better quality, improvements in housing, and the emergence of an aspirational consumer culture, allied to greater spending power and disposable incomes, created a sense that "the cultural eco-system was evolving much faster than in the past." Society was transforming itself for their benefit and "at their behest."

For many, this shiny new world of indulgence and imagination sat squarely in the middle of a patch of cleared ground, amidst the derelict industry and slum clearances. The bonfires and bulldozers that accompanied the remodelling of skylines and society created a stark backdrop against which fantasies of change played out. As community and industry withdrew, ahead of whatever change was set to come (or not), they left behind them vacant spaces primed with danger and possibility. Across Europe, from Liverpool to Hamburg, the seamier, exciting side of city life had burgeoned from the 1950s onwards though music venues and revue bars.

Around 1955 and 1956 the serious post war stuff of austerity, creating the NHS and the Welfare State, began to give way to more individualistic concerns. The years after 1945 had been filled with optimism about creating a better world, although this still occurred in the midsts and memory of the slaughter and destruction. At some point in the middle of the 1950s the mood shifted and Britain, whilst not forgetting the sacrifice, sought to pivot away from the past. The nation's cultural life began to reflect the new egalitarianism and this manifested itself across a range of artistic and creative practices. Alongside the emergence of the Independent Group in the visual arts, a new generation of playwrights and novelists, mostly from working class and lower middle class backgrounds, seized the nation's imagination with provocative works that spoke of and were from the lives of ordinary people. The fictional "coffee bar philosopher" in John Osborne's *Look Back In Anger* acted as a lightning rod. Unfortunately Osborne's views also attracted scorn from both the left and right of politics. Despite this rejection the gritty appeal of kitchen sink realism would come to supplant the charming stereotyping of the urban poor and working class previously found in British theatre, literature and film.

Jazz music, which had for so long been the dark force in popular youth culture, had a challenger to its crown in the shape of Rock 'n' Roll. The film *Rock Around The Clock*, released in 1956 and covering the rise of Bill Haley and the Comets, sparked mayhem and rioting in the nation's cinemas with its hypnotic beats and jive dance scenes. Rebellion had a soundtrack and a vernacular all of its own. The American film *The Blackboard Jungle,* released in 1955, had been the first to witness such scenes of mayhem. Commercial television arrived.

Not in Front of the Children

Teddy Boys, a long gestating working class youth tribe, whose origins lay in London's declining post war industrial areas, emerged in outfits that mimicked a vogue for Edwardian style clobber prevalent amongst the louche and wealthy "men about town" of the West End. Territorial and violent, their codes of behaviour and rituals were a response to a vacuum of relevant values. In many ways the first true manifestation of modern, post war working class youth culture, they rejected the traditions of their elders, eschewing the modes and manners that underpinned the station of working people for generations. Emerging from their communities to terrorise at will, they moved en masse, manifesting their power with impunity. Rioting, fighting, smashing shop windows and overturning cars, this wanton destruction was incongruously juxtaposed against expensive statement outfits that cost five times their weekly wage. Hair influenced by Hollywood's movie bad boys, brightly coloured, Edwardian gent inspired jackets, shirts worn with a bootlace tie, decorative waistcoats, tight fitting trousers and crepe soled brothel creepers - the look was a million miles from practical workwear or Sunday best.

Working class culture had always thrived away from the attention of genteel society for centuries, occasionally catching the attentions of the well-to-do when a King took an actress as mistress or a music hall song moved into the broader popular consciousness. Mostly the attention was associated with scandal and outrage and in attempts to close a venue down or drive out its unchristian elements. Temperance campaigners, churchmen and newspaper editors looking for a story to stoke the outrage of their readership saw the music hall as a threat to Victorian probity. Stories of drunkenness, assault and sexual abandon swirled around these venues and their cast of travelling entertainers, and this made them a focal point of perceived lawlessness.

Not in Front of the Children

Local papers were full minor tales of bad behaviour and intrigue. The story "Music Hall Scandal" carried by *The Sheffield Independent* is typical of these: Miss Lottie Collins, who was "well known in music hall circles" brought a complaint against Catherine Gurshon and Sarah Vandenberg, a mother and daughter, for an assault during which Miss Collins allegedly lost £7 and had her dress torn. It contained all the elements necessary to whet the appetites of the general public, with a wandering husband lured into infidelity by one of music halls' fallen women, assault, accusation and counter accusation - all provided by a cast of people who could be looked down upon. For the most part, however, these reported scandals tended to be more prosaic affairs, revolving around breaches of contract, absconding with monies and performing whilst intoxicated. In short they represented the minutiae of people's daily struggles writ large. A handy signifier for the ways of the urban poor, with their grubby behaviours and entertainments, they reinforced the otherness of the underclass for the provincial middle class whilst delivering a frisson of fear and dismay. Victorian values, underwritten by a disdainful paternalism, moral superiority and highhanded religious teachings, were built on an oppositional relationship between a lost and undeserving poor and the well-to-do - these stories only served to reinforce this.

Often growing out of public houses where a few turns would pan handle to punters, by the middle of the nineteenth century music halls had become the focal point of the first big commercial entertainment boom. Every town and city had at least one. The buildings were often, though not always, elaborate temples to mass entertainment, and full houses enjoyed a mix of magic, music, variety turns and pantomimes. Shows were designed to appeal to specific audiences, ranging from the saucy and raucous to the more family friendly. Participation, either invited or not, sat squarely at the heart of a good night out and this, alongside the drinking of alcohol, was why music halls gained a reputation for lawlessness.

This nineteenth century thirst for entertainment was driven by what could be called the first UK baby boom, with over half the entire population being under twenty years old in 1851. Like their descendants a century later these young people sought out entertainment and escapism, away from the firesides of their cramped and overcrowded homes or the dead hand of the church and chapel. A night at the music hall was a release from the unremitting drudgery of their lives.

Before 1843 strict rules regulated any establishment hoping to stage entertainments, but the Theatres Act of that year loosened regulations previously set out in 1737 Theatres Act. Incidentally, in an indication of how alive the establishment always were to the subversive nature of theatre, the 1737 Act was brought in when Sir Robert Walpole's sensitivities, both political and personal, were offended by the satirical plays of Henry Fielding. Fielding never wrote again for theatre. Although posited as a relaxation of the rules the 1843 Act served to consolidate licensing in the hands of either the Lord Chamberlain, within the Metropolitan area, or local authorities in areas outside the capital. One consequence of this was that all new plays or translations of old plays had to receive the approval of the Lord Chamberlain. Once approved, the scripts could not be deviated from. The Lord Chamberlain's remit extended to forbidding, without any leave to appeal, any performance or play seen to undermine the preservation of "good manners" or the "public peace". Oddly enough the office of the Lord Chamberlain appears to have developed a blind spot where music halls were concerned. This went largely unnoticed until 1912 when it became clear that the system of censorship, as applied to plays performed in theatres, could not be effectively used to police the increasingly subversive content of the country's music halls.

The Theatre Acts of 1737 and 1843 resulted in over a century of neutered British plays. The plays of the generation of Angry Young Men, like Harold Pinter and John Osborne, are seen by many as a reaction to the restricted, bland and formulaic products of this incredibly long age of censorship and repression. In 1968, however, responding to the changes occurring in society, a new Theatres Act abolished most of this censorship - though licences were still required. It had only been a short ten years since Wolfenden wrote "For some time the subject of homosexuality has been so widely debated, and written about, that it is no longer justifiable to continue the strict exclusion of this subject from the stage," but change did come.

It was also a mere blink of an eye since the passing of the Obscene Publications Act of 1959. This significant piece of legislation, which upended a longstanding legal position by shielding uncensored works of adult literature from obscenity charges, would be subject to the infamous *Lady Chatterley's Lover* test case of 1960. As important as Wolfenden, this case would pit Penguin Books and a host of expert witnesses against the rear guard action being fought by the British Establishment. DH Lawrence's novel may have been written thirty odd years before, in 1928, but until the Obscene Publications Act, and Penguin's decision to publish an unexpurgated version of the text, readers in this country had had to make do with their imaginations when it came to inter-class sex and earthy eroticism.

By the 1930s the arrival of cinema had done much to damage the world of music hall and variety theatre. Alongside this change came the first real distinct youth culture in the shape of the dance hall. A perfect place to meet members of the opposite sex, dance halls were often opulent and palatial, selling a fantasy of escapism and romance that mirrored the imagery found in the movies of the day. Drug dealing, usually cocaine, was widespread, with local criminal gangs adding an air of danger. Raids by the local constabulary and the resultant angry reaction by patrons would regularly bring dance halls to the attention of parliament. One particular incident, at Harworth Colliery in 1937, saw police officers enter a dance hall to arrest men connected to an ongoing strike. This incident, which occurred during an already bitter dispute, inflamed the situation greatly and pitched battles were fought in the street. Parliamentary questions were asked.

The presence of "six penny dance partners" in dance halls blurred the lines between someone to move around the floor with and someone who would provide a little bit extra. After the 1920s, when Mecca came to dominate the dance hall market, the position of these hosts and hostesses was formalised as professional dancers and strict rules governed the behaviour of staff and customers. However, beyond the organised world of Mecca Dancing and the grand palias de danse was a network of independent halls and night clubs where partners had to work for tips and drinks, paying over a percentage of what was earned to the management. Government *Mass Observation* interviews from the early 1940s describe a world where dance partners provided "company" whilst attempting to persuade customers to buy food and drinks. Sex, as it was a surefire way to get better tips, was also on the menu.

Beginning with the emergence of ragtime at the beginning of the twentieth century, and its impact as an exciting American import in the pubs and clubs of Britain, jazz shook up the staid world of winsome popular songs and formal waltzes. Truly alien in its sound, eschewing the expected in favour of syncopated rhythms, it symbolised modernity in Edwardian Britain. Within its beats ragtime contained its own sexual revolution. The restrictive women's dresses of the Victorian era had been cast aside and, as the American music trade magazine the *Musical Courier* wrote in 1899, "a wave of vulgar, filthy and suggestive music... inundated the land." Regarded as morally suspect, partly because of its origins in African American culture, partly because of what J. B. Priestley called its "fascinating, jungle-haunted, monstrous" sound, many called for it to be suppressed. Britain, like the United States, went mad for the cakewalk dance, with its body contact, embraces and, as the *Courier* opined, its "obscene posturings" and "lewd gestures".

The advent of radio from the 1920s spurred on this revolution, taking jazz beyond the confines of the world of the wealthy and the well-to-do into the lives and minds of the general populations. This was the age of large public dance halls, but the jazz intoxicant could be found wherever there was space to dance, in purpose built dance halls and village halls, even in the ample spaces of the municipal baths.

Ballroom dancing, an ever evolving thing in itself, which drew over the decades from each passing wave of fashion, also flourished. A "national dance culture" of ballroom, described by Allison Jean Abra in *On With the Dance*, gained popularity "due to its simplicity and originality", emerging from the end of the First World War to occupy the position of "primary dancing style". A standardisation of venues ran concurrently with the emergence of a mass marketing of leisure during the 1920s and 1930s, cementing ballroom's appeal across all classes and in all geographical regions.

Even as rock music and pop culture swept all before it during the 1960s, ballroom, dance bands and dance halls survived. The dominance of dance halls in British life led those who controlled them to take on the role of cultural guardians. As a result, when young men across the land sought to find an outlet for their Mersey Beat music inspired combos they found their local halls closed to their requests to play. Even though a good many of them cut their teeth playing simple rhythm guitar in show bands and dance bands their status as insiders meant nothing if they wanted to emulate the Fab Four.

Jazz also continued to evolve in its own way. In the tightly regulated world of the 1950s Mecca dance halls, where tea and cake had long ago replaced whiskey and cocaine, there was no place for non-conformity. You followed the steps prescribed or you didn't dance - there was no room for improvisation. Jazz offered an alternative, away from the corralled and codified world of the mainstream. Hundreds of clubs, many run by musicians in need of a place to play, operated across Britain. In the West End and Soho alone there were said to be around two hundred live music venues during the 1950s, each of them small, intimate and hidden away. For many musicians the day job was playing in the increasingly moribund world of the big band. If they wanted to experiment, stretch themselves and see what their fellow musos could do they had to go elsewhere. Jazz clubs were where it was at and places like Studio 51 and the Feldman Swing Club (later known as the 100 Club) gave a home to freedom and expression. These places rejected the sterile corporate commercialism of Mecca, instead placing an emphasis on self-reliance and self-organisation. This approach meant that the profile of the jazz club fitted perfectly with that of the young intellectuals who crowded the coffee bars of Soho to reinvent the left.

The expansion of education in the 1950s created a generation of politically engaged young people. This was particularly the case for those attending arts schools and universities where provocative intellectual ideas, particularly those emanating from the nascent New Left, caught their imaginations. Even the eager and idealistic minds in the nation's grammar school sixth forms were captured by this desire to know and to act. Just like the Teddy Boys this group sought out elements that would identify who they were and how they thought. Perversely perhaps, for a generation recently granted access to the hallowed halls of Britain's premier seats of learning, they sought to define themselves through the work of American writers like Jack Kerouac, Allen Ginsberg and William S. Burroughs. These Beat writers, who sought to redefine literature beyond the stultifying confines of academia and academic language, championed a more natural or speech based approach. With an emphasis on experimentation the Beat Generation's open attitude to creativity, drugs, sex and sexuality, as well as alternative spiritualities and lifestyles, would form the basis of the emerging agendas of the New Left.

The Beat Generation's eventual home, in sunny San Francisco, would come to be symbolic of their DIY ethos of self-reliance and personal fulfilment and would capture the imaginations of a later generation. Bizarrely, given its position as a point of origin in the story of a whole slew of youth cults, fifteen or so years after the Beats descended on SF, the journalist Ralph Gleason would suggest that the city could become the "new Liverpool".

Beatnik, a term which came from the sometimes acerbic pen of the *San Francisco Chronicle's* Herb Caen in the spring of 1958, was meant as a slur against the excitable, left wing Beat followers. A stereotypical image of goatee beards, berets and black turtlenecks had already solidified around a mass market version of this outré lifestyle. But like most pejoratively applied names, it stuck.

When the Beatnik craze emerged in Britain in 1960 the uniform had gone native - perhaps reflecting the colder weather in its duffle coats, anoraks and donkey jackets. Corduroy trousers, v-neck sweaters and either sturdy boots or suede desert boots completed an outfit perfectly suited to the rigours of marching for peace on a cold and wet British summer's day. A tartan drawstring duffle bag would be carried, serving as an ideal receptacle for a battered copy of *On The Road*, a thermos of tea and some sandwiches. The pipe, with its tools and its rituals, its slowness and its craft-like effort, was also an obligatory prop for male Beatniks.

In the way of much of what was to follow in youth culture, the Beatnik style defined itself through its opposition to or difference from what was around it - as well as through its own internal contradictions. Set against the smart world of adult fashions or the Brylcreemed hair and loud suits of the Teddy Boys, Beatniks exuded a contrived blend of intellectual seriousness, political earnestness and scruffy insouciance. Wrapped in their university scarves, they wore the colours of those academic institutions their Beat Generation progenitors had rejected. Signalling a membership of a broader club of individuals through their clothes, the books they read and the jazz they listened to, they massed around an emergent mood of individuality.

Over six or seven years from 1960 Beatnik youth would be mobilised en masse to protest against the bomb and American involvement in Vietnam, as their taste in music and clothes evolved. At its heart, through their wearing of workman's donkey jacket and their political posturing, there was a kind of fetishised kinship with an image of the working people that was already out of date. CND and other protest groups would come to provide the organisation through which most identity was found. These gave meaning and a sense of the possible to this generation of the new middle class whose parents had received their own vital leg up in the shake up of society that followed World War Two.

Not in Front of the Children

There may have been rioting at the Beaulieu Jazz Festival in 1960 but for a group of young people jazz just didn't cut it when it came to excitement. For those who craved a different kind of rush, rock 'n' roll still held possibilities. The Teddy Boys seemed rather anachronistic by the end of the 1950s but their outlook, and a good deal of their fashions and tastes, were continued by the Rocker tribe.

The racism and anger that fuelled much of the Teddy Boy violence remained. Fighting for kicks, for honour, fighting for territory, or simply because someone was different, became a hallmark of this band of self-consciously delinquent adolescents. Just as American movies had spawned the initial rock 'n' roll frenzy so the Rockers too took their cues from Hollywood films. Marlon Brando's Johnny Strabler in *The Wild One* and James Dean's Jim Stark in *Rebel Without A Cause* provided the template for both the look and the attitude. Leather, denim, often outrageously quiffed hair, and motorcycles (which usually demanded a good deal of manual attention to keep them going) provided the props for this mainly working class cult of the bad boy. The role of females in this group tended to be as trophies or possessions, offering adoration and support to their brave men and policed by the old fashioned, backward looking attitudes to women that were still prevalent in the working class communities they came from. Essentially romantic in their outlook, with their freedom underscored by the role of the motorbike as trusty steed, theirs was a fantasy of escapism par excellence. They rejected respectability, ostentatiously sneering at genteel middle class ways and the establishment, seeing themselves as permanently on the wrong side of the law simply by dint of their status as Rockers. Although primarily a London phenomenon, based around their spiritual homes of the Ace Cafe on the North Circular Road and Paddington's 59 Club, greasers, as they became known, would eventually be found across the land. Usually based around a cafe, often chosen because of its location on a route or because of the Eddy Cochran songs on its jukebox, their love of roadside cafes and Americana would earn them the derisive epithet coffee bar cowboys. They were also known as ton up boys. Ton is slang for one hundred miles an hour, a speed many Rockers claimed, perhaps fallaciously, to have reached on their unreliable British motorcycles.

Displays of machismo, whether through reckless speeding on their bikes or through fighting, made the Rocker perfect material for a press whose coverage of young people already verged on the hysterical. However, their role as a lightning rod for all the nation's fears about youth culture was made more marked by the almost simultaneous emergence of a vivid apotheosis in shape of the Mods. Swarms of Rockers wreaking havoc may have quickened the pulse of the average *Daily Mail* reader - but for a second violent youth tribe to emerge must've seemed like the end of days. National Service had ended in 1960. Many saw its end as being directly linked to the rise in youth delinquency. The loss of the discipline, respect and short haircuts that a spell in the forces provided would be lamented by many for decades to come. National Service was said to make a man of you and when the Mods came along an injection of manliness seemed all the more urgent.

Where Rockers were backward looking and old fashioned, with their resolutely mechanical motorbikes and rugged manly clothes, the Mods were not only new but alien. Working class boys in well-tailored suits, who cared more about their clothes than anything else? Where would it all lead?

Clean cut narratives about the origins of subcultures are appealing. Competing stories make for messy outlines, so it is understandable that this tendency or that faction is ignored or diminished, especially when an argument is being constructed. When it comes to Mods and their origins there are two possible roots, though in truth each is probably valid. One story has Mod emerging through East End based working class Jews whose parents worked in the rag trade. Another has Mod as being a West London phenomenon driven by the Anglo Irish working class. Similar narratives have their genesis as being in Soho with a group of fashion conscious young men who loved jazz and called themselves modernists. Others point to London's arts schools as being the source. The truth is probably a mixture of all of these.

At a point when Britain was banging on Europe's door with increasing futility, when swathes of the population were retreating into xenophobia and racial bigotry, the Mods looked to Europe and America for their style. This was group youth culture as narcissism, marked by an acute obsession with the sharp accoutrements of personal identity. Whether it was the exquisitely tailored Italianate suits, the hair styles, the scooters they rode, or the music they listened to, this was competitive consumerism, in a race to be considered a "Face".

Mod fashions evolved at a terrifying pace. To be part of it was to submit to a relentless and ever changing round of new styles - a commitment to the now. All of this was dictated by a seemingly invisible osmotic process of see and be seen, wherein a short window of a la mode opportunity existed between the appearance of a new cut of jacket or trouser and its relegation to squaresville. For the majority of Mods, who worked in low paid jobs to pay for their clothes addiction, the painfully short life of a garment was a price worth paying: the conveyor belt of expensive tailor-made or hard to get off the peg items was all part of the ostentatious consumerism that marked out this particular strand of alpha male oneupmanship.

The exoticism and the tailored style were not new in working class culture. To name just one example, the navvies who built the railways in the nineteenth century also had a penchant for sartorial showmanship. For some, who witnessed the consumerist, materialist frenzy, it all felt deeply depressing. In his autobiography *Just Me and Nobody Else* Neale Pharaoh expressed a mixture of Beatnik cynicism and world weariness when he commented on the disjunction between the relative affluence and "glossy package of the pop world" experienced by some young people and the "the hard realities beneath." Describing them as suffering from "an enforced schizophrenia" he saw the world of things that young people enjoyed as being purely superficial, sitting atop age old and unchanged moral codes.

For the Mods this contradiction did not matter. They gorged on the new, getting a buzz from it in the same way they got a buzz from the amphetamine pills they took. To criticise them for enjoying such things, for not wringing their hands or carrying placards, is to misunderstand the reality of their backgrounds and motivations. Just as the Rockers recognised their impotence in the face of "the Establishment" or "the law" so Mods understood that in order to find fulfilment they had to draft their own set of rules. The aspirational society made conflicting demands on the young people of the time. It offered them things but wagged a finger when they wanted or took them. At the same time it took those desires as proof of their degeneracy and shiftlessness. Work, save, borrow, spend - the invitation to define yourself through material things like televisions, fridges, washing machines and cars was also an invitation to long term drudgery. The Mods rejected all of this, choosing instead the immediate thrill of quick, circular and relatively instant gratification. As with all youth tribes, Mod was inherently contradictory. It celebrated authenticity, originality and individuality whilst simultaneously requiring those who followed it to conform to the strict diktat of an unseen and fickle street style god.

The music they listened to was also about authenticity and originality, with an obsessive commitment to new and obscure R&B and Soul sounds. Rare American grooves provided the backbone of a scene where, as one might expect, the purist held sway. From around 1963 onwards DJ Guy Stevens served as a conduit for much of this music, playing obscure platters at the Scene Club, another venue located in Soho, on his weekly R&B Disc Night. The see and be seen vibe attracted members of The Who, the Small Faces, the Rolling Stones and The Beatles, plus a good many more, who came to hear the latest sounds from the Motown, Stax and Chess record labels.

One of the main forces behind this music was Henry Murray's Sue Records. They had entered the UK music scene through a distribution deal with Decca's London Records, but a hook up with Chris Blackwell's Island Records greatly expanded their reach. Stevens was brought on board and oversaw a burst of chart topping R&B singles from Rufus Thomas, Elmore James, Donnie Elbert and Ike and Tine Turner and many more. Stevens' thirst for uncovering music would also see a number of releases from a host of small US independents - a decision that would complicate Blackwell and Stevens' relationship with Murray. Chris Blackwell, the owner of Island Records, was just one of a new breed of music industry movers and shakers that included Andrew Loog Oldham, who was closely associated with the Rolling Stones, the Small Faces, the Nice, PP Arnold and Marianne Faithfull; Mickie Most, who produced the Animals and Herman's Hermits; Brian Epstein, who was The Beatles' manager; and Shel Talmy who produced the Kinks as well as that quintessential British Mod band, The Who.

Not in Front of the Children

In many ways this short but by no means definitive list sheds light on the diverse nature of talents that flooded into Soho and the West End at the beginning of the 1960s. Guy Stevens was the product (until he was expelled) of one of the nation's post war experiments in broadening the scope and reach of education. Born in East Dulwich he was enrolled at one of the country's few local authority owned boarding schools, the London County Council owned Woolverstone Hall. Blackwell was related to the Crosse & Blackwell preserved foods dynasty and, on his mother's side, a rum and sugar fortune by way of a plantation in Jamaica. Loog-Oldham, who was the son of an American airman who was killed during World War Two and an Australian nurse, attended various prestigious independent and grammar schools, before cutting his teeth working as an assistant to the young Mary Quant and a music publicist in Soho. Brian Epstein was born into a family who owned a successful furniture dealership, Epstein and Sons, in the North West of England. Shel Talmy was born in Chicago, and later educated in Los Angeles. He began his career as a recording engineer at Conway Studios in LA in the late 1950s before moving to England in 1962, where he joined Decca Records.

The flip side of the Soho club scene that Guy Stevens made his own was found most visibly in the provinces in Mecca-land, where the by now sprawling ballroom empire had mutated to include record only club sessions. Recorded music was heavily resisted by the industry body, the Association of Ballrooms, but Mecca displayed no such sentimentality. Business was business and, faced with a growth in independent clubs and venues that played records, they brought in someone good at both self promotion and attracting a teen audience. Jimmy Savile, a man now notorious for his sexual crimes, was a native of Leeds who understood the relationship between music and showmanship. Lurid costumes, outrageously dyed hair, flags, even cycling tours, all figured for a man who established himself at the centre of a coterie of teenage admirers who attended his "lunchtime hops". His impact at Mecca, where he oversaw their entire estate of venues, was immediate. His success was such that, by the mid-1960s, Savile was working for the BBC, having moving there via Radio Luxembourg. Mecca would face competition from independent clubs like Manchester's Twisted Wheel, but their domination of the mainstream provincial music scene would continue throughout the 1960s.

By 1966, when Pharaoh bemoaned the lack of real change in the lives of young people, Mod culture had spread way beyond its place of origin in London and out into the regions. In the capital the Mod style, which sometimes saw men wearing make up or fashions usually associated with Soho's homosexuals, had become part of the broader Swinging London circus. Peddled to the masses as part of a carefully codified, cookie cutter offering it would mutate into something unrecognisable as the original Mod style made way for something very different.

Away from the obscure delights of hard to find R 'n' B and Soul sounds mainstream record sales boomed. Almost two hundred million of the seven inch black vinyl discs were produced between 1964 and 1966, in service of a market almost evenly split between teen power and parent power. This intergenerational battle royale, fought in the nation's charts, would continue throughout the 1960s and into the 1970s, as music amplified the already obvious divisions between the worlds of mum and dad and their errant teenage offspring. Worthy but dull offerings from respectable artists like Jim Reeves, whose September 1966 hit 'Distant Drums' would knock the Small Faces 'All Or Nothing' off the top spot, before tenaciously holding The

Who's insurgent 'I'm A Boy' at bay, symbolised an old world order unwilling to let go.

The post war revolutions in work and education broke the longstanding tradition that assumed that young people would do as their parents did: dressing like them, following them into the jobs they did, living life as they did. Young people were offered their own forms of cultural expression in fashion, music and outlook and, by the mid Sixties, no self-respecting teenager wanted to be like their parents. For the first time a generation of young people were being told that they deserved better and should expect better. However, they were being offered more than one alternative to what went before. On the one hand there was the opportunity being offered by the state, in training and education. This was the call to join the "white heat" of Harold Wilson's "scientific revolution" through education and training and, although exciting in many respects, it evoked a world of hard work and responsibility. On the other side, the alternative to Wilson's alternative, were the inspiring images from the world of the flâneurs of Soho, the artists, musicians, photographers and designers, with their exciting, leisure filled and creative lives.

Wilson's offering may have proved intoxicating to parents and those young people turned on by politics, but for the vast majority of teens the escapism found between the pages of youth magazines was much more alluring. Alongside the slew of around a dozen new or reinvented music focussed titles, such as *Melody Maker*, *Disc Weekly*, *Record Mirror*, *New Musical Express* and *Music Echo*, there was *Rave* magazine, with its intoxicating mix of in depth content and quality photographs. Covering everything from the glamour of the new James Bond movie franchise and pop star fashion tips, to interest pieces on established and upcoming bands, it was largely written by a new generation of women journalists. Writers like Cathy McGowan,

Maureen O'Grady and Dawn James offered intelligent perspectives that appealed to both sexes in a well-designed package that made good use of the work of exciting photographers like Terry O'Neill and Jean Marie Périer.

Vibrating with the spirit of a parallel age, the music, the fashions and the magazines outshone even the brightest light generated by Wilson's own overheated revolution. His attempts to harness these mercurial forces, by awarding the Beatles MBEs in 1965, would draw criticism from friend and foe alike. Such was the outrage amongst previous recipients of honours that many immediately returned their gongs in protest. Amongst their number were the former Canadian MP Hector Dupuis, a retired Squadron Leader called Douglas Moffit and Colonel Frederick Wragg, who sent back twelve medals. Even Tony Benn railed in his diaries against the "appalling mistake" of Wilson thinking "he could buy popularity". Four years later John Lennon would join Colonel Wragg and company when he deployed his own MBE as a weapon against government policy by returning it.

It is worth noting that for the biographer Philip Zeigler, Wilson's dalliance with The Beatles went deeper than mere opportunism, with his "affection" for showbiz bringing a veritable troupe of entertainers through the front door of Downing Street. From Gina Lollobrigida, the Italian actress and international sex symbol, to the nation's favourite wartime sing-a-long national institution, Vera Lynn, Wilson sought out the company of the most iconic stars he could find. Notwithstanding his undoubted love of showbiz, Wilson's reputation as a media savvy political operator dictates that any reading of these, always carefully documented, encounters should be done with caution. A showman, who understood the power of television from very early on, his image was carefully constructed to emanate modernity.

Alongside the glossy, carefully presented images of celebrity ran another, more subversive, current that suggested the revolution may be more than simply stylistic. When, in 1965, Bill Wyman of the Rolling Stones was prosecuted for urinating in public, and the rest of the band were criticised by the judge for insulting behaviour, a media firestorm of disapproval focussed on the band's inability to set a moral example for their fans. Andrew Loog Oldham, their manager, and the man credited by author Jon Savage as being the architect of their role as the anti-Beatles, capitalised on the scandal by drawing press attention to what he called "the band's image as longhaired monsters from the teenage Id..." However, in the midsts of the manufactured media outrage, all this ever boiled down to was marketing, or what Savage called "a new kind of showbiz".

For Jon Savage the release of '(I Can't Get No) Satisfaction' in 1965 was the moment The Rolling Stones pushed pop culture to become a teller of harsher truths. This was when they, as outsiders, became insiders and also the embodiment of change. The band's inner circle, the group of people who influenced them, had shifted over the course of the previous year, in a repeat of a process that had and would happen with each new wave of popular celebrity. As we have seen, Britain's new generation of wealthy elites woke to the power of mass culture early on. They found its possibilities intoxicating and worked to establish themselves at the centre of what and who was happening. The presence of persons from the elite, like old Etonians Robert "Groovy Bob" Fraser and Christopher Gibbs, in the lives of the Rolling Stones did not stem from the same paradigm that brought about Wilson's flirtations with the idols of the time. Although the stars were undoubtedly trophies to be collected, the creative influence of these elite beings cannot be underestimated. Fraser, for example, played a key role in the creation of the Beatles' iconic *Sgt. Pepper's Lonely Hearts Club Band* LP cover.

David Bailey's *Box of Pinups* from 1965, the artwork that was a cardboard box containing photographs of the then current cast of celebrity faces, operates as a kind of commentary on the desire of the elites to collect stars. The act of boxing the images denotes both ownership and storage, whilst emphasising the transitory nature of fame. Like many of the people featured in the Box, with their working class and lower middle class roots, Bailey's origins, allied to his talent as a photographer, had catapulted him into a lauded group of famous captives. Described as "this Debrett of the new aristocracy" by Jonathan Aiken in his 1967 survey of the times, *The Young Meteors*, that writer's enthusiasm for a "London scene" was somewhat tempered by wry cynicism. The artwork, and its celebration of a cast of characters "from two well known gangsters to Lord Snowden" is wryly dismissed as "selling surprisingly few copies". "Upward climbed Bailey's popularity rating," continues Aitken, sniffily consigning Bailey's achievements to the realm of the crass. Another fully paid up member of the nation's elite, old Etonian Aitken is alleged to have experimented with LSD in 1966, the year he stood unsuccessfully as a Conservative candidate for Meriden in the West Midlands. Apparently his experience was so bad that he immediately called for a ban. During the 1960s and early 1970s he worked as a war correspondent in Vietnam and Biafra and blazed a trail on the newly created Independent Yorkshire Television station. Elected as the Conservative MP for Thanet East in 1974, he was a one time boyfriend of Margaret Thatcher's daughter Carol, as well as an eventual apologist for Nixon. Writing in *The Young Meteors* that "if there is any moral virtue left in the youth of London, it has been brilliantly camouflaged," Aitken encapsulated the contradictions felt by those in the elite who were both attracted to and repelled by the changes occurring in British society.

In that box of pinups, alongside the Beatles, Terence Stamp, David Hockney and thirty six half tone prints of other examples of what Christopher Bray calls "working class kids on the make on the rise", was Mick Jagger.

Jagger, who operated as the pinhole in the camera through which everything about the Stones was inverted, was not the animal the media feared. And nor could he be. Despite being presented as a delinquent by the newspapers, those who cared to listen knew that he was thoughtful and intelligent. On one level Jagger's supposed degenerate behaviour was nothing more a theatrical rejection of the status quo; a shock tactic designed to create a space in which the Stones' music could generate sales. Through brushes with the law, by being busted for drugs, or by drawing down a withering criticism from one of the nation's many moral guardians, the band invited their young fans to experience a momentary glimpse of themselves in the role of anti-hero. Loog Oldham's approach sought to co-opt that energy, further legitimising the image of the Rolling Stones in the eyes of any would be fan.

On the other side of the table from Mick Jagger the angry working class iconoclast sat Mick Jagger the friend of aristocrats, who rubbed shoulders with the best sort of people. Implicit in this interplay of contradictions was a further complex offering - a box within a box. Jagger had become the insider, and for his fans his presence within the inner sanctum of respectable society gave them a glimpse of menacing possibilities. This added to the thrill.

However, despite their flouncing and sulking, despite the sneering rejection of everything their parents held dear, most teens still craved security. They needed to know that their rebellion could stop at tea time and that their socks would be washed. Though exciting, the idea of pulling everything down terrified them, because they were, at heart, a deeply conservative lot. This was a generation born into a nation, indeed into a cultural block if you consider the entire West, in a state of permanent physical and psychological revolution. In Britain, the slum clearances, the massive redevelopment of town centres, the falling away of old political and social certainties combined to create a maelstrom of uncertainty. Across the entire western world, similar forces were at work. Over all of this hung the bleak and ineluctable reality of a civilisation that stood on the brink of annihilation in a burning nuclear holocaust. Their anger, their fear, their hopelessness manifested itself due to a deep existential crisis that came from a projected future stripped of all certainties. Those born during the the early 1950s stood almost as immigrants in a new land, shorn of the reference points that, for previous generations, had both tethered and guided on the journey through life. This was the case across an entire generation, across all class divides.

In the post war years a scramble was underway to determine which ideas would have supremacy. In the fight over which political and social agenda would dominate a whole host of unforeseen consequences occurred. Complicated, schizophrenic, contradictory, the years after 1960 have been described in such dysfunctional terms because they represented a speeding up of chain reactions. The dissolution of the structures of working class life, the loss of deference and the symbols of prestige amongst the ruling elite, the collapse of the moral certainties of the bourgeoisie, these were all symptoms of the blind process underway.

The potential energy of rebellion, suggested by Jagger's admittance to the citadel, could not become kinetic. Like the Op Art paintings of Bridget Riley or the Pop Art Target paintings of Peter Blake, which caught the public's imaginations and mood, Jagger's capacity for revolution had to remain an abstract two dimensional idea in order to retain its potency. Like the higher purchase contracts their parents signed for TVs, the young had entered into an agreement that fixed them between the world of their teenage fantasies and the reality of their own futures.

Incidentally, two years after Bailey's *Box of Pin Ups*, Peter Blake would revisit the notion of two dimensional collections of celebrity on his cover for the Beatles' *Sgt. Pepper's Lonely Hearts Club Band* album. The Beatles had ceased to play live and would, henceforth, be nothing but images on a screen or magazine - a ghost or even spirit version of the band whose tours triggered mass hysteria. The *Sgt. Pepper's Lonely Hearts Club Band* sleeve would place John, Paul, George and Ringo amongst a mixed cast of spiritual gurus, Hollywood stars, pop stars, writers and sports people. These cut outs represented the ultimate flattening out of the celebrity image - prematurely placing the Beatles in the nostalgic scrap book of the past.

Despite this attention (or because of it) and the cacophonous call of contradictory invitations to come and break free, young people were unhappy. The sociological studies of researchers like Brian Jackson and Dennis Marsden had uncovered the rage of working class youth, whilst excavating the longstanding resentments that lay behind it. Memories of decades old mistreatment, meted out to working class communities during the days of high handed authoritarian paternalism, still lingered on. Mistrust at the shiny offer being made in the 1960s was compounded by the realties of most people's lives, as the images of possibility and plenty served only to highlight the grim anxiety of everyday life.

Although his contract as a member of the Beatles dictated much of what he did, John Lennon's cheeky scouser schtick was given a peculiar highbrow twist with the release of two books of poetry. 1964's *In His Own Write*, and

Not in Front of the Children

1965's *A Spaniard in the Works* were interspersed by Lennon's appearance on the comedy sketch show *Not Only... But Also*. Seen frolicking on Wimbledon Common to Vivaldi's *The Four Seasons* with Dudley Moore and Norman Rossington, Lennon's poetry is read in sombre but absurdist tones. If each of Vivaldi's *The Four Seasons* stood for a Beatle, then Lennon had chosen to be winter. But beyond that his association with a show by arch political satirists Peter Cook and Dudley Moore sent an early sign of future political intent. Although it is likely that Epstein, Lennon's over controlling manager, felt the Fab Four brand was insulated from any damage by Peter Cook's recent disavowal of politically inspired comedy, the nonsense poetry and pastoral clowning is undoubtedly charged with a targeted and acerbic wit. As with youth movements, the potency of modern forms of art come from their incongruous opposition to the status quo. At the time of filming in November 1964 Lennon was helping to spearhead the much vaunted British Invasion of America, had been celebrated in Parliament by politicians, and was soon to be honoured by the Queen. He was a member of Britain's foremost popular music songwriting duo, Lennon and McCartney, and was subject to the adoration of millions of screaming fans. In this context the poem, *Deaf Ted, Danoota & Me*, and its accompanying film could not be more different or unexpected.

Lennon, like many of his fellow musicians of the time, had been to art school. Unfortunately, for those seeking clear lines of sight through to his more avant garde creative work, he was a less than perfect student: he wore the then uniform of the delinquent and dressed as a Teddy Boy, was disruptive and was thrown out before his final year.

Lennon's bad boy antics aside, the impact of the arts school on the 1960s cannot be underestimated. The opportunity to study the arts had been extended to Britons in the aftermath of World War One, but the availability of courses had been greatly expanded after World War Two. Keith Richards, Jimmy Page, Pete Townsend, Ray Davis, Eric Clapton, Syd Barrett, Jeff Beck, Ron Wood, Eric Burdon, all key figures in the story of 1960s music, each experienced some level of arts education. Art schools operated as incubators of ideas throughout the 1950s, building on curriculum work done at the private Euston Road School by Victor Pasmore, Graham Bell, William Coldstream and Claude Rogers. D'Arcy Wentworth Thompson's *On Growth and Form*, Norbert Weiner's *Cybernetics* and the ideas of Walter Gropious helped to solidify an approach that found voice in the teachings of artists like Terry Frost and Alan Davie. The emphasis was on constructive experimentation, with the aim of developing an understanding of colour, shape, form and materials. As the Fifties progressed into the 1960s an emphasis on painting and sculpture gave way to an acceptance of the artistic validity of new media such as silkscreen printing, film, sound art and works involving light.

Art schools were not always places of such unfettered exploration. In the years immediately after World War Two the Ministry of Education's prescriptions were rigorously overseen, policed even, by panels of external examiners. The main changes began to occur in the late 1950s, initially under the National Advisory Committee on Art Examinations. An advisory council, under the chairmanship of the artist and educator Sir William Coldstream, published a report in 1960 that recommended an overhaul of the examination and certification of the arts. From this major change in the provision of arts education came.

The tradition of the artist as a force of nature, which emerged during the eighteenth century Romantic period, sat squarely at the centre of European modernism. As a result this philosophy was at the heart of the influential curricula developed by Coldstream and Pasmore. Seriousness of purpose, the romantic ideal of the artist, allied to a formal sophistication, underpinned the modernist teaching in art schools. This, allied to openness and an engagement with the constructive experimentation espoused by Pasmore et al, would create the conditions in which a generation of art school educated musicians could engage with and process the ever expanding range of influences they were exposed to.

Despite his rejection of art school it is likely that this time would continue to have an influence on Lennon's creative life. Indeed, his aggressive repudiation of the ethos inculcated by Liver School of Art during his early youth may have laid the ground for his later self-conscious embrace of a romantic artist stance. His activities in the spheres of poetry, satirical comedy, his openness to experimentation on *Magical Mystery Tour* and *Sgt Pepper's Lonely Hearts Club Band*, and later dalliance with conceptual modes with Yoko Ono, were a manifestation of the romantic ideal of the serious artist he had previously rejected. That, added to eastern mysticism, psychiatry, the experiments with LSD and the engagement with politics, activated the creative cyclone of Lennon's life from the mid-1960s to the early 1970s. In a few short years Lennon, perhaps more so than any of his contemporaries, compressed a lifetime's worth of intellectual and expressive engagement.

Those working class and lower middle class young men and women, the musicians, photographers, models and film makers, who found themselves playing a central role in the lives of elite society, were perfectly poised to absorb and process a cultural panoply that had thus far only been open to the ruling classes.

Perhaps the most obvious signifier of the cultural revolution of the 1960s was LSD. As Christopher Booker notes in *Neophiliacs*, the rise in popularity of drug use (or at least the image of it in the popular consciousness) did not happen overnight. Booker describes 1965 as being the point where "the growing ten-year long drugs craze was entering its prolonged climactic phase, as the pop-Bohemian demi-monde was swept by the vogue... for the fantasy drug, LSD". This pop-Bohemian demi-monde included both figures like Lennon and Jagger and members of the elite like Robert "Groovy Bob" Fraser and Christopher Gibbs as well as their counterparts in Europe and the USA.

Britain's elites were no strangers to psychotropic substances. Another old Etonian, Aldous Huxley, was a full ten years ahead of American Ken Kesey, his Merry Pranksters and their experiments. Huxley relied on the naturally occurring substance mescaline, rather than the artificially synthesised LSD that was used by Kesey, when he explored ways to reach spiritual enlightenment through drugs. Like RD Laing, who would deploy LSD to facilitate a breaking down of barriers in his psychiatric treatments at Kingshill, Huxley's 1953 experiments grew out of attempts, by psychiatrist Humphry Osmond, to use mescaline to treat schizophrenia. Huxley would write about his experiences in his book *The Doors of Perception* - a work that recounts his experiences in a hybrid scientific and philosophical tone.

Of course Huxley was just one of a long line of English gentleman experimenters, including Byron and Coleridge, whose activities stem from an innate acceptance that the ruling classes operated under different rules to the common man.

LSD would emerge into the mainstream around 1965 only to be banned a year later by the Home Secretary. John Lennon and George Harrison would encounter LSD, during that brief popular window in 1965, when their coffees were spiked by George's dentist, Dr John Riley. Use and possession of cannabis had already been criminalised by

1965, when it was proscribed in the 1964 Dangerous Drugs Act. This followed a global move, sponsored through the UN in 1961. Amphetamines were also criminalised in 1964 under the Prevention of Misuse Act. Latterly, doctors who were treating heroin and cocaine addiction would be required to notify the police. The law in relation to heroin, cocaine, morphine and opium had been tight for decades following the introduction of the 1920 Dangerous Drugs Act, but these drugs had very little appeal to the popular consciousness at the time.

Undoubtedly, the use of cannabis rose during the time, but LSD was always a more marginal drug, and much harder for the average citizen to secure. Even during the Summer of Love when, if the press coverage was to be believed, everyone was tripping, LSD was never easily available. For most UK teens drug use was restricted to amphetamines and cannabis. Although the situation in the USA was undoubtedly more visible, it is likely that, even there, the image of an entire generation embarking on a psychedelic journey is more about a triumph of record company marketing rather than actual drug consumption. The elites and their proteges in the rock bands of the age undoubtedly experimented with LSD, a substance referred to in the press at the time as "brainwash powder", but beyond their glamorous circle anything mind bending was still restricted to forty woodbines and a pint of mild. Yes, the Mods took amphetamines and barbiturates, but these drugs were more easily available - at least until they were criminalised. The media hysteria that occurred around LSD with brainwash powder and cannabis with reefer madness was a part of a concerted move to create the conditions for control and criminalisation. The placing of spectres in the minds of the general public laid the necessary groundwork to control substances that had gone wild and were in danger (at least in the minds of the establishment) of passing into popular use.

This hysteria, the blowing up of a small fragment of the countercultural identity by the press, also occurred around the issue of public disorder. However, despite pages of coverage about teen delinquency and violence in the press in the early 1960s the hysterical pitch was only really reached from 1966 and 1967 onwards. This shift in coverage came when the disruption that had previously occurred on the streets of provincial towns or working class neighbourhoods attached itself to what were apparently political causes.

Harold Wilson had refused to join the USA's war effort in Vietnam as early as December 1964. This was despite the fact that the US President Johnson required a symbolic number of British and Commonwealth troops to act as a fig leaf for world opinion. However, there were high levels of public feeling against Britain joining the war and Wilson, always a smart operator who understood the importance of covering all the angles, sought to deploy multiple reasons to justify his rejection of America's calls. He cited his position as co-chairman of the 1954 Geneva peace conference that partitioned Indochina as precluding any hope that Britain could involve itself in fighting in the region. Wilson also pointed to the engagement at the time of British forces in a counterinsurgency operation in Malaysia known as the 'Confrontation'. It is worth noting that Wilson's relationship with Johnson was never particularly good. Indeed the slow slide of Britain's prestige discussed in the last chapter went hand in hand with a withering assessment of the nation's leaders. In the run up to Wilson's victory Johnson had been presented with a pithy assessment of Britain's choice in the election as being between 'smart aleck and dumb Alec' - Wilson was the former and deemed as "someone who does not inspire a feeling of trust in many people."

Although Wilson was to come under intense pressure from his key ally he never wavered and British troops did not join battle against the communists in Vietnam - not even after the end of the 'Confrontation' in 1966, by which time Wilson was able to point to pressing matters at home.

Wilson may have refused but this appears to have fallen short of the requirements of a generation of young people whose newly engaged perspectives were suddenly more global. News coverage of the time was full of what Kissinger, the eventual key advisor to the future US President Nixon, called the "anguish of the younger generation". On the 28th of March 1967 twenty five thousand anti-war demonstrators descended on Trafalgar Square to hear speakers. The Trafalgar crowd was the sum total of two demonstrations, one organised by the Aldermaston March Committee and one by CND, and contained what *The Sun* newspaper called "anarchists" and "a soldier, in uniform and carrying a banner saying 'I refuse to Fight in Vietnam'." The solder was escorted away by military police. *The Sun* article leads with the violent disruption of the demo by the anarchist contingent, who "hurled smoke bombs at the speaker's rostrum and then tried to storm it".

There were further demonstrations in 1968. Much more violent, with more than two hundred arrests, they came on the back of months of increasingly hostile press coverage that sought to paint the protestors as lawless. Perhaps spurred by the reaction of the press, or motivated by well documented fears within the security services about the dangers of Soviet influence, the policing was heavy handed. In particular the use of horses to charge protestors appears to have angered and disturbed at least some politicians of the time.

Not in Front of the Children

The Labour MP Peter Jackson commented: "I was particularly outraged by the violent use of police horses, who charged into the crowd even after they had cleared the street in front of the embassy." However, despite the bricks that were thrown, the heads cracked by police truncheons and the arrests made, these demos never reached more than twenty five thousand in number. This figure pales rather when compared to US protests like the three hundred thousand who protested in New York or half a million who protested in Washington in the November of 1969. That is not to belittle or denigrate the British protests, which were undoubtedly genuine. However, this significant piece of the UK Sixties myth, of an exploding generation of politically active individuals bent on violent insurrection, is unfortunately largely a construct, something manufactured by the newspapers of the day to boost circulation. Of course the British establishment of the time were sensitive to the dangers of a Moscow directed civil disorder spiralling out of control and destabilising the country; however, unlike their US counterparts, they had an abiding sense of power over events. This not only stemmed from the innate confidence of the ruling elite but from the continuing deference, still felt by the majority of the population, towards the governing classes. The years following World War Two may have been tumultuous in terms of social and economic revolution, but the upshot was not an unshackling but the reverse. Bound by financial commitments to the things of the consumer boom and the aspirational society the majority of adult Britons were interested only in higher wages and better (or at least secured) living standards.

The global events of the late 1960s - the Prague Spring, the American civil rights and anti-war movements - broke upon a Britain fatigued by decades of slowly eroding power and already wrapped in a cycle of economic boom and bust that forestalled any attempt to look beyond the horizon.

Collective community impulses, the foundations of the Labour and trades union movements, had been diluted by reforms specifically designed to improve the lives of working people. Whatever broader politicisation there may have been had already been lost to a world of HP and colour TV.

At the end of the 1960s and throughout the 1970s, when this combination of aspiration and individualism came into contact with increasing economic insecurity, the results would be a new kind of union militancy. Local concerns, instead of national bargaining, would drive industrial action as shop stewards, buoyed by an increase in their power, responded to issues in a piecemeal way. Moderate trade unionism had held sway since the late 1920s, rejecting militancy and revolutionary ideas in favour of a more collaborative and conciliatory approach, underwritten by official recognition and acceptance. The ideals of democratic socialism called for democratic political solutions and this approach would be further cemented during the Second World War and the years that followed. Figures like Harold Tewson the General Secretary of the Trades Union Congress (1946 to 1960), Arthur Deakin the General Secretary of the Transport and General Workers' Union (1940 to 1955) and William Carron the President of the Amalgamated Engineering Union were moderate men who presided over a benign era in the economy and industrial relations. By the second half of the 1960s, however, a new generation of union activists would begin to make their presence felt. Jack Jones at the TGWU and Hugh Scanlon at the AEU, both elected in 1968, became known as The Terrible Twins, and represented a new form of robust trade unionism that would push back against attempts to limit their powers. Labour's white paper, 'In Place of Strife', which was presented by Barbara Castle in 1969, proved to be one last throw of the dice for Wilson's administration before they were ejected from office in favour Ted Heath.

The number of workers involved in strike action would rise from 530,000 in 1966 to 1,722,000 in 1972 as the carefully constructed compact between Labour and the unions unravelled. Incomes Policy, that carefully metered and managed solution that lay at the heart of Wilson's economic strategy, would run aground and break up over those few years, reversing a position of solid support for an economic strategy that included wage freezes and price controls. Echoing a broader global phenomenon of gathering union militancy Britain's problems were not unique. But in this country rising inflation, falling living standards and a loss of control by union authorities to local shop stewards exacerbated the situation.

When elected in 1970 Heath would find his government's lofty agenda quickly derailed as a fear of unemployment replaced the need to control inflation as the primary concern. By the September of that year a period of severe industrial unrest had begun that would spread throughout the economy. 1972 saw his Conservative administration introduce the most expansionary budget in the country's history, reversing its aims, stated only two years before during the General Election, of income tax cuts, drastically reduced public spending, increased competition in the economy and reduced inflation. Once great industrial giants, Rolls Royce and Upper Clyde Ship Builders, companies once considered the backbone of the economy, were rescued from collapse by a Conservative administration that had sworn itself against such intervention.

On the shop floor, in industrial relations, confrontation replaced conciliation as postal workers and miners twisted the government's arm until they caved in. Violence erupted on picket lines and power cuts became a fact of everyday life and British industry was crippled by the three day week. An attempt to implement a follow up to Castle's failed 'In Place of Strife', the 1971 Industrial Relations Act only served to exacerbate things by poisoning what good relationships still existed. The National Industrial Relations Court, the state registration of unions and the power to impose punitive fines were just some of the measures seen by trade unions as being part of a politically motivated attack on their ability to protect the rights of their members.

From the end of the 1960s and throughout the 1970s Britain was a nation riven by fragmented industrial disputes that, by dint of a broader militancy, were able to coalesce into a broader unrest. However, because national bargaining or collective bargaining had failed, the potency of these actions was always likely to be weakened.

There were, of course, exceptions. The miners, the eternal demon of the Conservative Party, had considerable industrial muscle - something Ted Heath would discover to his cost in 1974. But even the story of the NUM undermining a democratically elected government is just another extension of the union as convenient bogey man: Heath's government had already failed. With prices sky rocketing and inflation running at between fifteen and twenty percent he was already on borrowed time.

Perhaps the biggest consequence of the teenage revolution of the 1960s was the dislocation of the relationship between parents and children. Music and fashion played an increasingly important role in shaping the identities of the young people as they were drawn into their own version of the consumer world. Concurrently, parents were being shaped by the products they owned or hoped to own and the aspirations inculcated in them by the press and the burgeoning magazine sector. The difference, the estrangement felt by teens in the late 1950s, 1960s and into the 1970s, was a new construct designed perhaps to help clearly delineate them as a market sector. Alongside this, popular cultural reference points, disconnected, but seeping through from their points of origin in the work of people like Marcuse and R D Laing, proclaimed the redundancy of the family, painting it as a barrier to real experience and life. At the exact moment when the young identity was forming a schism suddenly appeared. Where, previously, family, work and apprenticeships would have consolidated the sense of self there was a gulf into which all their peers were being tipped.

Although an American programme, *Scooby Doo Where Are You!* speaks to the alienation felt by teenagers and their parents in Britain and the rest of the western world. The monsters that the gang chase, who are always men dressed in masks, are, in many ways, like the divided self that R D Laing wrote about. The gang, travelling in the van as a rock band who never do gigs, are divorced from their families, cast upon a world where they do battle with demons and monsters which, no matter how often they are revealed as a disgruntled janitor, always seem real. Like the whole teenage world of that time, they were in a perpetual state of suspended disbelief that meant their entire existence was one of blind terror.

Ontological insecurity was the key experience of the modern age - particularly for young people. In the US the spectre of the bomb, and the ballooning and terrifying war in Vietnam, which disproportionately sucked in America's black and white working class poor, alongside an awareness of the discriminatory nature of a society where black people were still denied the vote as late as 1965, were the main source of any insecurity about existence; as the dominant cultural power in the Western world, but particularly in relation to Britain, the concerns of America became the concerns of the world. Naturally, the spectre of immediate vaporisation in a nuclear holocaust was an equally pressing concern for teenagers in Britain and Europe - but the big stand off, between the USA and the Soviet Union, was always carried on above the heads of the British state. Not that that made the fear any less pressing.

Laing's approach to psychiatry was one manifestation of the prevailing approach that emanated from the New Left. The Marxist application of the pithily termed dialectical rationality to history and its processes had long ago highlighted the contradictions inherent in a society where the workers produced the wealth but had no share in it. Over the course of the intervening decades the myth of a fair society was examined and excised in the work of numerous political philosophers. By the 1960s, however, the New Left's reinvented analysis and prescriptions, as offered by Marcuse and others, offered a different framework. More pertinent to the new strain of post war capitalism, which merged consumer and popular culture, this new approach sought to address an increased sense of alienation, felt by ordinary people, that Marcuse identified. A manifestation of this alienation was a supposed false consciousness, brought about through mass media, popular and consumer culture, that inured the masses to the falsity of the proposition under which they lived - in effect keeping them in a perpetual state of suspended disbelief.

For many thinkers of the New Left, including Laing, the causes and consequences of this move were multiple. In his 1964 essay on Marcuse's book of the same year, *One Dimensional Man*, Laing laments the diminution of an academic and research language "purged" and "incapable of expressing any thoughts other than those furnished to the individuals by their society." A process which occurs whilst the "scholarship" and the "national purpose" are in "a state of permanent mobilisation for their own destruction" results in values that relegated to an "unscientific, unverifiable, subjective ideal realm that can be debated endlessly without validation". This in turn gives rise to what is described as "a phoney pluralism" where "un-freedom" and "un-happiness" are given a "veneer of freedom and fun" but where all choices - be they political parties or brands of soap powders - are nothing more than "phoney pluralism". This phoney pluralism of the "competing institutions" then serves to solidify the containing power of the whole over the individual. This whole, Marcuse suggests, is nothing more than irrational and driven by a need for growth and expansion whilst stalked by the spectre of continual war and the threat of imminent death.

1964's *One Dimensional Man* was bleak in its outlook, much more so than the earlier erotic idealism of 1955's *Eros and Civilization*. It was a project of hoped for hope, though denied by the intrinsic pessimism of circumstances in a world overwhelmed by the unending consequences of humanity's march towards spiritual and physical oblivion. The old remedies of dialectical theory were, for Marcuse, if not entirely rejected, by this time almost spent and useless - over a century of purpose undone.

During the 1960s the freedoms secured in the aftermath of World Wars One and Two, the quid pro quo for the sacrifice, the bribe instigated as a means of keeping revolution at bay, were given voice in the popular music of working class people. The rock 'n' roll that, in its various forms, emanated from the disappearing communities of industrialised cities spoke of the scintillating possibilities of those freedoms. As it merged with and then came to be part of a broader commercial business model it was able to reach bigger audiences and touch the lives of people in ever more sophisticated and complex ways. And the results of this process were indeed wonderful in terms of the music and its impact. However, as the power of this cultural force increased, its message was distorted and turned into a lurid caricature that could be used against itself. The hell of a permissive society of promiscuous sex and dangerous drugs emerged in the national press and popular culture, inadvertently or not, was turned into the canary in the coal mine that sang of a wider malaise and disturbing trends. It became the agent of its own destruction - with the excesses, which had hitherto only really been enjoyed by a minority of new aristocrats and elites, used to justify a clamp down or reversal of the reforms that had led the nation to where it was. Modern freedoms took on the role of a spectre or a terrorist, a bogey man or a monster that threatened to run out of control and undermine the security, peace and prosperity that ordinary people craved. In its final stages, in the years after 1970, the clamour for reform of the reforms gained pace. The image of a society of dangerous radicals and outrageous spongers grew and the blame for all of society's ills came to be placed on the permissive society and the things that had brought it about. In turn this would and still is used to justify every piece of regressive legislation that undoes advances made in education policy, housing reform or wider civic freedoms.

Footloose and fancy free Velma, Shaggy, Fred and Daphne epitomise the freedoms of an age that were, in truth, always out of reach for most young people. Coupled and travelling unchaperoned together, there is an implied sexual dimension to their existences that separates them from the small c conservative ways of the vast majority of people in the 1960s. There's a life of privilege and indulgence that finds parallels with the gentlefolk detectives of Agatha Christie or the precocious well-to-do children mystery solvers of Enid Blyton. There are no pressing demands on their time, no requirement for labour nor a need to earn - this is the ideal teen existence that places personal reverie over enterprise and industry but which, like the monsters they chased, never really existed at all.

Not in Front of the Children

Sources and Bibliography

Special thanks to:

http://www.toonhound.com

http://www.jedisparadise.com

Derek Gillard, http://www.educationengland.org.uk

Frank Mort, Capital Affairs, Yale University Press

Jon Savage, 1966 - The Year the Decade Exploded, Faber & Faber and Teenage: The Creation of Youth:1875-1945, Pimlico

John Grindrod, Concretopia: A Journey Around the Rebuilding of Postwar Britain, Old Street Publishing

The National Archives

The British Newspaper Archive,

https://www.britishnewspaperarchive.co.uk

Hansard, http://hansard.millbanksystems.com

Municipaldreams.wordpress.com

Hunslet Remembered, Hunslet.org

Jason Slack, South Leeds Life - Leek Street Flats A Social History

BFI Screenonline

Dave Haslam, Life After Dark: A History of British Nightclubs & Music Venues, Simon & Schuster

Further invaluable sources and resources:

http://moneyweek.com/22-september-1955-itvs-inaugural-broadcast/

http://www.screenonline.org.uk/tv/id/1321302/

http://www.turnipnet.com/whirligig/tv/history/history.htm

http://www.toonhound.com/alexander.htm

http://www.toonhound.com/ivorengine.htm

The History of Broadcasting in the United Kingdom: Volume IV: Sound and Vision, Asa Briggs, OUP Oxford.

Small Screens, Big Ideas: Television in the 1950s, Janet Thumin, I.B.Tauris

http://www.methodistheritage.org.uk/western-dales-railways-and-religion-1011.pdf

http://www.nrm.org.uk/railwaystories/railwayarticles/navvies

http://www.smallfilms.co.uk/ivor/history.htm

Regulating Lives: The State, Society, the Individual and the Law (Law and Society)1 Jun 2002

by Robert Menzies and Dorothy E. Chunn

Workmen's Compensation Act

https://www.gov.uk/government/uploads/system/uploads/attachment_data/file/329300/IIAC_history.pdf

http://pathetic.org.uk/features/secret_history/1949%201958/

http://www.cbrd.co.uk

http://motorwayarchive.ihtservices.co.uk

The Slow Death of British Industry - A Sixty Year Suicide Note 1952 - 2012 Nicholas Comfort.

Civil Society in British History, Ideas, Identities and Institutions, - Edited by Jose Harris, Oxford Press.

John Betjeman, the Euston Arch, and the Fight to Save London's Industrial Heritage - Dr Ruth Adams - Senior Lecturer in Cultural & Creative Industries

Department of Culture, Media & Creative Industries - King's College London

The British Environmental Movement: The

Development of an Environmental Consciousness and Environmental Activism, 1945 - 1975, Mark Wilson, Doctoral Thesis, University of Northumbria. The English Terraced House Stefan Muthesius, Yale University Press.

The Heart of the Empire, Charles Masterman, Book on Demand

Cities of Tomorrow: An Intellectual History of Urban Planning and Design, Peter Hall, Wiley-Blackwell.

Working Class Communities - Some general notions raised by a series of studies in northern England, 1968, Brian Jackson.

Concretopia: A Journey Around the Rebuilding of Postwar Britain John Grindrod - Old Street Publishing

Hunslet.org Hunslet Remembered

Benson, J.; Neville, R.G. (1976), Studies in the Yorkshire Coal Industry, Manchester University Press

South Leeds Life - Leek Street Flats A Social History - Jason Slack

http://www.sllife.leeds11.com/leek-street-flats-social-history-shared-facebook/

The Leek Street Flats Rocked - Facebook Group.

Stevenage Master Plan 1966 a Summarised Report of the Stevenage Master Plan Proposals Prepared by by Stevenage Vincent Leonard G

http://www.localhistories.org/preston.html

The Buildings of England: Yorkshire West Riding, Leeds, Bradford and the North, Pevsner & Leach, Yale University Press,

https://municipaldreams.wordpress.com/2013/11/05/stevenage-new-town-building-for-the-new-way-of-life/

Leodis.net

http://hansard.millbanksystems.com/commons/1946/may/08/new-towns-bill - NEW TOWNS BILL HC Deb 08 May 1946 vol 422 cc1072-184 Order for Second Reading read.3.37 P.m.

The new town story / Frank Schaffer ; with a foreword by Lord Silkin.

Coal Mining in Middleton Park, Martin Roe, Meerstone.

Author Schaffer, Frank, 1910- Published London : MacGibbon & Kee, 1970.

https://municipaldreams.wordpress.com/2013/02/26/leeds-the-quarry-hill-flats/

http://www.bdonline.co.uk/large-panel-systems-exposed/3046447.article

Advances in Building Technology, Part 2002 - by M Anson

Belle Isle Study Group. (1985), Belle Isle, Belle Isle Study Group

A Journey Through the Ruins: The Last Days of London - Patrick Wright

http://www.southleedslife.com/leek-street-flats-social-history-shared-facebook/

http://postwarbuildingmaterials.be/material/heavy-prefab-systems/

https://sixtiescity.net/Culture/cities.htm

https://thecharnelhouse.org/2011/09/20/the-sociohistoric-mission-of-modernist-architecture-the-housing-shortage-the-urban-proletariat-and-the-liberation-of-woman/

http://www.talkingnewtowns.org.uk/content/topics/developing-a-new-town/architect-raymond-gorbing-housing-density-stevenage-2

The Stagnant Society, Michael Shanks, Penguin Books.

The Likely Lads, Phil Wickham, Palgrave Macmillan.

State of Emergency, Dominic Sandbrook, Penguin Books.

Social Mobility Myths, Peter Sanders.

Driving Spaces: A Cultural-Historical Geography of England's M1 Motorway By Peter Merriman

http://www.concrete.org.uk/fingertips-nuggets.asp?cmd=display&id=684

Working Class Community, Brian Jackson, Pelican Books.

John Blenkinsop of Middleton, The Middleton Railway, John Bushell.

Education and the Working Class, Brian Jackson and Dennis Marsden, Pelican Books.

Communities in Britain, The Social Life of Town and Country, Ronald Frankenberg, Pelican Books.

This Island Now, G.M. Carstairs, Penguin Books. Concise Townscape, Gordon Cullen, Routledge

John Le Mesurier, A Jobbing Actor, John Le Mesurier, Sphere.

http://teaching.shu.ac.uk/ds/housing/hnc/year_1/course_material/housing_construction_and_property_management/HCPM101_00.pdf

http://www.urbanrealm.com/blogs/index.php/2016/02/05/dorran-and-dye-homes-for-the-future?blog=16

https://www.theguardian.com/society/2005/sep/14/communities1

http://www.1stassociated.co.uk/different-types-of-non-traditional-construction.asp

http://www.racfoundation.org/assets/rac_foundation/content/downloadables/car%20ownership%20in%20great%20britain%20-%20leibling%20-%2020171008%20-%20report.pdf

Britain's New Towns: Garden Cities to Sustainable Communities By Anthony Alexander

Municipaldreams.wordpress.com

A History of the Parish of Middleton and its Parish Church, Middleton Parish Church, Illing, Rev. E. J. (1971),

gordon cullen architectural review july 1953

Breaking up communities? The social impact of housing demolition in the late twentieth century Record of a study and information sharing day November 2nd 2012, York University

Alkimia Operativa and Alkimia Speculativa. Some Modern Controversies on the Historiography of Alchemy

http://www.historyhome.co.uk/polspeech/bank.htm

Beatrice   Hart

http://www.rfwilmut.clara.net/about/mpeg.html#list

https://en.wikipedia.org/wiki/Harry_Tate

http://www.fundinguniverse.com/company-histories/stoll-moss-theatres-ltd-history/

http://www.massculturalcouncil.org/services/BYAEP_History.asp

http://www.bbc.co.uk/news/magazine-21698533

https://discover.ukdataservice.ac.uk/catalogue/?sn=1405&type=Data%20catalogue

http://www.lloydsbankinggroup.com/globalassets/documents/media/press-releases/halifax/2010/50_years_of_housing_uk.pdf

https://workspace.imperial.ac.uk/humanities/Public/files/Edgerton%20Files/edgerton_white_heat.pdf

http://www.nationalmediamuseum.org.uk/~/media/Files/NMeM/PDF/Collections/Television/ColourTelevisionInBritain.pdf

http://thechels.info/wiki/Chelsea_2-1_Leeds_United_(1969-70_FA_Cup_Final_Replay)

The Dock Worker - by the Social Science Dept of Liverpool University

Coal Our Life - Dennis, Henriques, Slaughter

The Uses of Literacy - R Hoggart, Chatto & Windus

http://www.theguardian.com/news/datablog/2010/apr/30/union-membership-data

https://docs.google.com/spreadsheets/d/1kZfsrxfQVAQJQbb-CIUsE1GASXtTzwmtrOOkr4kugGQ/edit?pref=2&pli=1#gid=0 Trade Union figures

https://en.wikipedia.org/wiki/Altamont_Free_Concert#Death_of_Meredith_Hunter

'Let it Bleed', by Ethan A Russell Little, Brown

http://www.ukrockfestivals.com/my-iow.html

http://ultimateclassicrock.com/isle-of-wight-festival-1970/

http://www.live4ever.uk.com/2010/08/crushed-dreams-the-1970-isle-of-wight-festival-40-years-on/

http://jonimitchell.com/library/view.cfm?id=806

http://unesdoc.unesco.org/images/0004/000468/0468
88EB.pdf Record sales USA

http://www.recordcollectorsguild.org/modules.php?op
=modload&name=sections&file=index&req=viewarticle&
artid=44&page=1

http://www.ukrockfestivals.com/free-festivals-
menu.html

https://en.wikipedia.org/wiki/UK_Singles_Chart_reco
rds_and_statistics

https://orca.cf.ac.uk/13695/1/912.full%20Newton.pdf
Devaluation of the pound - Wilson '67

Scott Newton - English Historical Review English
Historical Review Vol. CXXV No. 515

doi:10.1093/ehr/ceq164

The Sterling Devaluation of 1967, the International
Economy and Post-War Social Democracy*

Leruez, Economic Planning and Politics in Britain
(London, 1975)

C. Schenk, Britain and the Sterling Area: From
Devaluation to Convertibility in the 1950s

(London, 1994)

Hirsch, The Pound Sterling: A Polemic (London, 1965),
Gollancz.

M. Stewart, The Jekyll and Hyde Years. Politics and
Economic Policy in Britain since 1964 (London, 1977),
Littlehampton.

Milward, The European Rescue of the Nation State
(London, 2000), Routledge.

S. Newton, 'Wilson and Sterling in 1964', Lobster, xlix
(2005

J. Callaghan, Time and Chance (London, 1987), Politicos
Publishing.

Trends in British Society Since 1900: A Guide to the Changing Social Structure of Britain. Edited by A.H. Halsey. Palgrave Macmillan 1972

National Archives
http://www.nationalarchives.gov.uk/wp-content/uploads/2014/03/prem13-28411.jpg - voter reform Wilson

USA 1966 Credit Crunch, A E Burger, 'A Historical Analysis of the Credit Crunch of 1966'
https://research.stlouisfed.org/publications/review/69/09/Historical_Sep1969.pdf

The forgotten credit crunch –
http://www.palisadeshudson.com/2014/01/the-forgettable-crash-of-1966/

http://biography.jrank.org/pages/1424/McKee-David-John-1935-Sidelights.html

http://www.telegraph.co.uk/news/uknews/8045026/History-of-the-Bowler-Hat.html

http://www.knownman.com/pinstripe-suits/

Troublesome Young Men: The Rebels Who Brought Churchill to Power and Helped Save England by Lynne Olson - Macmillan.

Scandal!: An Explosive Exposé of the Affairs, Corruption and Power Struggles of the Rich and Famous - Colin Wilson, Damon Wilson, Virgin Books

http://www.telegraph.co.uk/news/obituaries/1512656/John-Profumo.html

Reference: KV 2/4101 Serial 25a: record of BURGESS' interview with Guy LIDDELL about his indiscretions in Tangier. Serial 36a: BURGESS' letter to LIDDELL with his defence to the allegations
https://www.theguardian.com/politics/2001/apr/10/past.derekbrown

Handard - SECURITY (MR. PROFUMO'S RESIGNATION)

HC Deb 17 June 1963 vol 679 cc34-176 3.33 p.m.
Hansard - PERSONAL STATEMENT John Profumo
HC Deb 22 March 1963 vol 674 cc809-10
FBI Records Vaults - John Profumo (Bowtie) - Subject
Christine Keeler, John Profumo - Internal Security.
https://vault.fbi.gov
http://www.independent.co.uk/voices/comment/step
hen-ward-s-trial-was-disgraceful-there-can-be-no-
justification-for-it-9937083.html
Stephen Ward Was Innocent, OK' Geoffrey Robertson
QC
Macmillan: A Study in Ambiguity By Anthony Sampson,
Allen Lane.
Catherine R. Schenk Glasgow University paper The
Retirement of Sterling as a Reserve Currency after 1945:
Lessons for the US Dollar
The Brief and Turbulent Life of Modernising
Conservatism By Stuart Mitchell
Inside British Intelligence: 100 Years of MI5 and MI6 By
Gordon Thomas
http://nuclearweaponarchive.org/Uk/UKArsenalDev.
html
http://www.atomicarchive.com/History/coldwar/page
10.shtml
The Official History of the UK Strategic Nucl...
(Hardcover), Matthew Jones
The American People - Creating a Nation and Society,
Nash, Jeffrey, Howe, Frederick, Davis, Winkler, Mires,
Pestana, Pearson.
Report to JFK: The Skybolt Crisis in Perspective,
Richard E Neustadt.
Edward Heath, The Authorised Biography, Philip
Ziegler, Harper Press
Neophiliacs, Christopher Booker, Pimlico
Spy Catcher, Peter Wright, Viking

Education and Economic Decline in Britain 1870 - 1990s, Michael Sanderson, Cambridge University Press.

The Hadow Report (1926) The Education of the Adolescent

The Hadow Report (1931) The Primary School

Education in England: a brief history, Derek Gillard
http://www.governornet.co.uk/comprehensive-school.html#England_and_Wales

STERLING IN CRISIS: 1964-1967 Michael D. Bordom, Ronald MacDonald, Michael J. Oliver

Working Paper 14657

http://www.nber.org/papers/w14657, National Bureau of Economic Research.

The influential intellectual legacy of Dr JWB Douglas: originator and developer of the large birth cohort study research method, Michael Wadsworth PhD FFPH http://www.nshd.mrc.ac.uk/files/4414/4620/5868/Douglas_paper2.pdf.

The Home and The School - A Study of Ability and Attainment in the Primary School - JWB Douglas - Panther Modern Society.

Identities and Social Change in Britain Since 1940: The Politics of Method, Michael Savage

Family Newspapers?: Sex, Private Life, and the British Popular Press 1918-1978, Adrian Bingham, Oxford University Press.

Popular Culture and Working-class Taste in Britain, 1930-39: A Round of Cheap Diversions?, Robert James, Oxford University Press.

Winds of Change, Macmillan to Heath, 1957 - 1975, John Ramsden - Longman.

How a Soho coffee house gave birth to the New Left - Vanessa Thorpe - The Guardian Newspaper

Crosland and The Future of Socialism, GILES RADICE - 30 JULY 2010 - Policy Network

THE FUTURE OF SOCIALISM Anthony Crosland, Jonathan Cape

Sept 14 1957, International Congress on Clinical Chemistry, The British Medical Journal

Guardian Editorial - Crime and Sin Originally published on 5 September 1957

The World We Have Won: The Remaking of Erotic and Intimate Life, By Jeffrey Weeks

Wolfenden and beyond: the remaking of homosexual history, Jeffrey Weeks

Promise of a Dream: Remembering the Sixties, Shiela Rowbotham, Allen Lane.

The Beatles' Second Album, Dave Marsh, Rodale.

Come on Down?: Popular Media Culture in Post-war Britain, edited by Dominic Strinati, Stephen Wagg

Harworth Colliery Dispute, HC Deb 29 April 1937 vol 323 cc517-20

Harworth Colliery Dispute Tuesday 15 December 1936, Leeds Mercury

http://hansard.millbanksystems.com/commons/1937/apr/13/harworth-colliery-dispute

http://hansard.millbanksystems.com/commons/1937/apr/29/harworth-colliery-dispute

http://hansard.millbanksystems.com/commons/1937/feb/09/harworth-colliery-dispute

The Beatles in Hamburg, Ian Inglis, Reaktion Books.

On With the Dance: Nation, Culture, and Popular Dancing in Britain, 1918-1945, Allison Jean Abra A dissertation submitted in partial fulfillment of the requirements for the degree of Doctor of Philosophy(History) in the University of Michigan 2009.

Censoring Sex: A Historical Journey Through American Media, John E. Semonche, Rowman & Littlefield Publishers.

http://www.themodgeneration.co.uk

The Young Meteors, Jonathan Aitken, Secker & Warburg.

1966 - The Year Modern Britain Was Born - Christopher Bray.

http://fineart.ac.uk/home.html

1966 - The Year the Decade Exploded - Jon Savage, Faber and Faber.

Capital Affairs - Frank Mort, Yale Press.

Decade of Discontent - Nick Gardner, Blackwell.

Life After Dark - Dave Haslam, Simon & Schuster.

Never A Dull Moment - David Hepworth, Black Swan.

Murder Houses of London, Jan Bondeson, Amberley.

Prostitution, Women and the Misuse of Law, The Fallen Daughters of Eve, Helen J Self, Routledge.

Sixties Rock - Garage, Psychedelia and Other Satisfactions - Michael Hicks, Illinois.

San Francisco Nights - Gene Sculatti & David Seay.

Working Class Heroes - David Simonelli, Lexington Books.

Heterosexual Dictatorship: Male Homosexuality in Post-War Britain, Peter Higgins, Fourth Estate.

The Significance of Records of Crime, Thorsten Sellin, 1951 Law Quarterly Review.

White Heat - Dominic Sandbrook, Abacus.

Mapping Sexual London, The Wolfenden Committee on Sexual Offences and Prostitution 1954 - 1957, Frank Mort, New Formations, #37 Sexual Geographies.

Teenage - The Creation of Youth 1875 - 1945, Jon Savage, Pimlico.

Community and Organization in the New Left, 1962 - 1968, The Great Refusal - Wini Breines, Rutgers Press.

Postwar, A History of Europe Since 1945 - Tony Judt, Pimlico.

1965, The Year Modern Britain Was Born - Christopher Bray, Simon Shcuster.

Art Since 1940, Strategies of Being - Jonathan Fineberg, Laurence King Press.

Sex, Politics and Society, The Regulation of Sexuality Since 1800, Longman

The Bag I'm In, Underground Music and Fashion in Britain 1960 - 1990, Sam Knee, Cicada.

Bubblegum Music Is The Naked Truth, edited by Kim Cooper & David Smay, Feral House.

1968, The Year That Rocked The World, Mark Kurlansky, Vintage.

Wilson, The Authorised Life, Philip Zeigler, Weidenfield Nicolson Publishing.

The New Barons, Stephen Milligan, Temple-Smith Publishing.

Rotten to the Core? The Life and Death of Neville Heath, Francis Selwyn, Routledge.

Social Mobility and Class Structure in Modern Britain, John Goldthorpe, Clarendon Press, Oxford.

New Towns as Prototypes, Colin Boyne, The Listener

Slow Death of British Industry, Nicholas Comfort, Biteback Publishing.

The Way We Live Now, Richard Hoggart, Pimlico.

A Short History of Twentieth Century Technology, Trevor Williams, Oxford University Press.

In Praise of Commercial Culture, Tyler Cowen, Harvard.

The Profession of Violence - The Rise and Fall of the Krays, John Pearson, Bloomsbury.

Villains Paradise: Britain's Underworld from the Spivs to the Krays, Donald Thomas, Murder Room.

Retromania, Pop Cultures Addiction to its Own Past, Simon Reynolds, Faber and Faber.

10 Rillington Place, Ludovic Kennedy, Chivers.

In Their Own Write, Adventures In The Music Press, Paul Gorman, Sanctuary Publishing.

Acid Bath Murders, The Trials and Liquidations of John George Haigh, History Press.

Fools, Frauds and Firebrands, Thinkers of the New Left, Roger Scruton, Bloomsbury.

Songs in the Key of Z, The Curious Universe of Outsider Music, Irwin Chusid, Chicago Review Press.

The Saga of Hawkwind, Carol Clerk, Omnibus Press.

Outsider Art, Spontaneous Alternatives, Colin Rhodes, Thames & Hudson.

Making Sense of the Troubles, A History of the Northern Ireland Conflict, David Mc Patrick & David McVea, Penguin Viking.

Dick Emery, Ooh You Are Awful but I like you!, Fay Hillier, Sidgwick & Jackson.

Manson, The Life and Times of Charles Manson, Jeff Guinn, Simon & Schuster.

States of Emergency, Cold War Nuclear Defense, Tracy C Davis, Duke Publishing.

The Electric Kool-aid Acid Test, Tom Woolfe, Black Swan.

The Greening of America, Charles A. Reich, Penguin.

Between the Avant-Garde and the Everyday, Edited by Timothy Brown & Lorena Anton, Berghahn Books.

The Empire Strikes Back, Race and Racism in 70s Britain, Centre for Contemporary Studies, Hutchinson University Library.

Strange Days Indeed, The 1970s: The Golden Age of Paranoia, Frances Wheen, Public Affairs Books.

The Motorway Achievement, Building the Network in the North East of England.

Tony Benn, Office Without Power, Diaries 1968 - 1971, Arrow.

Living In Cities, Ralph Tubbs, Harmondsworth.

Tony Benn, Against The Tide, Diaries 1973 - 1976, Arrow.

Not in Front of the Children

Festivalized, Music Politics and Alternative Culture, Ian Abrahams & Bridget Wishart, Gonzo Multimedia.

British Science Fiction Television, A Hitchhikers Guide, Edited by John R. Cook & Peter Wright, IB Tauris Books.

Edward Heath, Philip Zeigler, Harper Press.

Nice to See It, To See It Nice, The 1970s In Front of the Tele, Brian Viner, Simon Schuster.

What Went Wrong, Working People and the Ideals of the Labour Movement, Jeremy Seabrook, Victor Gollancz Ltd.

Glam, Bowie, Bolan and the Glitter Rock Revolution, Barney Hoskins, Pocket Books Music.

Crisis What Crisis? Britain in the 1970s, Alwyn Turner, Aurum.

War Plan UK, The secret truth about Britain's "Civil Defence", Duncan Campbell, Paladin.

A 1970s Childhood, From Glam Rock to Happy Days, Derek Tait, The History Press.

Seasons In The Sun, The Battle for Britain 1974 - 1979, Dominic Sandbrook, Penguin.

The Verdict of Peace, Britain Between her Yesterday and the Future, Correlli Barnett, Macmillan.

The Railwayman's Pocket-Book, Instructions for Drivers & Firemen on the Great Railways, Conway Press.

In Plain Sight: The Life and Lies of Jimmy Savile, Quercus.

Unzipped, Suzy Quatro, Hodder.

The Railway Navvies, A History of the Men Who Made the Railways, Terry Coleman, Head-Zeus.

The Steel Highway, Railway Planning & Making, Cecil J Allen, Longmans.

Trains and their Control, Cecil J Allen, Longmans.

Fire & Steam, A New History of the Railways in Britain, Christian Wolmar, Atlantic Books.

Not in Front of the Children

Teddy Boys: A Concise History, Ray Ferris & Julian Lord, Milo Books.

Diary of a Teddy Boy, Memories of the Long Sixties, Mim Scala.

Mod! A Very British Style, Richard Weight, Random House.

Society and the Homosexual, Gordon Westwood, Gollancz.

We Are The Mods: A Transitional History of a Subculture, CJ Feldman, Lang.

The Teds, CS Perkins, Richard Smith, Traveling Light/Exit,

The Young Edwardians: race, authority and the formation of a subcultural identity 1953-1959, University of Wisconsin- Madison.

The Grand Hotel Abyss, The Lives of the Frankfurt School, Stuart Jefferies, Verso.

Shock & Awe, Simon Reynolds, Faber & Faber.

Bread Butter and Architecture, John Summerson, Horizon.

This Ain't the Summer of Love, Steve Waksman, University of California Press.

The Teds: a political resurrection, Tony Jefferson, Centre for Cultural Studies University of Birmingham.

Coming Out, Jeffrey Weeks, Quartet Books.

The Divided Self: An Existential Study In Sanity and Madness, RD Laing, Penguin.

Destructive Generation, Second Thoughts About The Sixties, Peter Collier and David Horowitz, Encounter Books.

Sanity Madness and the Family, RD Laing, Routledge.

Reason & Violence: A Decade of Sartre's Philosophy, 1950-1960, RD Laing & David Cooper, Routledge.

The Book - On the Taboo Against Knowing Who You Are, Alan Watts, Souvenir Press.

Not in Front of the Children

A 1970s Teenager, Simon Webb, The History Press.

The Home and the School, A Study of Ability and Attainment in the Primary School, JWB Douglas, Panther Modern Society.

Education and economic decline in Britain, 1870 to the 1900s, Michael Sanderson, Cambridge University Press.

London's Gangs at War, Dick Kirby, Pen & Sword.

The Survivor, Blue Murder, Bent Cops, Vengeance, Vendetta In 1960s Gangland, Jimmy Evans & Martin Short, Mainstream.

The History of Education in England, Derek Gillard, educationengland.org.uk.

Education in Britain 1944 to the Present, Ken Jones, Polity.

Ghosts of My Life, Mark Fisher, Zero Books.

Urban Regeneration in the UK, Phil Jones and James Evans, Sage.

Militant Modernism, Owen Hatherley, Zero Books.

British Family Cars of the 1950s and '60s, Anthony Pritchard, Shire Books.

Britain, Modern Architectures in History, Alan Powers, Reaction Books.

A Local Habitation, Life and Times 1918 - 1940, Richard Hoggart, Chatto Windus.

Austerity Britain 1945-1951, David Kynaston.

The Making of Modern Britain, Andrew Marr, Pan.

Sexuality, J Weeks, Taylor Francis.

Sex, Politics and Society: The Regulation of Sexuality Since 1800 (Themes in British Social History), J Weeks, Routledge.

The Spiv and the Architect: Unruly Life in Postwar London, Richard Hornsey, University of Minnesota Press.

Moments of Modernity?: Reconstructing Britain - 1945-64, Becky E Conekin, Frank Mort, Chris Walters, Rivers Oram Press.

https://www.lambiek.net/artists/r/ryan_john.htm

http://www.telegraph.co.uk/news/obituaries/culture-obituaries/tv-radio-obituaries/5899923/John-Ryan.html

http://www.toonhound.com/marymungomidge.htm

http://www.imdb.com/title/tt0804422/ John Ryan

http://www.britishclassiccomedy.co.uk/mary-mungo-and-midge

http://www.thechestnut.com/mary/mary.htm   Mary Mungo and Midge

http://nostalgiacentral.com/television/tv-by-decade/tv-shows-1960s/mary-mungo-midge/

http://www.jedisparadise.com/2/Mary_Mungo_and_Midge.htm

http://www.captainpugwashexhibition.co.uk/mary-mungo-midge-tv/

http://www.plymouthherald.co.uk/news/local-news/mr-benn-childrens-tv-classic-354642

https://www.theguardian.com/culture/2017/mar/07/how-we-made-mr-benn-david-mckee-ray-brooks-interview?CMP=Share_iOSApp_Other

Jedi Paradise

http://www.jedisparadise.com/2/Mr_Benn.htm

https://www.doyouremember.co.uk/memory/mr-benn

http://www.bbc.co.uk/news/av/entertainment-arts-41000907/the-magical-world-of-mr-benn

https://amp.ft.com/content/0e435544-6724-11e7-8526-7b38dcaef614 Finacial Times Mr Benn Insurance Ad.

https://www.dailyrecord.co.uk/entertainment/magic-childrens-tv-hero-international-11105953.amp

https://www.simplyeighties.com/mr-benn-cartoon.php#.WmT-zebLehA

Toon Hound

http://www.toonhound.com/mrbenn.htm

http://www.tallstories.org.uk/the-extraordinary-adventures-of-mr-benn

Seeing Things, Oliver Postgate, Canongate Books
smallfilms.co.uk
Ivor the Engine 1958 IMDb
Ivor the Engine 1975 IMDb
BFI Screenonline - Ivor the Engine 1954-1964
BBC Wales Arts Ivor the Engine
http://www.bbc.co.uk/wales/arts/sites/children/page
s/ivor-the-engine.shtml
Clive Banks An Interview with Oliver Postgate
www.clivebanks.co.uk
The Guardian, Bagpus creator Oliver Postgate in his
own words - 9/12/2008
http://www.jedisparadise.com/5/Ivor_the_Engine.ht
m
http://www.toonhound.com/ivorengine.htm
http://www.turnipnet.com/whirligig/tv/children/ivort
heengine/ivortheengine.htm
http://nostalgiacentral.com/television/tv-by-
decade/tv-shows-1950s/ivor-engine/
http://www.walesonline.co.uk/news/wales-news/lost-
ivor-engine-reels-found-1893448
The Independent, Ivor the Engine chugs again - on
video, Kate Watson-Smyth, 30/04/2000
Official Scooby-Doo Website,
https://www.wbkidsgo.com/en-gb/scoobydoo
Big Cartoon Database
https://www.bcdb.com/cartoons/Hanna-
Barbera_Studios/S/Scooby_Doo__Where_Are_You_/
Scooby-Doo, Where Are You! IMDb
Scooby-Doo, Where Are You, tv.com
www.bcdb.com/cartoons/Hanna-
Barbera_Studios/S/Scooby_Doo_Where_Are_You
webarchive.org
http://scoobydoo.wikia.com/wiki/Scooby-
Doo,_Where_Are_You!

http://tvtropes.org/pmwiki/pmwiki.php/WesternAni
mation/ScoobyDooWhereAreYou

https://www.inverse.com/article/15431-scooby-
dooby-doo-where-are-you-why-are-your-animated-series-
so-short-now

http://www.dccomics.com/comics/scooby-doo-
where-are-you-2010/scooby-doo-where-are-you-61

https://www.britannica.com/biography/Hanna-and-
Barbera

https://www.illustrationhistory.org/artists/hanna-
barbera

http://www.cleveland.com/entertainment/index.ssf/2
017/07/60_years_of_hanna-barbera_cart.html

My Life in 'Toons: From Flatbush to Bedrock in Under
a Century, Joseph Barbera, Turner Publishing

Hollywood Cartoons: American Animation in Its
Golden Age, Michael Barrier, Oxford University Press

American Animated Cartoons of the Vietnam Era: A
Study of Social Commentary in Films and Television
Programs, 1961 - 1973, Christopher P Lehman, McFarland
& Co.

Saturday Morning Fever, Timothy Burke and Kevin
Burke, St. Martin's Griffin.

University of the West of England Construction Website
-
https://fet.uwe.ac.uk/conweb/house_ages/council_housi
ng/section3.htm